JUST TELL HER TO STOP:

Family Stories of Eating Disorders

always have HOPE

Becky

"A wonderful reference for all families and friends who have a loved one struggling with an eating disorder in order to provide hope and excellent information in how to navigate the rough waters. I really believe it will be a must-read for all my families. Becky has compiled this well researched resource that is full of sound, practical advice."
—**Susan Buesing L.M.F.T., L.D.**

Just Tell Her To Stop will help enormously in exposing and exterminating this manipulative, isolating, and dangerous illness. In my recovery journey, a constant image spurred me on—that of extracting the eating disorder from the darkness of my mind. The families in this book write from the heart, bravely and candidly exposing the reality of eating disorders. Their words are a bright light shining, a beacon, a pathway, for anyone caught up in an eating disorder."
—**June Alexander,** Australia, Author of *My Kid Is Back: Empowering Parents to Beat Anorexia Nervosa* (collaboration with Daniel Le Grange) 2010; *A Girl Called Tim: Escape from an Eating Disorder Hell* (memoir) 2011; and *A Collaborative Approach to Eating Disorders* (co-editor Janet Treasure) 2011. Member: ANZAED, AED Patient-Carer Task Force Committee

"I have worked with many brave, compassionate, and wise parents, and find their commitment to helping their child recover from an eating disorder has been both humbling and inspiring to witness. After many years of feeling alone, these parents now

have the support of the clinical community and other parents, such as yourself, as they accompany their child on the road to recovery. I will recommend your book among the resources that parents and families might turn to for information, along with organizations like NEDA, FEAST, AED, and foundations such as the Anna Westin Foundation. Congratulations on this tremendous accomplishment. I am most grateful to have it as a resource."
—Bethany Helfman, Psy.D., Bloomfield Hills, MI

"Great job of telling families' personal stories and giving them a voice, hearing those stories can provide much encouragement and comfort to friends and families finding themselves in the role of supporting a loved one with an eating disorder."
—Melinda Parisi, Ph.D., Program Director, Eating Disorders Program University Medical Center at Princeton mparisi@princetonhcs.org

"You fought and won to get your traumatized brain back, then fought to win your joy back and have bravely marched out of the dark forest of eating disorder heartbreak. Then, armed with knowledge, experience and hindsight, you turned around and went right back in, to bring the rest of the families lost in the darkness out into the sunshine again. I'm so proud of you. If we, as your family had this book to guide us back when you were lost in the forest, we would have been more equipped to walk with you through the nightmare."
—Your Sister, Karen

"Becky Henry's book tells it like it is for parents whose child has an eating disorder. Now I have a book that I can recommend to parents by a parent who has been there. I enthusiastically endorse this book."
—**Marcia Herrin, Ed.D., M.P.H., R.D., L.D.,** Herrin Nutrition Services, 367 State Route 120, Unit B-8, Lebanon, NH 03766; Email: marcia.herrin@dartmouth.edu; Website: www.marciaherrin.com; Tel: 603-643-7677; *The Parent's Guide to Eating Disorders* (Gurze Press, 2007); *Nutrition Counseling in the Treatment of Eating Disorders* (Brunner-Routledge, 2002)

Just Tell Her To Stop is a page-turner! From the very beginning, the message enticed me, and I knew that I was not alone in the struggle. So comforting, even though people die, it is still comforting.

Any reader can gain from these important and significant family stories. The tips at end of each chapter were helpful and insightful, giving us concrete ways to deal with things. Often parents feel "blamed," and these stories tell us that even if a parent said something that wasn't the best to say, it's not your fault—take from the experience and move forward.

Everyone who is struggling can relate to all of the different stories—the good, bad, the ugly—and the tragic. You get a front row seat to what people had experienced! I read this important and phenomenal book from beginning to end."
—**Dawn Hynes, M.S.W.,** CEO, and Co-Founder of Eating For Life Alliance (ELA) www.eatingforlife.org

"Living with an eating disorder is extremely challenging and Becky Henry has found the perfect way to share beautifully written family and patient stories. Each contributor shares a list of recovery TIPS at the end of their story, and they contain

particularly valuable "positive living" information. *Just Tell Her to Stop* is already a classic in the field of eating disorder treatment and recovery. Great value for both families and anyone who works in the eating disorders field."
—**Janet Nestor, M.A., L.P.C., D.C.E.P.,** Author of the mindfulness handbook, *Pathways to Wholeness,* Holistic Mental Health Therapist, Center of Well-Being, Winston-Salem, NC

"With *Just Tell Her to Stop* is a much-needed resource for those who truly stand on the front lines of the eating disorders recovery battle—the parents and families of a sufferer. A parent-turned-activist herself, Ms. Henry has experienced firsthand the power and value of having access to a parent support network. This book takes aim at popular myths that parents cause eating disorders, and deliberately chooses a different approach—to educate and support families so they can then better support the sufferers in their lives as well."
—**Shannon Cutts,** founder of MentorCONNECT and author of *Beating Ana: How to Outsmart Your Eating Disorder and Take Your Life Back*

"Every journey of recovery from an eating disorder is unique, but a common necessary ingredient is courage. Be it anorexia, bulimia or binge eating disorder, this journey is a perilous, yet possible, one. There is little that is more valuable to families and partners than stories from those who have been there before. The journeys revealed in *Just Tell Her to Stop* by Becky Henry offer the most precious commodity to both survivors and their supporters: hope."
—**Amy Pershing, L.M.S.W., A.C.S.W.,** Founding Director, Bodywise Binge Eating Disorder Recovery Program, Annapolis MD and Ann Arbor, MI.

Just Tell Her to Stop

FAMILY STORIES OF EATING DISORDERS

Becky Henry

Infinite Hope Publishing • Minneapolis

Published by Infinite Hope Publishing
Becky Henry, President and Founder, Hope Network
www.HopeNetwork.info
www.JustTellHerToStop.com

Cover design by Alan Pranke, amp13design, and
Alan Michael, Alan Michael Design
Interior design by Dorie McClelland, Spring Book Design

ISBN: 978-0-9845489-0-3
Printed in the United States of America

16 15 14 13 12 5 4 3 2 1

A portion of the proceeds from the sale of this book will go to Eating Disorders Coalition for Research, Policy & Action.

This book is dedicated to all of the incredibly brave individuals who daily reclaim their power over eating disorders, to the families who lovingly walk alongside them, believing in full recovery and reclaiming their own power over fear and panic, and to all, including health care providers, who are passionate about resolving eating disorders issues for all people. My intent is that these stories will give you peace and hope, as well as the tools to effectively support your loved one through recovery.

CONTENTS

FOREWORD

If the title of this book, "Just Tell Her To Stop," makes you shake your head with recognition, then you are probably a family member of someone with an eating disorder. How we respond to that title, and that idea, will tell you a lot about loving someone suffering from anorexia, bulimia, or other eating disorder. Nearly every parent of a child with an eating disorder has heard it, and it says so much about the public misperception of these dangerous illnesses.

Yet it is also true that we cannot "Just Tell People to Stop" saying these things. The public doesn't have a good understanding of what eating disorders are, what they can do to a family, or how they can be treated. That is why this book is so important. You can't "just" do anything with this illness: you have to do a lot of things. This is a book that offers so many of the ways people fall ill, get support, and the different outcomes that can happen. No one story is sufficient to illustrate the pain, the bravery, the love, and the many pathways toward recovery.

There is hope here, and helpful advice for families and their friends. Not all these stories end happily, but that is a reality that must be faced. Patients who do not recover are no less worthy, no less loved, and no less courageous—nor are their families. Not all of these stories follow the same path: there is no one way to pursue recovery.

It is my hope that this book, written by a loving parent, will find its way to not only other family members facing eating disorders but to our communities and our leaders and educators. It is not sufficient to just discuss eating disorders when it strikes people we know. We need to bring this illness into the open for the public good.

Eating disorders have for too long been hiding in a cul-de-sac of our own making. Separate from other healthcare issues, other mental health issues, other community issues, we have allowed ourselves to be ignored and misunderstood. Through stories—real stories—of families and individuals facing this illness, this is the best way to bring needed light and openness to a topic too long kept apart. This is not an issue just for the families impacted directly. This is an illness that goes undetected and untreated in our schools, clinics and in our neighborhoods: misunderstood and even stigmatized.

The news is good on eating disorder treatment. Evidence-based treatments are making their way into practice and public education is improving thanks to organizations like the Academy for Eating Disorders, the Eating Disorders Coalition, BEAT, The Butterfly Foundation, the National Eating Disorders Association, and others. My parent-oriented organization, F.E.A.S.T., is a more recent addition to advocacy and we stand on the shoulders of many before us.

I am grateful to Becky Henry for offering the gift of family stories; voices that can animate and transform your view of eating disorders. This is one of the most frequent requests F.E.A.S.T. gets—examples of other families—and I look forward to shar-ing this book with that community. These stories are filled with experience, painfully gained wisdom, and hard-won insight. These stories will startle and, with luck, move you to take action. Whether you are yourself dealing with an eating disorder in your family or hoping to understand the needs of another family you will find help here in this book.

Laura Collins Lyster-Mensh
Executive Director
F.E.A.S.T. (Families Empowered and Support-
ing Treatment of Eating Disorders)
FEAST-ED.org

INTRODUCTION

When our sweet, adorable, competent and very responsible teen-age daughter dramatically changed, I knew something was horribly wrong. The difference in her personality was so drastic I knew it couldn't just be teenage hormones. I began searching the Internet, looking for clues as to what could be going on with her. My research led me to suspect that she might be depressed or might have bulimia, or maybe both. I naively trusted that our pediatrician would know how to recognize both disorders so I was surprised when she told me my daughter had neither of them. I persevered and took her to one psychologist, then another, but they also discounted my instincts.

Two very long chaotic years later, in spite of my best efforts and being ever vigilant, I still didn't really know what was going on. Then one day her friends nervously told me the complete story. They were quite concerned about her sometimes-dangerous erratic behavior and they confirmed my suspicion—she was bingeing and purging.

At that point my husband and I were actually relieved, thinking we could finally get help. We said, "Okay, now we *know!* The doctors will fix it. We can handle this. All we need is love." With apologies to the Beatles, we soon learned that love was *not* all we needed. We needed help—from the medical community, from our family and friends, from the world in general. We did get help—some, but not enough, from the medical community, more from family, more or less from friends (some were great, some we lost and many others just couldn't understand). The world? Not so much. Eating disorders are still misunderstood, discounted by many, and not taken seriously by even more.

It was 2002 when my daughter was officially diagnosed. By this time, because we were not able to get her diagnosed and treated earlier, she was seriously ill. After she had been in treatment for a while, I asked her why she thought the pediatrician and psychologists had missed the diagnosis. She laughed as she said, "Mom, I *lied* to them!"

It was not, and still isn't, a laughing matter to me. I now know the pediatrician and psychologists lacked the training to recognize the shame, secrecy and lying that people with eating disorders use to hide their illnesses from those trying to uncover them.

At the time, most physicians were responding from limited outdated research. There were huge gaps in knowledge about eating disorders in the medical community and there were few treatment facilities. For us, there was an immeasurable amount of frustration, isolation, desperation, hopelessness, and fear until we found real help for our daughter—and ourselves.

The gaps have narrowed a bit but many health care providers still believe that a person must be severely underweight to have an eating disorder. This is not only wrong, it's been a hindrance to proper diagnosis for far too many people.

Another yawning gap in knowledge was that for many years, the medical community blamed parents, especially moms, for the eating disorders, so they pushed parents aside during treatment, an approach that's been called a "parentectomy." That, too, has been debunked by research but that message still needs to reach many physicians and therapists.

Families are *essential* to the recovery of someone facing these illnesses and we need skills, tools, support, and knowledge to withstand the assault eating disorders bring to our families to be able to support our loved ones in their recovery. I have heard from those who have recovered that having their family stand by them gave them the courage to keep trying to recover.

I am often asked, "What causes eating disorders? Is it really just about being thin?" Of course, body image (a person's perception of how she looks) is the number one reason girls and women of all ages are so self-obsessed about their weight and how they look. But the causes are much more complex. Eating disorders are multi-faceted bio-psychosocial illnesses. How's that for complicated?

The latest research shows the causes to be a combination of social, interpersonal, psychological and biochemical factors with an underlying genetic link.

This does not mean that researchers believe that there is a particular eating disorder gene. Rather, they think that some people inherit a vulnerability for traits such as anxiety, compulsions and perfectionism that may, combined with certain stimuli, lead to the development of an eating disorder.

The bottom line, though, is no one really knows the causes of eating disorders, though much more research is finally occurring. What researchers seem to agree on at this point is that *eating disorders are brain disorders;* what they don't agree on is what that means.

The research is so young that even the medical community hasn't fully determined what to "label" eating disorders. Some call them addictions, others call them mental illnesses; still others use that more generic term, brain disorders.

The *Diagnostic and Statistical Manual of Mental Disorders* (DSM), which is published by the American Psychiatric Association, is relied upon by a wide range of professionals, from researchers and clinicians to insurance and pharmaceutical companies, and even policy makers, to provide the criteria for classifying mental disorders, including what is and what is not a mental disorder. The following eating disorders are listed in the order of their most common occurrence.

NOTE: "Compensate/compensatory measures" mean that the person is trying to balance out what she has just consumed.

- Eating Disorder Not Otherwise Specified (EDNOS)— EDNOS is a clinical diagnosis given to people who don't fully fit the specific criteria for other eating disorders such as binge eating disorder, bulimia or anorexia. In spite of the unfamiliar name, it is a serious disorder. People with EDNOS might have the majority of the diagnostic criteria for bulimia or anorexia, but if they don't have 100% of them, they can't be diagnosed as having those eating disorders, and insurance companies will often deny payment for treatment.
- Binge Eating Disorder (BED)—A type of eating disorder not otherwise specified. It is characterized by recurrent binge eating without the regular use of compensatory measures to counter the binge eating.
- Bulimia Nervosa (BN)—A serious, potentially life-threatening, eating disorder characterized by a cycle of bingeing and compensatory behaviors, such as self-induced vomiting, designed to undo or compensate for the effects of binge eating.
- Anorexia Nervosa (AN)—A serious, potentially life-threatening, eating disorder characterized by self-starvation and excessive weight loss.

As of 2010, Binge Eating Disorder (BED) is not technically an eating disorder according to the DSM-IV so for insurance purposes doctors must currently diagnose it under Eating Disorder Not Otherwise Specified (EDNOS). BED impacts millions of women and men worldwide and is expected to be in the next DSM, DSM-V, which will be published in 2013.

Many people may be surprised how these disorders are listed. It's been commonly believed by many (even health care providers) that anorexia is the most common eating disorder and, as mentioned above, that a person can't have an eating disorder unless he or she is "stick thin." But an eating disorder is when *a person has an abnormal relationship with food due to underlying genetic factors.* These people can be any size, even overweight, and experience a life-changing eating disorder that needs treatment.

One analogy I use when I talk to families and health care providers is, "A Chevy is always an automobile but an automobile isn't always a Chevy. Anorexia is always an eating disorder but an eating disorder isn't always anorexia."

More than ten million females, and at least one million males in the United States alone and an estimated 70 million world-wide (according to the Alliance for Eating Disorders Awareness) suffer some kind of an eating disorder. If we broaden it to include those who have symptoms of eating disorders then we see numbers go up to approximately 10% of females. AN and BN occur about nine times more in women than in men when looking at strict numbers. But definitions are changing as to what AN and BN look like in men. With BED the occurrence is about the same with men and women.

Eating disorders are potentially life-threatening conditions that strike women and men of all ages, races, and socio-economic backgrounds. Lifetime prevalence estimates of DSM-IV anorexia nervosa, bulimia nervosa, and binge eating disorder are 0.9%, 1.5%, and 3.5% among women and 0.3%, 0.5%, and 2.0% among men. These estimates are relatively constant across Western nations. Despite the serious nature of these disorders, to date there is little research available to help practitioners recognize, diagnose, and treat them. —Cynthia M. Bulik, Ph.D., FAED, Director, University of North Carolina Eating Disorders Program, Chapel Hill, N.C., and Nancy D. Berkman, Ph.D., MLIR, Senior Health Policy Research Analyst, RTI International Research Triangle Park, N.C.

For simplicity's sake, this book most often refers to daughters and their parents but it is for all people who care about someone who is being lost to an eating disorder, whether it's a son, daughter, friend, grandchild, partner, co-worker, or employee. When you read, insert your own words for that person as you find the skills, tools, and hope needed to navigate this challenging journey.

I mostly use "her" throughout the book because the majority of those who suffer from eating disorders are girls; however, I want to stress that it's becoming quite common for boys and young men to need treatment. They can be genetically pre-disposed as well. Some boys told me that their eating issues began with trying to "make weight" for a wrestling team, or trying to be faster for the swim team or cross-country team. Sadly, it's time for treatment centers to develop more programming for the growing male clientele.

Diagnoses can be complex and so is treatment for these disorders. As much as we would wish it to be so, there is no one-size-fits-all treatment. Treatment is complicated by the fact that eating disorders morph—anorexia can morph into bulimia, bulimia can morph into binge-eating disorder, and then they can morph back, or elsewhere. It is also common for there to be co-occurring disorders, ranging from anemia to alcoholism and drug addiction to the very serious diabulimia, which occurs when someone with type-1 diabetes also has bulimia.

A wide gap exists on treatment approaches and perspectives between the eating disorders field and the substance abuse field and as a result there is no collaboration yet between these professional communities. This needs to change.

Treatment options include, but are not limited to, traditional psychodynamic therapy, cognitive-behavioral therapy (CBT) and family therapy. Some of these have been studied more than others and more comparison of the various treatments needs to be done to understand what is most effective. One approach, recommended by the American Psychiatric Association as the first line of treatment for anorexia, is being called the Family-Based Maudsley approach. It's also proving to be helpful for other types of eating disorders. Unfortunately, it is often unfamiliar to many physicians.

There is no right or wrong treatment. What's most important is to find the right treatment for your loved one. Several treatment centers are named in the stories that follow. This book is not meant to endorse them, but to let you know about them.

If you are a parent/loved one reading this you are most likely coming out of the denial stage. You may want to stay there, hoping to prove to yourself that your loved one doesn't have an eating disorder. Please know that denial is very common and part of the process. I ask that you not stay there very long as your loved one's life depends on getting help—sooner rather than later. Just like any other illness, outcomes improve with early treatment.

This book was written because I don't want any other family to go through what my family went through. I also hope to reach health care providers, to show them the "other side," to help them understand that though they may see their patient for 50 minutes a week (at most), families, mainly moms and dads, are on the front lines of these illnesses the other *10,030* minutes each week.

Let me be absolutely clear: THIS BOOK IS NOT A MEDI-CAL REFERENCE. It's a book of stories about real people dealing with all aspects of these diseases. You will see how real families and real health care providers handle the experience of these illnesses very differently and sometimes not well.

It's also a book of hope. As you will see, people do recover and go on to live full lives without further sign of their eating disorders. And it's a book of truth: Some people die from eating disorders. Some of those stories are also in this book.

Learn from these families and follow your instinct about what will and won't work for your family or your patients. Keep an open mind. You will meet people who have recovered and some who are in varying stages of recovery. Learn from all of them.

Even though sometimes the one telling his or her story in this book seems to be talking to the person with the eating disorder, please keep this book away from your loved one as there may be statements that could be "triggering" (another term you will learn) to their eating disorder. The stories in the book could "teach the eating disorder" new tricks to further compromise your loved one's health. My editor was shocked when I told her about Pro-Ana websites . . . yes, there are websites where people suffering from eating disorders teach other people ways to help hide their eating disorders, i.e., how to be more effective at having an eating disorder. As a care provider it is important to know that those sites are out there—check your loved one's computer history to find out if they are visiting such sites.

Many people with eating disorders feel that their lives are out of control and believe that controlling food or the amount of food they allow in their bodies gives them back control. As a family member or friend, it's easy to think this is their choice when in reality they are not able to make reasonable choices due to the combination of the brain biology not working properly and the malnourishment. It is challenging to separate the individual from the illnesses when we are living with them and see such irrational behavior. When these often very intelligent people tell us it gives them a sense of control, we believe them.

When you read the following stories, you will learn that one way to separate the individual from the illness is to name the eating disorder. "Ed" and "Bully" are the most common. In fact, many people with eating disorders will describe "hearing" from their eating disorder that they need to purge, exercise, or in some other way discharge the calories they just consumed—thus redeeming themselves at least in the "eyes" of the eating disorder. Family members using this tool will find it easier to be angry at the eating disorder instead of the person exhibiting "behaviors," another term you'll learn in reading the stories. For example, as you'll see in some of the stories, it's a little easier to take verbal abuse from Ed or Bully, than to think the awful words are coming from your child.

You'll also read about one of the most important tools I learned. Our family therapist introduced me to the concept of "letting go with love." It took me about a year to even grasp its meaning but now I coach families to use this important skill to give their loved one a sense of empowerment as well as to help themselves to regain their own freedom. The basic idea is continuing to participate and engage without needing your loved one to like it and to own your own feelings. It's much easier said than done when you are scared that your child/loved one is dying or may try to commit suicide. It does *not* mean that you aren't still actively involved as a part of the treatment team. It's learning to not join the loved one's fear and anxieties but remain active in seeking and following through on treatment without being overbearing.

I didn't get it at first. I disengaged instead of detaching. When done well, it is a healthy way to care for yourself and accept the ups and downs of the process while being a caregiver to your very ill loved one.

I interviewed people who have recovered, are in recovery and their family members for this book. In the majority of the stories I have changed the names and identifying characteristics to protect the privacy of the people concerned. Some of their stories were combined to give the reader a better understanding of a certain idea or concept.

There are five stories in which the people wanted their real names used because they are doing advocacy work in the eating-disorder field. Those are: Patrick Bergstrom, Carolyn Costin, Dexter Godbey, Kris Henderson and Kitty Westin. All of the other names have been changed.

The stories I heard were so powerful I chose to write them in the first person. Each chapter has an introduction in my voice followed by my interpretation of their story in their voice.

These are stories of families across the world where young girls, women, boys, and men of all ages and sizes worry about their body image.

Every parent, spouse, friend, sibling, or neighbor who sheds a tear over the potential loss of these lives can open the lines of communication and work together with their loved ones to help them on their brave paths to recovery.

Though each story in this book is unique to that family, there is some general advice that families going through this health crisis have told me they want others to know:

- Avoid being judgmental.
- LISTEN (this means don't talk and try to fix—use your ears more than your mouth).
- Remember, this illness is not just black and white; it has many areas of grey.
- Be supportive (ask what we need).
- Keep in mind that there is no right or wrong way to do treatment.
- Know that we are doing the best we can with what we have.
- Be mindful that we are experiencing and grieving major secondary losses.
- Understand that we often feel powerlessness over the severity of the situation.

- This illness and all of its complicating factors are putting a huge strain on our marriage/relationships, finances and health.

- Fear is our constant companion—this makes us a little jumpy and irritable—and also affects our cognitive functions, including memory. This is normal in our situation; please cut us some slack but don't panic.

Waiting Rooms

Tiny little rooms
Like jail cells
All taupe and fluorescent lights
Nothing to look at
A symbol of the jail I feel ED has put us in

So scary
So incredibly alone
So helpless—losing hope
Knowing I'll have only a few minutes
Of some professional's precious time
To ask our questions.

Want to jump out of my skin
So trapped, so tired

Will they ever help us?
We must help ourselves
Sad
Sadness
Hopeless

Is this how all parents of chronically ill children feel?
I am the parent of a child with an eating disorder
And I need a hug!!

—Becky Henry, 2002

1

Becky Henry's Story

Learning About Eating Disorders Is Necessary for the Family

I wrote the poem "Waiting Rooms" when I was sitting in the very tiny space allotted to family members waiting while their loved ones were being evaluated for eating disorders. It had taken two years to get an accurate diagnosis and many more weeks trying to find someone/someplace that could help us determine what our next steps needed to be to save our daughter's life.

Looking around the sterile square room I would have been happy to have had just one colorful poster to distract me. The bare taupe-colored walls only served to make me feel that parents were not important. I kept staring at the blank wall, wondering, *Why don't they just have a big poster with some bullet points about what is going on, what to expect, what to say, what to do, how to get help for my daughter, for me, for my family? Wouldn't it help my daughter if I were informed?*

After so many trips to so many doctors, after trying so hard for so long to get answers, I wanted action. I wanted to know what was happening. The longer I waited, the more negative my thoughts. *Maybe they want to keep me in the dark so she stays sick longer and they'll make more money? Oh, am I that cynical? Have I lost my mind? Or is it the system that is messed up and needs fixing?*

That was in 2002, over eight years ago. I've learned a lot since then; some have even called me an "expert" in eating disorders. I'm still not sure there are "experts" because there is still so much to learn but if I'm in any way an "expert," I am an unwilling expert due to being the mother of a child with an eating disorder. I didn't choose to know this disease any more than my daughter chose to suffer from her eating disorder. I don't have all the answers. No one does. I do have my own set of questions, a list that seems to get longer instead of shorter. But I have learned one thing for sure. Talking to others in the same situation really helps, if only to realize *you are not alone.*

This long, incredible journey has made me determined to make sure no family is alone and without some answers when the uninvited guest I sometimes call "The Bully" appears in their lives. It has become my passion to help other families through their healing. In my coaching I help families more effectively support their child, spouse, sibling, parent, etc., who has an eating disorder while also helping the families learn how not to let the eating disorders define their lives. As you will see in the following stories, this can happen.

The families I work with often have very similar questions. They want answers to questions that range from the simple to the unanswerable:

- Why is this happening to *our* family?
- Where can one mother talk to another mother?
- How soon will she get well?
- What works?
- What doesn't work?
- How can we have a normal family meal?
- Where do we turn when we're being torn apart?
- How do I pay for this?

- If she is out of high school, but too sick to go to college, will our insurance cover her?
- What do we tell family members?
- How do we *not* neglect our other children?
- How do I know if the treatment center near us has had good results?
- How do I recognize a relapse?
- How do I stay calm and supportive when a relapse occurs?
- What can I read to learn as much as possible?
- How do we keep our marriage/family together during this illness?
- What do I tell my son's grandparents about this illness that used to be considered a female illness?
- What do I tell my friends about what is going on with my mom?
- Is she going crazy?
- Am *I* going crazy?

Research is ongoing and there is still a lot we don't know but we do know that *people don't "get" an eating disorder because of how they've been treated by their parents.*

The old idea often was: This poor sweet girl has a demanding mother who wants her to be perfect; that's why she has an eating disorder. The "then" thinking (and too often yet today) was: It's the mother's fault.

Grasping for causes, the reasons for the illness, doesn't justify blaming the family. We have learned from the treatment of families impacted by alcoholism and drug addiction that this simply isn't effective for anyone.

One major difference in the treatment of alcoholism/drug addiction and eating disorders is that much more is known about treating alcoholism and drug addiction, treatment is much more readily available, including many more treatment centers, and insurance coverage for treatment usually isn't as much of an obstacle.

We wondered at times if it wouldn't have been easier to find suitable treatment for our daughter if she had, in fact, been addicted to drugs or alcohol. I've heard parents who have had difficulty finding a treatment program for their daughter say, "Well, she could get into a great twelve-step program if she also had a drug or alcohol addiction." This needs to change—we cannot wish such awful things on our children in the desperate search for good treatment.

As you read the sometimes heartbreaking, sometimes heart-tugging results of my interviews, you will see similarities and differences in the way ill people, and their families, handle day-to-day living.

Each family has tried different things to just survive these ever-changing illnesses, finding what works for them as individuals, as couples, and as whole families.

Many told me that, on some occasions, they knew they were "connecting with their daughter" and could reason with her, but at other times they knew that the eating disorder occupying her head was distorting every single word they said and every gesture they made as it grabbed another inch of control over their child's mind and body.

I have met many amazing and truly special people in the life-coaching profession; they are the main reason I am coaching families now. They showed me how to listen and, most importantly, acknowledge a person for who he or she is and what he or she is experiencing. It took me awhile to understand that acknowledging *who* a person is, is not flattery; stating what you see in that person is one of the most validating human experiences there is.

Looking back through several years of healing and recovery for my family, I'm at a point where I know our experiences can help others. We are now a healthy enough family I can objectively look at what we went through during the *slow* recovery process.

I didn't do it alone. Ann, a colleague, was one of the angels who helped me. I want to share some of the most compassionate words I heard during my darkest days, when I was consumed with fear for my daughter's life. Early in our journey I was working on a project with Ann and I shared some of what we were experiencing with our daughter. Ann sent an email of encouragement. I replied: "This parenting a child with an eating disorder is harder than I thought it would be." I shared that my daughter's eating disorder was directing anger toward me—and the pain of having my child hate me, which was what it felt like at the time, was excruciating.

I have read Ann's response many times when I needed support.

Becky—

I don't have any direct experience with what you're dealing with and can only imagine how painful it must be. What I do know from my days in youth development research is that if you can hang in there and keep loving her and expressing your love, more often than not it will make a difference. You're getting an adolescent double whammy—not just the usual disdain, but active anger. But kids who had parents that hung in there and didn't disconnect and kept coming back with love, no matter how far they tried to push the parent away (how's that for an easy challenge) were the ones who ultimately got through all of the troubles of adolescence more easily. But man, how hard!

And how hard to be the easiest target to blame, but even though none of us are perfect parents (even if that is what you are being faulted for!) it's not your fault. It really, really isn't. You are a

beautiful, clear, shining light (even when you don't feel like one),
and she's awfully lucky to have you for a mom as she goes through
this. I wish there were something more I could do or say, but please
know you have my support and if you need to vent or be coached or
be reminded of your magnificence, please call me.
    Very fondly,
    Ann
    Ann Betz, Coaching, Training, Leadership
    www.BeAboveLeadership.com

    Here's a novel idea: What if every treatment center in the
world would simply say Ann's words to the hurting families who
are bringing their loved one into their centers—actually make
it a required part of the assessment process? They would have
instant allies who would be much more supportive of the work
they are doing.

    Or maybe it could be made into posters to hang in waiting
rooms all over the world. My hunch is that the recovery rates
would be much better.

BECKY'S TIPS:

1. Prepare stock responses for people who don't know how to
   support you. Then, when you are emotionally and physically
   wiped out and caught off guard, you can retrieve your memo-
   rized comment/answer. For example, when someone says,
   "Can't you just tell her to stop?" You could reply, "Right now
   we just need love and support." Or if you hear: "I didn't think
   boys got eating disorders." A stock answer could be, "Unfortunately more than you would believe. We can use good
   thoughts."

2. Be prepared for people (anyone, whether they are friends,
   family, or care providers) to say insensitive things. Have

another stock response ready for the really insensitive ones. For instance, if your loved one has overdosed or attempted suicide and someone says, "Well, you know it was just a cry for help; she wasn't really trying to kill herself," it might be the right time to say, "That is so incredibly unhelpful, I just need your compassion please."

3. Worry isn't necessary. Worry is a choice, an option and a waste of time because most things we worry about don't happen.

4. Getting pulled into drama is optional.

5. You have a choice about how you react to challenges.

6. You can actively choose to let go of suffering (I'm not saying this is easy).

7. Find a way to tap into your fearlessness—it may be facing the worst-case scenario that frees you.

8. Practice separating the person you love from the eating disorder. It isn't easy, but it will help you both.

9. You can be happy, even if your child is not, but you have to work at it.

10. Keep looking until you find the treatment that works for your family member—there is no one treatment (so far) that works for everyone.

It appears that including parents and families is important in the treatment of adolescents with anorexia nervosa. It also seems that giving parents direct control over the management of disordered eating and other behaviors associated with anorexia nervosa is an effective strategy for helping adolescents with this disease. In published follow-up studies from the Maudsley group, overall outcomes suggest that up to 90% of adolescents who received family treatment using this model recovered. In contrast, studies of the overall prognosis of anorexia nervosa suggest that fewer than 50% would be expected to recover.

—James Lock, M.D., Ph.D., Dr. Lock is the coauthor of *Treatment Manual for Anorexia Nervosa: A Family-Based Approach,* which further describes the Maudsley approach and ongoing research by Dr. Lock and his colleagues at Stanford University.

2

Laura's Story

Family-Based Therapy—Currently Our Most Effective Intervention

Parents are not to blame and can be a major help in recovery. The Maudsley Family-Based Therapy Approach (FBT) includes the family from the beginning and empowers them to take an active role in recovery. It is hard for me to understand why utilizing parents as a valuable resource in their child's eating disorder treatment can still be considered a unique concept by some. Equally challenging is that this approach which has been around for over twenty years, has recently been called, "obscure."

Having been on the receiving end of the old-fashioned "parentectomy" model of blaming and excluding parents in eating disorders treatment, you can imagine my thrill when I found out about Maudsley Family-Based Therapy.

I first learned of the family-friendly Maudsley approach when my family was in the midst of our frustration with ineffective treatment. At that time, though, it was being used successfully only with anorexia and since we were mainly facing bulimia I didn't give it much more consideration. By the time I saw the University of Chicago call for clinical trials for bulimia patients we were deeply involved in a program that seemed promising. If I allowed myself to play the "What-if?" game I'd fantasize about how my daughter might have recovered in a year or two if we had traveled to Chicago and given that study a try. But it is useless to play that game and I am allowing myself to simply be grateful that Dr. Daniel LeGrange at the University of Chicago and Stanford's Dr. James Lock have been finding success using these methods with people diagnosed with both bulimia nervosa and anorexia nervosa.

As with any treatment there are different levels of care. Utilizing the family as part of the treatment team can be a part of many approaches to recovery. Some treatment providers are slow to embrace this concept even though a big shift in thinking about the role of parents came about in 2006 when the American Psychiatric Association published its Practice Guidelines for the Treatment of Patients With Eating Disorders (Third Edition) http://www.psychiatryonline.com/pracGuide/pracGuide-Topic_12.aspx. The APA said "No evidence exists to prove that families cause eating disorders" (Section II.A.3.), and that for children and adolescents the Maudsley approach "is the most effective intervention" (Section, I.B.3.a).

In the September 2007 issue of *Archives of General Psychiatry*, a University of Chicago Medical Center team reported that almost 40 percent of participants in family-based treatment had stopped bingeing and purging compared to only 18 percent of those who received supportive psychotherapy, the standard therapy.

"Parents are in a unique position to help their adolescents," says Dr. le Grange, "yet treatment typically excludes them from the process. Now we have the evidence that we need to bring them back in."

The trial, conducted at the University of Chicago, involved 80 adolescents, aged 12 to 19, with a diagnosis of bulimia nervosa (typically characterized by binge eating and purging) or partial bulimia. Although the family-based approach produced good results, the research isn't clear whether it was the family involvement or the focus on eating behavior found in family-based treatment that was responsible for the improved outcomes.

In the following story, an Australian mom, Laura, shares the success her family has achieved using Maudsley Family-Based Therapy (FBT) to treat her daughter's bulimia.

SAVING OUR VIOLET

Violet soared off the high dive with the sky as the backdrop. She looked like an angel floating down to us. Allowing Violet to compete internationally in springboard diving has given our family the opportunity to travel the world with her team and enjoy many fun times together. With so many reports suggesting that teens involved in sports do better in school, get into less trouble and are healthier, my husband and I encouraged and supported Violet's participation in diving.

Springboard diving seemed to give Violet's delicate teenage self-esteem the boost it needed. We never suspected it could lead to a life-threatening illness.

Her father, Mike, and I know it is useless to blame the sport; we'll never know for sure what triggered Violet's bulimia, which quickly progressed into a serious illness when she was 16. Still, we often wonder *What if.* What if she was not in such a body-focused sport? Would the eating disorder still have happened?

When I started to learn more about eating disorders I found that much has been written about how eating disorders are found in all sports, but athletes participating in activities that emphasize leanness for performance and appearance are at a significantly greater risk. Thus, gymnasts, long-distance runners, divers, jockeys, figure skaters, wrestlers and others are more prone to developing eating disorders and related problems than those who compete in non weight-restricting sports such as volleyball or football.

I was surprised to learn that jockeys embark on extreme programs to reduce their weight with a method known as "wasting," which can include a combination of starvation, dehydration, excessive sauna use and self-induced vomiting or "flipping." Our daughter's experience with bulimia was similar. Violet also reacted much like the jockeys in that she was more depressed and anxious when trying to achieve a certain weight.

We know three things: we can't blame one particular thing such as sports; *we* are not to blame (as we were initially led to believe); and no one chooses to have this illness. Society treats these girls like they are obsessed with their bodies but in Violet's case, that wasn't true. She was not obsessed with her body; she was obsessed with diving, so much so that we moved from one city to another so she could train with the national program on scholarship at a well-known sports institute here in Australia.

It was about the time of the move in 2006 that I became concerned about her moods and lack of coping skills when dealing with stress. I knew two girls on her dive team had eating disorders and the competition to be lean was tremendous.

There were red flags but more than two years went by before I was convinced Violet was purging. On four separate occasions I asked her if she made herself throw up (I had found evidence on the toilet) and she stared me in the eye and said, "No Momma, I would never starve myself—I love food too much." I think now she was lying, trying to throw me off track.

This wasn't the only red flag that we witnessed. Mike often commented, "Oh, the time that girl spends in the shower, what could she be doing?" She finally admitted to us, after she had begun treatment, that she often threw up in the shower.

Violet had two episodes of severe stomach pain but both times it was thought to be a virus. Then she became very ill with a kidney infection that left her in the hospital on IV antibiotics for four days. She was very concerned about eating the hospital food, so I would go home to prepare meals for her. One day I was delayed getting back to the hospital and she rang, in a bit of distress, to see where I was. That same day I took her to get a frappe (shake/smoothie). When she learned they were out of the flavor she wanted she broke down. At the time, I chalked it up to her emotional distress.

One day in 2009, though, I made a loaf of banana bread the same day my employer sent a basket of chocolates to the house. In less than a day both disappeared. At that point I sat her down and told her she had to tell me what was happening with regard to her eating as I was becoming very worried. I said to her, "You have to tell me what is up." Suddenly she was like a very small child and said, "Momma, I have been making myself sick." We made a pact that day that we would get through it. I wasn't angry but I felt sad that she hadn't told her dad and me. Violet told me she hadn't said anything because she didn't want us to think we were bad parents.

Her coach had made comments about her size. She is tall (5'5") for her sport, and he was constantly reminding her that she was one of the "biggest" divers. When an athlete gets to the level of pre-training for Olympic tryouts the competition becomes so cut-throat that anything goes and all the coaches care about is peak performance, no matter what it takes.

Violet had seen a sports psychologist at the sports institute who referred her to the institute's sports dietician. When the dietician put her on a 1700-calorie-a-day diet (much less than the amount she really needed while competing) she felt like a total failure because she couldn't stick to those few calories. She told us she gave up and gave in to the bingeing and purging. She admitted she had been sporadically bingeing and purging for about two years. Unfortunately, she was not reviewed, after the initial visits, by either the sports psychologist or the sports dietician and was never counseled to tell her parents.

Once we realized how intense her anxiety was we started her on a treatment called Pfieffer Therapy that helped her step back and reassess a situation. She found that it helped her day-to-day anxiety levels drop from 7 out of 10 to a 4 out of 10 and though in stressful situations her anxiety can be as bad as ever, she feels that it has helped as a layer of treatment that includes pharmaceuticals and supplements. She takes vitamin B6, which keeps her calm when she is on the right dose (one doctor made a mistake and put her on too much; she had an incredible outburst). Another supplement she takes is Sam-e; after taking Sam-e Violet told me it was the first time she felt calm. She now tells us she recalls feeling anxious as far back as age 4.

She also saw a doctor who specializes in people with eating disorders. After an electrocardiogram (EKG) and blood work, we learned that Violet had a low potassium level. The doctor mentioned that Violet had to eat certain foods to increase her serotonin levels but there was no real nutritional advice.

I suspected that some days the only thing she kept down was breakfast—and Violet concurred. Sometimes I wonder if the only way she made it through 28 hours of training a week was due to the nutritionist who told us to do shakes with whole grains, fruit and lots of good protein.

We did Cognitive Behavioral Therapy (CBT) for two months. It was terrible. My daughter went to them as a bulimic who had a good relationship with her parents and became someone who was more severely bulimic, aggressive and blaming, and lied to her therapist about her bingeing and purging. The therapist actually said, "I really think Violet should be getting some CBT away from her parents" to which I angrily responded, "Violet has sustained a biological brain injury from malnourishment. She does not need to be separated from her parents." As her mother I sensed that this was far more serious than anyone realized.

Through my research on bulimia I learned that mood swings during recovery are pretty normal but we have found it hard to cope at times. Bulimia Nervosa (BN) can make these kids uncaring, self-centered and just plain untruthful.

Things between us got worse quickly. At times Violet was great company and would tell us she was relieved to be getting support. Then she would be quite aggressive. After one of her attacking outbursts, saying awful things to me, I thought, *And this is the same girl who wanted to go out for coffee yesterday.* She called the next day and apologized.

Once we knew about the bingeing and purging we discovered how much money she had gone through buying "binge-foods" then replacing the foods she had purged. We discovered that to support the binges, she had been stealing money out of an account we used to pay our bills—well over $5,000! Mike had given her the password so she could have money while she was off at competitions. We knew this wasn't our kid—it was the eating disorder, the compulsion, shame and secrecy.

I began searching the Internet for help and wasn't making progress. I was becoming increasingly worried about both my daughter's moodiness and a concerning relationship she became involved in. So I sought a counseling appointment through an eating disorder organization, FEAST-ED. I first logged on to the site on Christmas Eve, 2009. This is where I learned about Maudsley Family-Based Therapy (FBT).

A basic summary of Maudsley Family-Based Therapy is that it is a three-phase approach beginning with refeeding to restore health. In the second phase, responsibility for feeding is returned to the adolescent (who may now be an adult). The third phase is establishing a healthy identity in the patient.

Violet's second sports psychologist told us that Maudsley FBT only works with very young girls with anorexia (AN), not BN or older girls. He told us she had to do this recovery on her own and wouldn't refer her for therapy. Actually, both practitioners told me she had to "go it alone." I have to ask—*If my daughter was able to recover on her own, why was she asking for help?* The "help" we got was not only outdated but also entrenched her symptoms. She got worse and we wasted time that could have been helping her instead of hurting her further.

Soon after, I fortunately happened to see a sign advertising FBT and through that we found a therapist trained in FBT. We got started on Phase I—refeeding, which required three meals and three snacks each day. That regimen gave Violet the power she needed over the eating disorder for the first time. The theory is that those with bulimia get too hungry from holding off and then end up bingeing and purging. Following the three meals/three snacks rules gave her self-esteem and took away the shame, guilt, desperation and feeling she had no control.

Our therapist sent Violet off for an energy expenditure test, which showed that while we were in the Phase I of Maudsley refeeding her metabolism was fast. The test indicated that just to have enough energy to get out of bed she needed 2,400 calories a day. The nutritionist we found, who specializes in treating eating disorders with this approach, told us that due to her high metabolism rate (130%) she needed close to 3,000 calories a day.

Violet became very worried about gaining weight as we began the refeeding. The therapist helped her by drawing stick figures showing her as tiny and the eating disorder as much larger. He said that until we made her as big as the eating disorder she would be governed by it. He also drew stick figures representing Violet and her possessive, controlling boyfriend, saying that until she felt larger than him she would still be controlled by him. At this time, however, she is still with him. It is baffling to me that she can't see she is being controlled by him. One of her friends told me that Violet said that she wants someone with money and we know this isn't her value. It's fair to say some disordered thinking still occurs.

I learned from Becky that many fathers are reluctant to share their stories. So often women will talk and get things off their chest and men will go into their cave, so to speak. I think mothers often take on the role of refeeding and fathers are sidelined. That's not true in our family.

My daughter is very fond and affectionate with her father. His opinion of her matters a lot. I truly believe my husband has done all that is in his power to do for his children. He is a wonderful, gorgeous man who has always prepared meals and discussed recovery with Violet. He has also held his role in her recovery to be really important. Currently, he is taking part in a father's study at Kings College that is looking at the role of fathers in this situation. I wish more men understood how important they are in their daughter's lives.

To an outside observer it may seem odd that I didn't confront Violet when I first began suspecting she was entering a danger zone with her exercise and eating behaviors. Looking back, I see that if this happened now I would intervene earlier and firmly. I didn't confront her because I thought she would be ashamed. The shame involved with bulimia nervosa (BN) is incredibly powerful and I didn't want to set that off and cause more problems.

Now in Phase II and learning to reclaim feeding herself, Violet can still be governed by her compulsions. As I write this she has been binge/purge-free for 28 weeks. Ever since beginning Phase I and eating three meals and three snacks each day, she has not binged or purged. Up until about 16 weeks I wasn't sure that she would never binge or purge again. Then after 17 weeks Violet said she knew there was no going back. She said, "Until we did Maudsley, I thought I would never get better."

Things can still be volatile during times of stress. She is still on the diving team and tryouts for different events can cause distress. The feelings she used to suppress with bingeing and purging are now erupting and can create this volatility, which is normal in the recovery of the illness. We are continuing to be patient and it helps that she is still seeing the same FBT therapist to address how she feels while she learns new coping strategies.

We have found support and help anywhere and everywhere we can. For instance, even though my mother-in-law and I have not always seen eye to eye, she was fantastic when Violet was in Phase I and would help out so I could have a break. We told Nanna that she was to give Violet the 3+3 and the most choice that Violet could have would be: "Do you want cheese and biscuits or yogurt?" This gave Violet time to connect with her nanna in a way that was really honest. Nanna would prepare the meals and Mike and I were grateful that we could come home and simply have a meal.

Gradually, we have progressed to where Violet is measuring out her food from larger sized containers instead of having the portion sizes and individual servings prepared and given to her. She is even able to manage the "fear" foods such as ice cream. Just last week we were able to go back to the large size tub of yogurt, without fear she would eat the entire tub in one sitting.

We have celebrated each week of staying on track and being free of bingeing and purging. At week 14 we got little bottles of bubbles and blew them while we sat at the table; during week 19 we played the Steely Dan song, "Hey 19"— little things to mark the progress of another week of recovery. We have also kept our sense of humor as much as possible and have joked about the line from the movie *Napoleon Dynamite*—"Just Eat the Food, Tina!" Keeping this sense of humor has also been important for all of us.

We are so grateful for Maudsley family-based therapy and the eating plan that helped Violet. She now realizes she doesn't have the normal cues for hunger and satiety so she needs to stick with a plan. I feel that for the rest of her life she will have to have food available at all times, such as a protein bar in her bag.

Marcia Herrin, Ed.D., M.PH., R.D., L.D., an expert in Maudsley FBT, has said that one thing that makes Maudsley so good for families with BN is there is an awareness in people with bulimia of wanting to change the illness that isn't usually present with people who have anorexia. Marcia's work has shown that those with bulimia have a higher sense of self-awareness that what they're doing (bingeing and purging) isn't a good thing to be doing and that they are ill. She also says that since girls with BN tend to be more compulsive and rebellious, these very characteristics combined with their often strong-willed nature will help them recover. We're counting on it.

LAURA'S TIPS:

1. If you suspect an eating disorder trust your parental intuition and pursue medical attention.

2. Research different types of treatment and find one that fits for your family situation.

3. If your child is in a body focused sport be aware of the messages they are getting from their coaches and counter negative messages.

4. Since most eating disorders begin with a diet, have conversations with your child as to what he/she is hoping to accomplish by dieting.

5. Household chores have been shown to be important in improving a teen's self-esteem. Make sure that your child plays an integral role in chores.

6. Try to keep a sense of humor alive while supporting your child in recovery.

7. Find little ways to celebrate the milestones in recovery.

8. For teens in elite sports or training for the Olympics, make yourself familiar with the IOC guidelines for coaches.

3

Tia, Sadie, and Kathy's Stories

Recognize the Differences in the Three Most Common Eating Disorders

Remember, Eating Disorder Not Otherwise Specified (EDNOS) is the *largest* group of eating disorders. It surprises many to learn that anorexia is the least common eating disorder.

I find it particularly frustrating that many people, including an unfortunately large number of health care providers, don't understand that a person of *any size* can have an eating disorder. Too many people have had treatment delayed because they were told that they "couldn't have an eating disorder" because they were not "sick enough" or "too heavy." These erroneous comments will feed the eating disorder's voice and give it the opportunity to grow stronger while its host body grows weaker.

"She doesn't look like she has an eating disorder" is an all-too-common statement. It's like saying someone doesn't "look" like they have a heart defect.

The following stories are grouped together to highlight the fact that EDNOS and BED are the most common eating disorders. The three women I interviewed for this chapter are still in varying stages of recovery. I wanted you to hear the voices of people who were recently, or are still actively, using disordered eating behaviors.

It's important to understand how the person still in recovery might hear or misinterpret things that are said. For example, most of us would have little or no reaction to someone making a statement about a particular food being "too rich," but for someone with an eating disorder, hearing that could trigger destructive behaviors or, in the lingo of the eating disorder world it could, "be a trigger."

These three women all shared with me very painful, personal experiences, hoping that families everywhere might become better equipped with what to say, and what *not to* say to most effectively support a loved one in recovery. This can vary depending on the type of treatment chosen. For instance, the more traditional treatment programs have a paradigm in which they suggest the family not talk about food, whereas a more family-based approach, e.g., Maudsley Family Based Therapy (FBT), encourages discussion about food.

BINGE EATING DISORDER (BED) AND BULIMIA NERVOSA (BN)

Many people wonder why binge eating disorder and bulimia are two different eating disorders. Hopefully Kathy's story will help to sort this out. The two illnesses can be very similar and yet BED does not have the purging characteristic. Purging can take many forms—over-exercise, laxative and diuretic use, as well as vomiting. Kathy's story highlights the fact that a person can have more than one eating disorder.

KATHY'S STORY OF BINGE EATING DISORDER (BED) AND BULIMIA NERVOSA (BN)

When an addiction begins, a person can stop developing emotionally, a direct result of the body and mind being deprived of proper nutrients. Though the jury is still out as to whether or not eating disorders are addictions, I know I stopped developing emotionally when, at age twelve, I went on what the girls in my dance class were told was the "Diet for Dancers," a completely fat-free diet.

The brain needs some fat to thrive, function, and grow. Since my brain wasn't getting *any* fat, I stopped growing emotionally and didn't develop certain life skills. Frankly, I know I still have a lot of growing to do, even though I'm now in my 20s.

I was heavy as early as elementary school. In fifth grade, when the zipper on my favorite pair of jeans broke, one boy asked, "Why is her zipper down?" A second boy answered, "Because she is fat." At age 10, this was so painful and embarrassing, I wanted to curl up and die. I had never heard anything like that before and had no clue how to react—and I don't remember how I did react. At that moment I believe the seed was planted that I was different, and it wasn't okay to be me. I got the clear message—I wasn't good enough.

It didn't help that even though my family wasn't wealthy, I grew up in a very well-to-do suburb where the girls were really, really mean. I was a dancer and skater, two of the more dangerous sports for people at risk for eating disorders. Most of the girls were skinny, and I started comparing myself to them. I wasn't skinny, didn't have designer jeans, blond highlights in my hair or wear makeup at age 12 like the rest of them. It didn't take long to notice that the skinny girls got chosen to compete in the higher levels and, being fat, I was in the lowest level.

I felt I was "different" at home too. My dad and sister are slim and very much into exercise. I was chubby and into food.

It seemed I never felt full. When I reached for dessert or a second helping at dinner, my dad would ask, "Do you *really* want that, Kathy?" "Do you *really* need that?" Then he would look at me as if he was ashamed of me. The spoken and unspoken messages told me what I was doing was wrong and, just as important, I continued hearing that there was something wrong with me.

No one really knows the exact causes of eating disorders, but I lean toward believing that I have a genetic predisposition to addiction, which, fueled by the fat-free diets, teasing, shaming, and feeling "wrong," all led me down the slippery slope toward an eating disorder.

When the eating disorder slowly crept into my life, I noticed that when I was "in my disease" (as I say to describe the times when the eating disorder was in control), I didn't feel anything, which felt good.

I was desperate for something to take away that feeling of being "wrong" or different from everyone else. I am sure that is confounding to a family member, hearing that the eating disorder is not about the food (although, as so many experts in the field will tell you, food is the "medicine" we need to get well).

For me, using the eating disorder behaviors or symptoms gave me the escape I craved. With the eating disorder, nothing mattered, not my family or school, nothing. I felt hollow, not caring if I lived or died. Even though I became dangerously ill, living without feelings was so much better that for a few years it was a fairly effective coping mechanism. Eventually, I learned a very high price is paid that outweighs the benefits.

From age 12 through my junior year in college, I used the eating disorder to cope with the deep-seated pain of feeling worthless and "wrong." When I was finally in recovery and learning how to feel again, I asked my dad, "Why does it hurt so much to grow?"

Sometime during the years of extensive purging, I lost my gag reflex, which resulted in a turning point for the eating disorder and me. During my junior year of college I was using a spoon to help purge, and accidentally swallowed the spoon. It had to be surgically removed.

For another year and a half, I still didn't admit I had a problem, even though I drank heavily. As a dance major I was so used to seeing disordered eating patterns that I somehow was able to normalize what I was doing. I thought I had things under control since I had a dietician, I was going to an outpatient program, and I was seeing doctors regularly.

I switched majors and began studying for my doctorate in physical therapy. During this time, I relapsed for another seven months, at which time my school forced me into treatment.

I had become hypersensitive, over-reactive, and was so dramatic that I would numb out to escape these emotions. I went into treatment in the South, which is where I realized the role the eating disorder played in all this.

In this new treatment program, I was empowered by daily support to learn to deal with my emotions and life changes without putting down or picking up food. I learned that, together, with the help and support of others in recovery, we could do it. I had previously tried to do it all by myself. Alone, I couldn't admit defeat or climb the first step toward recovery.

This treatment center's 12-step program saved my life. With the recognition that I am an addict, I am now able to see that it is my nature to be irritable, restless, and discontent. I have learned to live with those qualities and love myself. I have built relationships, created a career, and embraced being 100-percent myself, which has allowed me to have many wonderful facets to my life, including a boyfriend.

Another huge part of my recovery has been a branch of Overeaters Anonymous (OA) called OA How, a very aggressive 12-step program for compulsive overeaters. OA How has been the greatest gift in so many ways. It has brought a relationship with God that I had always wanted, which fills the void I had been trying to fill with the eating disorder, just like many other addictions.

It has also allowed me to have healthy relationships with other people. Without OA How, I wouldn't have my job, friends, successes, gifts, or boyfriend.

Many people have a negative reaction to the intensity, structure, and time commitment required for OA How. At first glance, it looks like you're trading in your addiction for an addiction to measuring food, calling your sponsor, and going to meetings.

I weigh and measure all of the food prescribed by my dietician and I do daily reading and writing. In addition, I report to my sponsor each morning for 15 minutes, eat six times a day and make three daily calls to others in my group. I report everything I eat to my sponsor. It sounds like an enormous commitment; it is. And it saved my life and has given me a life that is fulfilling and joyful.

OA How is intense, takes a lot of work and is not for everyone. But before you judge it, please go to an open meeting in your town and see how it has liberated the amazing people you will meet there.

Becky told me that when she visited an open group she was absolutely blown away by the courage, strength, and tenacity of the members. So when you see someone weighing their food on a tiny portable scale, you can give them the gift of support by acknowledging that you admire their commitment to their health. One last benefit I will mention about OA How: it is free. As you know, if you love someone with an eating disorder, you can go broke paying for treatment. This is an option that anyone can afford.

Everyone around me is so helpful and supportive of the OA How program I am in. If I'm going out, I usually bring my food with me. At home my mom will make a separate meal for me, weighing the portions.

Tonight I am going to dinner with my boyfriend at a spa. I called the spa yesterday and asked them to weigh and measure the food for me in the kitchen, and they were very happy to do that. I also ask to have food steamed or grilled with no oils or sauces. I have found many places to be very accommodating of my requests.

It might be useful to know that at times my weight was much too high; at other times, much too low for me to maintain health. My recovery team and I have found that I need to abstain from sugar, alcohol, and white flour, as those seem to combine in my body to create a drug that leads to loss of hunger cues for me. This is not for everyone, but it works for me.

Currently I am reading *Anatomy of a Food Addiction: The Brain Chemistry of Overeating,* which is helping me to understand the physiology of addiction and accept that I am powerless over food. I have learned from my past that I have lost the ability to make good decisions about food.

I know the scale doesn't lie. The same amount of food one day can seem like too much while the next day it can seem like not enough. I used to base my intake on emotion. Now I don't worry about the amounts. If the scale tells me to eat that amount, I know my body can handle it. Using the scale takes away a lot of pressure.

For over a year now I have maintained a weight that my care team says is acceptable. I don't want to share too many particulars about my weights, sizes or coping behaviors, because I know that people still in recovery may find their eating disorder sees those as milestones that it will then try to meet. Often the eating disorder will taunt the person with "See, she got to *that* weight and didn't die—you can do it too."

For parents/family/friends, my advice to you is to live by example. Exercise moderately and eat healthy, well-balanced meals. Don't make food the emphasis or the reward. For instance, when you go for a walk, let that be the treat, not the ice cream you stop for at the end. Let it be the movie, not the popcorn. This is not always easy if this hasn't been your habit, so get help figuring out how to walk this fine line. Have family dinners and spend time together having fun, living well-balanced lives.

I am now a doctor of physical therapy and wish my story brings you hope for your loved one and yourself.

KATHY'S TIPS:

1. Live by example. Exercise moderately and eat healthy, well-balanced meals.

2. Check out 12-step programs in your community—Al-Anon has helped families of those with eating disorders to cope.

3. Talk with your family about bullying and teasing people about their size. Try not to comment on anyone's size; model being respectful, not judgmental. Realize that even young girls hear the (unintentionally) negative messages from their parents and family.

4. Even if you don't understand your loved one's treatment program choices, try to support them by asking how you can help.

5. Learn as much as you can about eating disorders so you can be as supportive as possible of your loved one's complex illness.

6. Different treatment programs work for different people; recovery is not a "one size fits all." Keep trying until you find what works for you—it may be that the program is failing you, *not* you failing it.

7. Until your loved one is ready to admit his or her addiction, share your concerns using "I" statements such as "I am concerned about your health." Be prepared to show them some resources for help.

8. Medical researchers are working hard around the world to find out what causes these disorders and how to help people recover from them. There are often free research studies to participate

in that may help you and further the needed research. If an Internet search doesn't show what you are looking for, try the major universities with medical centers.

9. Be gentle with yourself as well as your loved one.

EATING DISORDER NOT OTHERWISE SPECIFIED (EDNOS)

In my experience, EDNOS can involve food restriction, over-exercising and bingeing, any and all of which can change, depending on moods, stress levels or sometimes for no apparent reason. Tia has BED and has been diagnosed with EDNOS.

For most people who are not living with an eating disorder, the idea of bingeing and then purging, throwing up food you've just eaten, is simply gross. Bingeing is also gross for those who live every second with an eating disorder. It's important to realize that, emotionally, many find it more difficult to binge than restrict food.

TIA'S STORY: WHAT HELPED AND WHAT DIDN'T HELP

My eating disorder started when I was about 12 years old. By high school, I was bingeing and restricting—and the bingeing really scared my family. They watched as I added over-exercising to the destructive behaviors. How much I did of any of the three really depended on how stressed I was at the time.

It was always easier for me to be "happier," at least on the outside, when I was restricting what I ate. I tended to be more depressed after bingeing because I felt it meant I'd lost control, again.

So, why did I do it? That's the 10 million dollar question. Each person is different; in my case bingeing my way through my cupboards became a way to cope with my emotional pain and the purging eased my guilt about the binge and helped me regain a sense of control (albeit false). Afterward when the depression set in as it always did, I felt guilty about what I had just done. This is what happened to me, but I have heard of other binge eaters who purged constantly just to try to lose weight. As I got better, ironically I became more irritable and unsatisfied. Why? My therapist explained that because I was giving something up I missed the sense of control that the eating disorder had given me, which made me cranky.

In spite of being in "recovery," the eating disorder so badly wanted to stay alive in me, *we* became hyper-vigilant, thinking every raised eyebrow, word, and action was a criticism so I often struck back. Soon people didn't know what was okay to say to me.

It was sometimes helpful to hear someone say, "You're doing better." However, my reactions would vary, based on my mood that day. It has really been a two-steps-forward/three-steps-back process. To play it safe, I suggest avoiding saying someone looks like they are doing better because it may empower the eating disorder.

I appreciated it when people would ask me directly, "When I say, 'you look a lot better,' does it help you?" But it would depend on the person and the way they said it.

My mom is never sick, is quite calm and seldom exaggerates. For my dad, though, everything is always a big deal. After I was diagnosed my parents found it helpful to occasionally see my therapist without me. With her help they learned to separate fact from fiction, and how to recognize the symptoms. It helped to take the mystery out of my eating disorder. They also learned how to communicate better with me. Before each appointment, we discussed what they could and could not talk about with my therapist.

I ended up in a traditional treatment center in the Midwest

while I was still in high school. In treatment the message I heard was to not talk about diet, appearance or food, but at home my health conscious mother was always on a "diet," talking about cellulite and making other body comments. "Innocent" comments like hers can have an enormous impact on someone with an eating disorder.

When I went off to college in the Southeast, ED was my constant companion. The college environment was a tough transition for me: strong competition, studying, lots of stress, drinking, and crazy sleep patterns. I would eat pizza late one night and forget to eat at all the next night.

During high school, I had been in a very structured treatment program. College presented freedom and choices. At college, my ED was really strong, and I ended up in treatment again, this time near the college. I was far away from family and friends and learned quickly that this treatment center's philosophy was quite different from the first one in the Midwest.

The Midwest center looked at how they could get me back to normal, get rid of the ED and the accompanying thoughts. The center near my college tried to minimize the effects of the ED, and help me live with it. This change in philosophy was very difficult and confusing for me.

Here is what I learned from my bingeing:
- I was going to do it—or not. No one else can prevent it.
- Stress, emotions and anxiety affected that. For example, I could have a delicious array of food in front of me, and not binge.
- Don't take away the special foods, for me Oreos and ice cream were my special foods. Instead, help your loved one deal with the emotions behind it.
- I came up with creative ways to avoid bingeing. When I bought Oreos, I repackaged them into smaller packs. I found

when I have a whole package in front of me, it's easier to overeat—again tied to my emotions.
• Portion control is essential. I now know what a healthy portion of food is.

As the treatment center near my college taught me to minimize the effects of the eating disorder and helped maximize my positive qualities I became aware of the role self-control had been playing in my eating disorder. Self-control is usually thought to be a good thing. For people with certain personality traits such as perfectionism, inflexibility, discipline, doubt and the need for order, it can become dangerous. [Note from Becky: for example, athletes with one or more of these traits can become too dedicated to their sports and spiral out of control when they get hurt or have to quit for other reasons. The transition to inactivity can be very difficult as a result of these traits.]

My recovery has progressed and I've learned it's important for me to schedule meals with people—even if I have to "fake it" during the meal. Eating alone is really hard, but when eating with others, I tend not to over- or under-eat.

I like it when I can be with people who do not know about my eating disorder; I can just hang out without them watching my every move. Some people in my life have to know, but it's nice to have other friends who don't know about the "elephant in the middle of my plate."

I've learned it's important to be able to cook and have a good relationship with food. As my dietician says, "If you eat to live, instead of live to eat, you are creating a healthy relationship with food."

As I get further into my recovery, I couldn't care less what other people say about food. But earlier on, while learning to have a healthy relationship with food, it was not helpful to hear my family's comments about food. I know they didn't realize what they said—or how it was interpreted by my eating disorder.

Shopping for clothing was always a pain; during high school my mom would bring the same jeans to the changing room in several sizes. I never looked at the size, just how well the jeans fit. I keep clothes in different sizes because my weight fluctuates. Whatever size I am, I wear clothes that fit, because clothes that are too tight make me constantly conscious of my body. Shopping with friends is hard because there is always so much conversation about "size" so I avoid it.

Grocery shopping can also be very stressful and cause anxiety. If I make a list ahead of time, and stick to it, I need to make fewer choices while shopping and it's less stressful.

After my first treatment program, my parents did a lot of things that were very helpful. They understood that:

• This was a *real struggle* for me.
• Just because I attended a month-long treatment program, I wasn't "all better."
• I might slip/relapse during recovery. Recovery, they learned, can take a long time, which is hard for some people to accept.
• They did a good job of saying: "Well, you didn't have a good day today, but that's okay. Tomorrow is another day."

Recently, I've seen how an eating disorder can affect family members. My friend Pam's older sister has developed an eating disorder and Pam is really angry. From her point of view, her sister's behavior is irrational, selfish and has upset everyone in her family. Pam's reaction has shown me how important it is for family members to talk to someone openly and honestly (like a therapist) to learn how to deal with the eating disorder.

This vantage point, seeing another family from the outside

looking in helped me take responsibility for the impact of my eating disorder on my family.

I am about to graduate from college—another transition—and am hoping that, without the college environment, things may actually get easier for me. To be around so many students who are constantly dieting is really low-hanging fruit for my eating disorder to grab onto. I look forward to having a more structured schedule and being around people who are focused on more important things than what they look like.

TIA'S TIPS:

1. Remember that most of us with eating disorders cannot see the grey areas.

2. It is not the family's job to prevent a binge; we are either going to do it or not.

3. Seeing products in the house that say "diet" or "low-fat" can be extremely challenging until we are recovered enough to address these realities.

4. Your loved one in recovery doesn't understand what is going on so don't expect that you can understand.

5. Phone, email or texting may be an easier form of communication for someone in recovery than face-to-face communication.

6. Try to reinforce the messages that your loved one is getting in treatment—this involves open communication. Having a family therapist who has signed permission to talk with care providers can support this effort. Then the family can ask during a therapy session what they can be doing to support the treatment messages.

7. Understand the philosophy of the treatment center.

8. Recovery takes a long time. This is hard for families to accept. Get support for yourself.

BINGE EATING DISORDER (BED)

BED (Binge Eating Disorder) is America's most common eating disorder, affecting more people than anorexia and bulimia combined (an estimated 3.5% of American women and 2% of American men, and those are just the ones who are diagnosed).

As a family member or friend of someone in the grips of an active eating disorder, you may be finding the whole thing very difficult to understand. You probably have many questions such as:

- *What is going on?*
- *Why is this happening?*
- *What will help him or her to get well?*
- *What can I do to help?*

Some experts say that understanding isn't as important as 1) accepting what is, 2) learning your role, and 3) doing those things that your loved one finds supportive. That approach makes sense to me. I support the idea that it's not necessary that the family understand the eating-disordered behaviors to be able to support their loved one's recovery.

Many people who have recovered granted permission to their families to "not understand." Yet, I find that many families *want* to understand, for their own well-being.

As we mentioned before, historically, parents, especially mothers, have been blamed for causing eating disorders in children. This is simply not true. There's no question that some parents do a lot of abusive, neglectful, hurtful things that cause a variety of problems and damage that might make any of these illnesses worse or more difficult to recover from, but *parents cannot cause a brain disease.*

Eating disorders are complex bio-psychosocial illnesses that don't have one direct cause. Think of it as the perfect storm with genetics playing a key role with other *individual* traits contributing. Within families, no matter what is going on with weight issues, it is rare that all of the children develop eating disorders.

That being said, some people in the early stages of recovery are typically so "into" their disorder, which they don't understand, they desperately want someone or something to blame—for their disorder, for their incredibly mixed-up feelings, for their guilt. This is very common, and you may find yourself the target of that blame.

In her story, Sadie says some things that sound very blaming of her family as she shares how her eating disorder developed. She is not yet fully recovered and as I was interviewing her, I could hear her wanting to find something or someone to blame.

Understanding how the mind of a person with an eating disorder works can be elusive—though not necessary for successful treatment, it can be quite helpful for the family. Many of the other stories in this book are directly about hope. The following story about Sadie's journey with Binge Eating Disorder (BED) provides hope in a different way.

This painfully honest portrayal will give you some insights and answers, and will help you realize that you are not alone in the mayhem that eating disorders bring to all the lives affected by them.

SADIE'S STORY

My parents found it difficult to support my interests since I preferred books and theatre to sports. It was much easier for them to relate to my brother because he was good at sports.

As a young girl, going to hockey games with my family was not my idea of fun. Reading and quiet intellectual activities suited me better; I didn't really fit in with the rest of my family. Because we're so different, I didn't particularly like spending time with them. To entice me to hang out with them, they'd say something like, "Let's go to a hockey game; we'll get you food there." They knew I liked to eat and it was an effective way to get me to go with them.

Food was one thing we had in common—something I was actually good at. Mealtimes provided lots of memories, especially with my dad. Sometimes, when veggies were left in the pan, I would sit on Dad's lap as we joked about who could eat the veggies in the fewest bites. This was fun as a kid but, as an adult, I realize I was rewarded for overeating. What seemed like harmless fun as a child, became a problem for me later on.

Biting and thumb sucking were other oral habits that gave me comfort and calmed me. My dad tried very hard to get me to stop; I kept track of where he was in the house so he couldn't catch me sucking my thumb or biting my brother. I sucked my thumb until I was a teenager, even in front of other kids. I became so accustomed to teasing I stopped noticing.

Food became my major link to comfort. During elementary school, when I was the first one home I'd sit in front of the TV and eat an entire box of macaroni and cheese. It didn't seem like a problem at the time; it sure never ruined my appetite for dinner. It's hard to know how much was simply physical appetite, or what void that food was filling.

I eat because I'm: happy, sad, angry or I feel good. I can just as easily binge on sushi or other healthy foods as anything else.

Because I showed such strong abilities scholastically, my parents encouraged me to take the higher-level classes in school. Although they were probably just trying to help me be the best I could be, and saw my potential when I couldn't, the pressure was intense. For example, when I was in sixth grade and had back surgery for scoliosis, I used it as an excuse for a lot of things. A report was due the last day of the school year but I didn't turn it in. Getting away with something was my goal, and I played up the whole "I've been in the hospital" thing. When my dad found out I didn't turn in the paper he came into my room and said, "You are writing that paper or you are not going to do another thing this whole summer!" I quickly finished the paper but this is what I mean by high expectations. He wouldn't let me get away with laziness. He had his point of view of certain ways to live one's life.

Because he didn't understand that there was more than one way to do things, I got frustrated. I feel a lot of my eating disorder has to do with my parents' high expectations. Maybe when I am fully recovered, I will see it differently.

My mother was also concerned about my weight. When I was in junior high school she took me to Weight Watchers. It was one of her attempts to be a good parent. She wasn't evil—Weight Watchers can be a good plan with an excellent nutritional structure, but it *is* a diet and *is* a diet mentality. Most eating disorders begin with a diet.

I keep wondering if things would have been different if, when I was 16, someone had told me that I was perfect just the way I was. Would I have felt good about my body? I've heard that some researchers think eating disorders are genetically based illnesses. I don't believe that.

My eating disorder began with compulsive eating and then Binge Eating Disorder (BED). By college I was regularly sneaking food from other people. I can remember a couple of people making comments, not on how much I ate but the fact that I tried to cover up how much I ate. It wasn't always junk food. Sometimes I would eat six grapefruits, an entire bag of apples or a box of oatmeal. Regular dieting would stress me out, and then I'd go on a food binge and feel bad about myself.

It's hard to tell if the depression came first or was a result of being overweight. Now that I'm an adult, I realize my college issues were about anxiety and not fitting in, not meeting standards (my own as well as other people's). In a typical 24-hour period, I would go over and over my day, and then not be able to sleep. I still blame this partly on worrying about my parent's high expectations.

For a short time in college, I experienced exercise bulimia. Even though I'd never been athletic, I found myself exercising to the extreme, trying to balance out all I had eaten. During this health food and over-exercise phase, I saw a psychiatrist who asked, "Why are you wasting my time when there are *real* sick people?"

I felt like the therapists were laughing at me. Being paranoid was one thing, but having health care providers make insensitive and disrespectful comments only made things worse.

When I visited a highly respected gynecologist for the first time, she clearly had no experience with the poor, overweight or depressed populations. She suggested I go to Weight Watchers without any consideration whether I could afford it. Then she suggested I see another doctor, which I did because during the exam she said, "If you want to lose weight, go over to Asia because they don't have the disgusting weight problems we do in the U.S."

I didn't even realize she was criticizing me because she was so sweet about the way she said it, but when I did realize it I felt she told me *I* was disgusting. She casually mentioned that no doctor would be willing to work with me because if I ever became pregnant I would be a high-risk pregnancy.

By this time I was married. My husband has been so supportive but we have always enabled each other with food, which obviously didn't help either of us except that we were in it together. When it became a medical emergency (a gall bladder attack), he became even more supportive and willingly changed the way he ate too. No matter what, he has always loved me. I have never had the feeling from him that "If you lose weight, I'll love you more." Working so hard as an adult to be okay with myself has yielded me many benefits, including knowing that my weight isn't related to how much my husband loves me.

When I had my gallbladder attack, I didn't want surgery. My husband and I read about a natural way to deal with it, which resulted in completely changing my diet. I started eating vegetables, fruits, and salads, while avoiding fast-food hamburgers and butter. I haven't had a gallbladder attack since.

Another medical problem was Polycystic Ovarian Syndrome (PCOS). Doctors kept telling me I had PCOS but I found a very good doctor who diagnosed Metabolic Syndrome. We don't know if I am overweight due to the Metabolic Syndrome or if I have the syndrome due to being overweight.

I was trying to get pregnant. Unfortunately, doctors kept telling me that if I would just lose ten percent of my body weight, I would become fertile again. My response was, "If I exercised, I would lose weight, but I'm not interested in exercising."

I kept waiting for someone to give me an answer, to give me some help, but I kept hearing, "You just have to keep trying harder." Another doctor, who was also overweight, told me, "Here's the 2,000-calorie-a-day diet—if you want all 2,000 calories in a Snickers, go ahead."

It seemed like I tried everything, including Overeaters Anonymous (OA), which worked for a while. In OA I learned to be okay with the number on the scale, who I am, and my body size. The number doesn't scare me or disgust me anymore. In fact, I have such a healthy sense of my body that when I pass a window and catch my reflection, I am surprised and think, *Who is that?* And then I think, *When did I get so fat?* This interesting dichotomy is a double edged-sword—even though I know my compulsive overeating is dangerous and unhealthy, I also know that being okay with myself, the way I am, is good for me.

Even as an adult, when I become anxious, I want to bite things. Joking with my husband, I'll say, "I'm going to bite you!" It's not really anger, but rather anxiety that creates the urge to bite. It's a way of releasing energy that I don't know how to release. Though I can still fall into my old habits of coping, my anxiety is now controlled well with medication.

Learning to deal with external stimuli has also been a benefit. Much to the surprise of my friends, if I see chocolate chip cookies I am not necessarily going to binge on them. Speaking of cookies, I learned from the book, *Potatoes Not Prozac,* by Kathleen DesMaisons, Ph.D., that I can have cookies—I just need to have them *with* my dinner. When I move the sugar to a meal, my body metabolizes it properly.

It has made a big difference for me to let go of the power to be neurotic about tracking my food in intense detail. The second I go into diet mode, it throws me into neurosis. Diets have been more destructive to me than a lot of things, even the teasing.

Paying so much attention to everything I eat, starting with diets in junior high, was definitely one of the worst things that could have ever happened to me.

Even though I am not currently going to OA due to job changes and a move, I learned about what I call OA 301. It helped me the most with structuring my eating. Here is what it looks like:

3 meals a day

0 snacking

1 day at a time

Saying I'm having three meals a day, no matter how much I eat, works for me. It's about learning when to start, when to stop, and when to wait. Most of us food addicts are pretty good at stopping, and really good at starting. But waiting until the next time to eat is the trick.

Eating protein at the right times of day with the right carbohydrates really worked for me . . . until I lost my job. Getting started again is too hard, and I don't know where I am with recovery right now. Not being sure which end is up is okay; I have a great attitude about it.

Food will always be an issue for me. When I stop having a great attitude, the trick will be finding a new way of being great—new components, a new experiment. It all depends on how much I want to work at it.

Support from those who love me comes in many forms. My dear, lifelong friend, Jan, is an alcoholic who has stopped drinking. Jan wonders aloud to me how one tells a food addict to stop eating. I really appreciated it when she said, "I don't envy you: giving up alcohol was nothing compared to what you have to deal with." It's not that we compare our suffering, but I understood that she felt empathy for the complexity of my food-addiction challenges.

My Overeaters Anonymous sponsor has also been really important. We still correspond via email. Knowing she is out there at any time, and that she can relate, is comforting.

I hope my experiences give you insights so you can be the best possible support person during your loved one's recovery.

SADIE'S TIPS:

1. Comments about weight from anyone—doctors, nurses, family, or friends—are not helpful. Even if you think you are doing someone a favor, it creates more shame.

2. Just having my family listen helps me. If you can simply listen, you will be helping. Trying to fix it doesn't help. Thinking you have the answer doesn't help.

3. As annoying as it is, I have to be patient with myself while I wait to be ready to do it again.

4. I would like my loved ones to say to me, "Here's the solution— a pill that takes this away." But seriously, it is always great when they can say they love me just the way I am.

5. Pressuring people into having weight-loss surgery is not okay. There is so much more to our issues than losing weight.

6. I found the book *Potatoes Not Prozac,* by Kathleen DesMaisons, Ph.D. very useful. Her website is: radiantrecovery.com

7. Sometimes our medications make us feel sick and like we need to throw up, and sometimes they make us gain weight. When we go off our medications, please don't get angry. Ask us what made us go off of them, and then help us find a doctor who will find a better medication without those side effects.

8. Know that even if we are paranoid, we may really be hearing very hurtful comments from our care providers, and it might be useful to come with us or find us new care providers.

4

Chris's Story

Eating Disorders Affect the Parents' Marriage

Walking up to Chris at a coffee shop, I was a bit surprised to see how composed she appeared. She had shared briefly on the phone about the many trials she was facing in addition to her daughter Mary's eating disorder.

Occasionally, her coral-colored lips quivered as she spoke, but her calm, matter-of-fact manner was almost unnerving as she casually spoke of circumstances most of us could barely comprehend. Only sporadically did a tear or two escape from her tired eyes, one of the few giveaways of the toll being taken on her life.

She currently lives with her own health issues as well as the constant worry that her daughter will die from her eating disorder. This is her greatest fear.

I kept having to manage the thoughts going on in my head while interviewing her: *How can she be so conversant? A person walking by would never suspect the stress this woman is under. Why do we feel such an intense need to hold it together when our lives are falling apart? Is there so much stigma attached to eating disorders we can't let others know about the extreme pain we are in?*

It is amazing how we are sometimes able to keep our outer shells so put together when our hearts are breaking. We all do the best we can to manage the blows that life throws at us and Chris was doing a beautiful job of holding it together even though no one had guided her in the essential skills needed to help herself or her daughter.

In a closer-to-perfect world, a parent with a seriously ill child would not face additional challenges. But they do continue and we are not handed just one challenge at a time; too often the challenges snowball. A lot of people lose their jobs, friends and family members die, car crashes happen. Even minor mishaps like the furnace breaking down can easily overwhelm us in a time of crisis. Soon the shoulders start to slump and our heads duck as we anticipate the next drama, the next upheaval.

Chris' story may be a useful tool for family members to share with friends or family who want to be supportive but are having trouble grasping the formidable challenges that exist during this illness.

CHRIS' STORY

One of my biggest frustrations is that I know my daughter Mary's eating disorder is much more serious than my husband Tom thinks it is. Hearing Becky say that she hears this often when speaking to mothers instantly reduced my feelings of isolation. Even though I know men and women experience trauma differently, it has been lonely not having Tom acknowledge the seriousness of her situation. Seeing Mary lose interest in her friends, school, hobbies, and activities has been like watching my child emotionally shutting down before my eyes. When I try to talk with him about how very ill she is, he just says, "She looks okay to me. I don't know what you're so worried about all the time."

When I am lying awake worrying about Mary, I wonder, *How can he just fall right to sleep? I feel so alone.* My annoyance has started to turn into resentment. My logical brain tells me

Tom is dealing with this frightening situation his way but the emotional side of me perceives his reactions as a lack of sensitivity and empathy.

Mary got married young and within months her new husband had found someone else. He made a point of telling her that his new love was slimmer.

The day after her husband left, Mary came over to our house. All Tom did was pat her on the head before walking out of the room. I was beyond frustrated.

Like so many parents who are trying desperately to save their children's lives from these illogical eating disorders, I find it helpful to do research. It is a coping mechanism that is helpful for me, as knowledge helps me reclaim some of the power and control the eating disorder stole when it invaded our lives. Even though some of what I learn is frightening, overall, I feel that being informed helps me support Mary more effectively and helps me know what my role needs to be. There is little else I can do as a parent to help my child.

I am often told by my husband and friends, "Don't do that research because you'll just freak yourself out more." This kind of statement just increases my feelings of isolation and helplessness. I wish they could understand that researching helps me support Mary as she regains her health.

The failure of her short marriage was the beginning of Mary's long downhill journey into sadness, pain, and self-destruction. She is a kind, loving, sensitive, caring person; all she ever wanted was to be married and have kids. After her new husband made it clear that this newer, sleeker woman was what *he* really wanted, Mary became obsessed with how she looked.

She became very negative about all aspects of her appearance. Nothing was good enough—her hair wasn't right, her clothes made her look "fat," etc. Then she stopped wearing makeup and wouldn't even shower regularly. It was quite apparent she was becoming depressed.

She wouldn't see friends, then lost her job and wouldn't even look for a new one, so needed to move in with us. About the time we thought things couldn't get worse she was diagnosed with the eating disorder.

Mary had been so secretive about her odd eating behaviors that it took quite awhile to get her to a doctor who could properly diagnose her. Tom and I had hoped that once she was seeing some treatment providers she would improve, but it has been a slow, painful process.

Today, Mary is trying to keep a job and go to school but things keep happening that make it impossible for her to maintain her schedule and stick to her commitments. Sometimes she cannot force herself out of bed; other times she is so down and dragged out from the medications that she just can't function. We see her daily struggles, and it just breaks my heart.

It is a challenge to not feel guilty about any role Tom and I may have played in this. Is it genetic? Did we give her genes that caused this? In addition, it appears that she inherited polycystic ovarian syndrome (PCOS) from me, which, ironically, is a condition common in people with eating disorders.

It hasn't helped that some of the "professionals" seem to know less about eating disorders than I do. One doctor actually said to her, "Just push away from the table," which did so much damage. Yet that comment was not as hurtful as when the doctor said to me, "If she had anorexia it would be much worse. You don't have as much to worry about with bulimia." Unbelievable. It may be true that more people die from anorexia than bulimia, even though more people have bulimia, but this doctor obviously has not seen the way bulimia sucks the life out of its victims and steals our loved ones from us. Our daughter deserves treatment that works.

Right now the daughter I knew is gone, replaced by a shell of her former self. I miss her terribly and my broken heart grasps for the slivers of her that randomly appear. One Sunday afternoon we played cards. Her mind was sharp and she was actively engaged in the game. It was fun and we all even had some laughs. Then, just as quickly, that glimmer of her former self was gone; the zombie that had taken over my daughter's mind, body and soul was back. Those rare glimpses of her former self keep my hope alive and tell me that she's still in there somewhere.

I don't know if our marriage can withstand this. Tom and I are both so tired and at a loss because it seems there is nothing we can do. I already have lost so much of my daughter—I can't lose my husband too. The frustration, fear, and helplessness have us grasping at straws and we fight about what to do next. Something as simple as cleaning up after dinner can spark a major disagreement as I freak-out about Mary's plate left filled with food while Tom just brushes it off.

With the current job and unemployment stresses (I recently had shoulder surgery and can't work), what little energy I have left is focused on keeping Mary alive. Tom also lost his job a few weeks ago but we still make time to spend a few hours together free of eating disorders conversation so we can have fun.

Most people would never know that this is yet another of the challenges facing families fighting these unrepentant disorders. People have no idea why we have found it hard to maintain a social life or even keep up the garden. The constant tension, arguments, and continual attempts to motivate her drain us. Some days, just getting food on the table is a great accomplishment—and even then the battles begin again.

Through my research I've learned that relationship coaches and therapists can give some insights into how to maintain marriages and respect the male-female differences in reacting to a crisis. In the meantime, I think it is essential to give ourselves permission to stop trying to get the men in our lives to grasp the seriousness of these illnesses. We need to find support elsewhere for ourselves as well as our loved one.

I have one sister in-law who is sympathetic, because she has a niece who had severe anorexia. My sister-in-law and a woman at work are the only people, besides the therapist I see, who are able to give me any comfort, sympathy, or empathy.

I have found it useful to spend extra time with girlfriends as well as consciously remembering what attracted me to Tom in the first place. It has also helped that Tom and I have agreed to not play the blame game and respect our differences. We are determined to save our marriage from being a casualty of this illness. We know we both love our daughter: we just have different ways of responding to her illness.

Here are some tools I've read about that couples have found helpful:

1. Date night—have a firm rule to not talk about the ill child during the entire date.
2. Family therapy—find a competent therapist (preferably one who understands eating disorders) that the entire family can see regularly.
3. Get yourself individual therapy—or an objective third party to talk to.
4. At home (not just date night), have a time block set aside with no discussion of your ill child or illness.
5. Give one another backrubs or foot massages.
6. Exercise together or agree to individual exercise.
7. Find a fun hobby to do together.
8. Read to one another about eating disorders (or share books).

9. Take warm baths.

10. Weekend getaways—if they don't cause added financial burden.

11. Meditate or practice yoga.

12. Listen to your favorite soothing music.

13. Go to a comedy club or rent funny movies regularly.

14. Talk with other parents of seriously ill children who "get it."

15. Tag team when the child is extra challenging to be around.

16. Consciously choose to be a "united front."

5

Patrick Bergstrom's Story

Men and Boys Getting Into the Game, Victory Is Definitely an Option

Advocates come in all shapes, sizes, colors, genders and socio-economic levels. Patrick writes about his experience in a piece he calls, *A Fallen Athlete*, which can be found on his website. During treatment for his eating disorder, Patrick Bergstrom continues to courageously remove the stigma so others, including males, will receive the treatment they need. Approximately one percent of all males in the United States are living with their own eating disorders and this growing epidemic is hitting males worldwide and across many age groups.

Patrick has been in what he terms "full remission" from his eating disorder for over two years as I write this. He has come very far in his recovery and in the outreach he is doing to help those who are still silently suffering find another chance at life. As the founder of I Chose To Live, LLC, Patrick now speaks throughout the country, sharing his hope-filled story of recovery as he promotes awareness and provides education about eating disorders.

I have heard from several mothers whose sons are in treatment that the treatment facilities have not caught up with the needs of males. A boy is often the only male in the center, and may find the activities include knitting and painting fingernails. Many boys are uncomfortable (to say the least) with these activities, but a few boys have told me they didn't mind; in fact, they feel they will be better boyfriends/husbands/dads as a result of learning traditionally female skills and hearing the girls' stories.

Patrick's story highlights what so many parents are seeing—coaches who put a heavy emphasis on maintaining a set weight for their athletes, especially in dance, skating, swimming, track, wrestling, cheerleading, and gymnastics.

A lifelong athlete, Patrick uses sports analogies to describe his recovery process and to motivate others through their recovery. He believes in full recovery and describes where he is today as the "overtime" part of his recovery. In his analogy, the treatment process was the first four quarters of the match, during which he was given the resources and knowledge to reach his final victory.

As you will read, it took awhile for Patrick to reach out for help. But now he says, "Friends and family are your biggest fans." As family members, we can find comfort and encouragement in this. Even when our loved ones in recovery may not sound like they appreciate us, we do play a very integral role; our love and support are the driving factors that help them change their lives.

Since Patrick is an activist in the eating disorders world, he has asked that his real name be used in this story.

PATRICK'S STORY

Running down the lacrosse field, my body was flying with a great sense of freedom. This power and freedom on the field gave me the high I craved and provided an escape from the realities of life, school, and girlfriend problems. Nothing could touch me there.

Expressing myself through this sport was my art, and a way to channel the perfectionism that constantly drove me. It seemed to be a healthy outlet for my personality.

Before a practice or game all I could think about was how I

could be faster, stronger and perform better. Constantly being told that I wasn't big enough or fast enough, I made up for it with heart, drive and self-discipline. Eating didn't figure into this equation.

The game of lacrosse and my need to be a better lacrosse player consumed me, literally. Both my dad and my brother were lacrosse players who helped me become the athlete I am and I felt the competitive pressure to be as good as them—or better.

College is already an ideal atmosphere for eating disorders. By my sophomore year, the late-night pizza and beer parties, crazy schedules and lack of meal planning started to catch up with me. Erratic eating patterns were formed. Toward the end of my junior year, I kicked up my training routine so I would be in top shape for my senior year.

My senior year found me struggling; the pattern of not eating and pushing myself physically was taking a toll on my body and on my performance on the field. After two playing-field concussions, my coach was doubting my playing ability, and I didn't get much field time.

Watching my team from the bench was not how I had planned to spend my senior year. This was difficult for me because I had always done well in everything I undertook and had never been doubted before. I was restricting my eating to keep my weight down and it was working, albeit temporarily. Physically, I was excelling, finishing first in sprints during practices. Yet even though my performance was good, I wasn't getting the opportunity to start in games. I didn't know how to handle failure. Hugely disappointed, by spring of 2005 my life was out of control. My obsession with lacrosse led to poor decisions and ultimately drove me into my secret battle with anorexia.

Fast forward to the final game of my senior year. What should have been a crowning moment for an elite athlete was, instead, a traumatic experience—a pivotal moment in my life. I put the lacrosse stick down and didn't play again for four years.

With lacrosse no longer providing an outlet—an escape route from reality, the eating disorder started to get worse, though I still didn't recognize it as an eating disorder.

Having majored in business with a concentration in marketing, after graduation I looked for a big-time marketing job. After numerous interviews and hearing again and again that I had great potential but lacked the necessary experience, I took an inside sales job doing cold-calling eight hours a day. I hated it. It really beat me up. Struggling financially and emotionally, eating just one meal a day became the norm, which I didn't see as a problem.

For years, when training and competing in lacrosse, I pushed my muscles, even when it hurt—to improve my abilities. I used the same method to meet my new challenges. All of my focus was on work and doing my best, but for the first time, I didn't have a sense of control. I had no way to cope with the challenges I faced without my escape mechanism, lacrosse. I substituted a three-mile run after work and felt better while I was running, but not afterwards as my body was depleted and my problems had not gone away. When I got home from work and running, I thought about eating, but instead I would just go to bed. Hunger was felt to a point but then my body just broke down and didn't know that it was hungry. After a while I no longer felt hunger.

On some level, I definitely knew I was struggling but I felt I couldn't tell anyone what was going on because I feared their reaction. Even *I* didn't know what was going on. Both my mind and body were a wreck but I kept up a good front.

Struggles with body image are universal and yet I thought it wasn't about body image for me. Even though my weight kept dropping, I wasn't concerned. Strangely, when I hit another low point on the scale, I would think that the number was way too low, but I didn't see that reality in the mirror. Then the number crept even lower.

Somehow seeing those lower numbers felt good, but I was sick and malnourished. Looking back, I can see it was clearly a control issue. I felt satisfied when I saw I was able to "control" my weight. Obviously, I wasn't thinking clearly; my starved brain was thinking, *Restricting calories and over-exercising will take care of all my problems.* Binge drinking became a problem as both my physical health and mental health continued to deteriorate. It became painful to eat and I became afraid to eat.

Now it all seems absurd. I hope that telling you this will give you greater insight into the wildly distorted thinking that goes hand-in-hand with an eating disorder. Understanding this may help you gain a sense of compassion to replace the fear, panic, and frustration that can lead to anger and resentment toward someone struggling with an eating disorder.

Fear of people finding out my "secret" kept me from calling my family. They were only an hour away, but we no longer saw each other as often. When they questioned how I was and why I didn't visit, I lied and said I was fine, just stressed out from work. In reality I was isolating myself to protect the eating disorder. I knew they would make me get help. Now I know keeping them in the dark was frustrating to them and empowering to my eating disorder.

Even living with my girlfriend and two other friends I still felt alone, drifting away from everyone. Everything and everyone was neglected as I became consumed with trying to take care of myself without letting anyone know I had a problem. The eating disorder made me think I was good at being sneaky. I was wrong.

My girlfriend, who became my fiancée on one of the happiest days of my life, tried to get me into therapy but at the time

I didn't even know what an eating disorder was. To help manage my stress, I was now purging after eating. My girlfriend was so disturbed by my behaviors that after telling me she had lost herself in my illness, she soon left. I had no idea that she even knew what was going on. She later came back when I first got into therapy.

My therapist said I was not having body-image issues and didn't have an eating disorder. We dealt with my binge drinking and I got a new job. Being told I didn't have an eating disorder gave me the excuse to continue my behaviors. It wasn't long before my fiancée walked away again, and we haven't spoken since. Back then, there was no way for me to know how devastatingly painful these illnesses are for the family—but I get it now.

Eventually, reality got me to take myself to a doctor, but these are complex illnesses and doctors have little training on eating disorders. I still was not diagnosed. The doctor told me, "Guys don't struggle with eating disorders." Even though my weight was very low, it wasn't low enough to fit the diagnostic criteria for anorexia nervosa. And I lacked another "important" criterion as well. I hadn't missed a menstrual period!

I wasn't eating, just drinking coffee and energy drinks. I was so weak each morning I could barely get out of bed, but the caffeine and the eating disorder kept me running three miles a day.

I finally broke down, crying, "I can't do this anymore." It was at this point, I was finally able to ask for help. My family helped me find another doctor who diagnosed anorexia nervosa, purging type. This doctor was clear: "You'll be dead within a year if you don't get treatment."

I chose to live.

Once you choose to live and thus cry out for help, the recovery process has begun. You have now admitted, to yourself and to the world, that you have a problem and you need help.

Two weeks later I entered into a treatment center that would take a guy and met the criteria I needed. It had been a four-year battle before I was finally diagnosed and got real treatment. I went into treatment one month before what was to have been my wedding day.

Openly asking for help was all it took but that was the hardest step in my recovery. However, no one can do it alone. Telling just one person can make all the difference. Speaking up can open many avenues.

Intelligent, successful, competitive people fear telling their families and friends. There is often pain, shame and embarrassment in asking for help, maybe especially for males.

A guy doesn't come to mind when most people think about eating disorders. As I mentioned, I shut people out of my life and didn't talk about what was happening. I held back from telling anyone about the eating disorder out of fear that I would feel abandoned and rejected again. Added to that was the fear of change and of the stigma of mental illness, which stops multitudes from obtaining help.

Luckily, my guy friends don't talk much anyhow so it wasn't a big deal. However, they were amazingly supportive when they found out. To this day they don't grasp what I was dealing with, yet they all came to my house after my diagnosis. I broke down in tears.

Families often wonder: *How much of an impact do we have? How useful are we?* My family and friends are the best part of my recovery; they were incredibly helpful to me. Even though they had never heard of males with eating disorders and didn't understand, they were supportive. Unfortunately, many thought I would be "all fixed up" right away.

When I was in treatment, I learned that the majority of guys with eating disorders begin their treatment in a hospital instead of a therapist's office because they don't realize they have a problem until they are dangerously ill, often with cardiac problems. Too often, though, the hospitals don't know where to send these boys and men after the immediate problem has been solved, so treatment for their eating disorders is further delayed.

An eating disorder is about your past, the positives and negatives. No one just wakes up and decides to starve himself or binge and purge. An eating disorder is about feelings: lack of confidence, pain, trauma, low self-worth, or feeling out of control.

Not all eating disorders are the same. The only common factor is that food is the "drug of choice" or the coping mechanism that is used (either eating it or not eating it) when struggling with problems. Your mind wants you to believe that food is a quick fix for the pain and suffering. The eating disorder wants you to think that all these negative or abnormal food behaviors are "normal and healthy."

In reality, whether you choose to restrict the food you are eating, or binge and purge, you are just feeding your addiction, giving the eating disorder more control. Living a life in which an eating disorder controls every aspect of your existence is not truly living. This must first be accepted, and then the decision must be made to change it. The reality is if you have an eating disorder, you are slowly killing yourself.

It destroys you, little by little. Whenever you purge or restrict the amount of food you allow yourself, the disorder grows in strength.

Food, of course, is necessary for survival, so we must face our food fears. Alcoholics can learn not to drink, drug users can refrain from drugs, but we can't stop eating food. One simple technique I learned is claiming and honoring the food that your body consumes. This approach was introduced to me when I ate my first meal at the Canopy Cove Treatment Center.

What worked for me was a partial treatment program. I had my own apartment and went to treatment all day. These programs are definitely directed toward girls, using art and music therapy, so I was out of my element, which humbled me. But they helped me learn to enjoy the basics of life. It opened my eyes to new experiences: that was a big part of what I needed. I had been a super athlete, but that's *all* I'd done. In treatment I learned how to enjoy other kinds of experiences and settle down my over-active thinking.

Yoga was something I'd never done and the first day I fell all over the place. The next day I was really sore. It was a great experience! Being out of my element and trying new things definitely helped me get better.

Another major help was listening to other people's experiences. Most guys aren't openly emotional and hearing the girls share their stories helped me open up. Listening to one girl's story made me realize I didn't have it so bad. She had been sexually assaulted, raped and beaten, and had dealt with the pain for fifteen years! She had a wonderful smile and kept trying to cheer me up, which woke me up and inspired me to get well. She deserves a lot of credit for my recovery.

While I was in treatment I wrote my story, which turned into my book, *A Fallen Athlete*. I also wrote poems and created a website, things I had never even thought of doing before. So I really didn't mind that the treatment was female oriented, but by the end of treatment I was antsy for sports—even a soccer ball.

As we look for solutions to eating disorders, it's natural to wonder about the causes, and often that's when blaming happens. Sometimes people have traumatic events as my friend in treatment experienced. Often, though, many of us have had wonderful childhoods. My parents were great; I had a good childhood and a picture-perfect life until the end of college. Knowing this has helped my recovery. I couldn't blame my parents because *I* was my own worst enemy so I blamed myself. Overall, though, I have found blame to be useless.

Those of us who have been affected by these illnesses are typically sensitive, often well mannered, searching for recognition and usually wanting to please others. Most of us want to get well.

My experiences have shown me that the willingness to ask for help affects how long the eating disorders can last. Like any serious illness, the earlier it is treated, the better the outcomes.

I am excited about my future and have forgiven myself for my past. I am truly "alive" again, and will have a full recovery. How do I know this? Because I still carry my team with me. When you leave recovery, your team goes with you. I keep in touch with my therapists at Canopy Cove and I am still connected with the others I met there. These teammates will never leave my side. To me this is probably the most important part of the recovery process. I also meet with my therapist once a week just for a little extra "fan support." Remember, your friends and family are your biggest fans.

I started by telling one person, and it turned into sharing my story on a national level. Now I am very open with my story and struggle. There is still a huge stigma around eating disorders, which is part of what kept me from treatment for so long. I am often the first person people will tell because they know I won't judge them. Eating disorders destroy other lives in addition to the life of their hosts. I hope to spare others some of that destruction.

PATRICK'S TIPS:

1. When you are in recovery, others who have been through treatment are your best resources for success.

2. Follow your heart, believe in the decision, and don't give up. (I wanted to leave treatment after the first day and fought with everyone for the first three days!)

3. Even in your darkest hour, if you follow your heart, you will get it done.

4. Trust is another key part to the recovery process. Trust the system, and trust your teammates. Be honest with yourself and hold nothing back. By expressing myself, I was openly telling my eating disorder, "You will take no more from me." Today I live by these few words.

5. Family and friends are essential members of the recovery team, and can be your biggest fans, supporters and source of encouragement.

6. Sometimes exercise can become an unhealthy quick fix for emotional problems.

7. Males don't always have the same distorted body image as females.

8. Sometimes we learn more from losing than we do from winning.

9. Determine your needs and find the treatment that can meet your requirements.

10. Try different avenues. Be willing to interact with others and receive support from anyone.

11. Try to find others who can understand and relate to what your family is going through.

12. While in treatment, find something that you can connect back to. At Canopy Cove, the safe place was an area on the

property we called "The Great Oak Trees." This was the place where eating disorders could not touch us. This is now where I go, sometimes literally, sometimes figuratively, when I feel a trigger or when I want to escape from the world. The eating disorder cannot find me there.

13. Believe in yourself but be a team player and you will have the ultimate victory.

6

Melissa's Story

To Be Fearless, Put Your Oxygen Mask on First

As Melissa shared the impact of her daughter Tracy's eating disorder, I got a clear picture of amazing strength and courage as well as Melissa and her husband Bobby's love for one another and their daughter amidst great fear. For years this family faced each day knowing their beloved daughter's pain and deep depression could lead her to yet another overdose on painkillers.

Not being consumed by the fear became almost as big a task as keeping their daughter from being consumed by the eating disorder. Melissa shared many details of her family's struggles and I hope they will help you as you navigate your own unplanned journey with eating disorders.

Their story is an example of what is frequently referred to as "treatment failure" and tells what doesn't work and what to do when what is being done isn't working.

When this was happening to them no one in their area had heard of the Maudsley Family-Based Therapy approach that involves the family in every aspect of treatment. Research on this evidence-based approach has increasingly shown its effectiveness in not only anorexia but also bulimia.

The eating disorder had moved in and taken control of their lives. Little by little, it became a part of every decision they made.

Melissa and Bobby lived with daily verbal battles, stealing, and lying and lost all trust in their daughter.

Melissa and Bobby had many heated discussions about what to do next and how to speak with Tracy. There was no guidance from the treatment team on what to say or do. On top of all the stress was the weight of guilt about spending so little time having fun with their young son. The financial impact of the eating disorder only added more stress as they spent thousands of dollars on treatments that didn't appear to help at all. They were completely drained by the powerlessness, stress, fear, exhaustion and lack of support they experienced.

MELISSA'S STORY—THE SECOND TRIP TO THE ER

My husband Bobby, our 11-year-old son and I were enjoying a lovely dinner at home. That alone was unusual, as dinnertime had become yet another minefield we traversed daily. At this point in a "normal" day, dinner meant we'd already made it through many challenges, including waking Tracy, our 16-year-old daughter, who was so drugged by her prescribed medications that just getting her out of bed was a major accomplishment. Then we supported her through the drama of choosing clothes she felt good about wearing for the day. We tried to leave her to herself, but most of the time she showed up crying, telling us that her clothes made her look ugly or fat.

Each day that she made it to the bus on time was deemed a success, but this didn't happen often. Getting a good breakfast into her was always a challenge, but after all the clothing, makeup, skin breakouts and drama, there usually wasn't time for her to eat. This was stressful, of course, because her nutritionist's meal plan included specific foods for breakfast.

We'd hold our breath all through the school day, hoping we wouldn't get a call from the school nurse to pick up Tracy. We wanted so badly for her to be able to have a normal school day and be able to keep up in her classes.

The physical pain the eating disorder caused Tracy showed up in various parts of her body on different days. Most often it was headaches or severe stomach pain; sometimes it was neck and back or joint pain. Other random pains took their toll on her young body. Our 16-year old, with all her accompanying aches and pains, often seemed like an old woman.

Many of us don't realize the depression that often accompanies eating disorders causes real physical pain in addition to the related severe emotional pain. After school each day I became Tracy's cheerleader, coach and counselor, trying to lift her back up from the challenges of her school day. This was a heart-wrenching exhausting process for us both.

Tracy's eating disorder had been diagnosed just a few months before. Even though we knew things weren't "right" for quite some time, it took us over two years to get her diagnosed.

Many days included trips to various care providers, which meant frequently pulling her out of classes to attend these appointments. Tracy, Bobby and I placed so much hope on these appointments, which seemed to only increase her anxiety and, as a result, ours. Often on the way to her appointments with doctors, therapists, nutritionists, and others, she would say something like, "I hope this person will help me." But they didn't.

She and I both tired of the fruitless appointments that interrupted our days, and I couldn't help but wonder how honest she was being with the therapists, doctor and dietician. At the same time, I felt the professionals were aloof and disinterested in helping my child. There were too many other serious issues to address so I never did ask if they had become hardened to the suffering of the people impacted by this illness.

At the end of each of these long, trying days, we all felt like the mythological Greek figure Sisyphus who rolled the boulder up a steep hill, only to have to push it up again and again and again.

Once home, the evenings were usually filled with tears, arguments and navigating eating rituals that were beyond anyone's ability to understand. Bobby and I tried not to worry when we heard the shower running after dinner, hoping Tracy was not throwing up the meal we had so carefully prepared to meet her dietician's requests.

We were depleted physically and emotionally as we continued to do our best to support Tracy in the face of her continual anger, often misdirected at us. Life became an act of survival—earning money, getting food into the house and having clean clothes were the only things we expended energy on. All of our remaining energy went into keeping Tracy alive, supporting her recovery, and giving some attention to our son.

We no longer invited friends or family to our home and rarely went to their homes. Trying to explain our new, unchosen, lifestyle to friends was pointless. Most didn't understand and more than one even asked, "Why don't you just tell her to stop?" Each time I heard that question I felt like I'd been kicked in the gut. I sometimes wanted to reply, "Gosh, why didn't I think of that?" but I didn't. I knew they had no way of understanding the seriousness of this illness. We felt totally isolated.

So that evening, knowing Tracy was out with friends, we were happy and hopeful she was having fun. Sitting at the dinner table chatting with our son, Bobby and I were relaxed for a change.

Then the phone rang. A security guard from the mall told us our daughter had overdosed on Tylenol and was in an ambulance on the way to the hospital.

This wasn't Tracy's first acetaminophen overdose. Her first attempt to stop the pain had occurred several months earlier. We felt confident that it had been a one-time cry for help, and since we had found treatment providers for her in the meantime who were guiding her recovery, it hadn't occurred to us that it would happen again.

Bobby had made the first emergency room trip with her, while I stayed home with our son, so we decided I would go this time. Bobby doesn't like to talk about emotions and hadn't shared many of the details of that first event with me. I was completely unaware of what lay ahead of me that night.

Tracy was already in a bed in one of those little curtained ER areas. Nothing in my mostly rosy life experience had prepared me for what I encountered. When a nurse walked me over to Tracy I was immediately confused. *Who is this large man sitting at the foot of her bed? What is he doing here and why does he have a badge on his coat? Why are her lips black? She isn't speaking. She looks blank.*

I asked the nurse about the man. "He is the hospital's security guard, and this is a requirement in an overdose."

My confusion as to why a security guard was needed must have been apparent. The nurse added, "So she doesn't harm herself or try to leave."

"What is the black stuff on my daughter's lips?" I asked.

"Oh, that's just from the charcoal that she had to drink to neutralize the pills in her stomach. We always give that to the overdoses."

Did she just call my daughter an overdose?

The nurse scurried away and I was left by myself. *What do I do now? Was this a true suicide attempt or another attempt to rid herself of the immense pain? Do I chat with the security guard? There's no privacy to talk right now with him sitting there. Can't he leave now that I'm here? When and how will my brain process all of this?*

I tried to talk with Tracy but she couldn't carry on any type of conversation. She was out of it—vacant. She didn't seem to know I was even there. I didn't know what to do.

I didn't want to cry in front of her. Out of desperation, I excused myself, saying, "I'm going to go stand over there for a bit, honey."

Outside the curtained area, I clung to a support column as tears began to run down my face. *Maybe while I'm standing here crying someone will tell me what to do next, how to handle this. There must be someone who is here to comfort the parents of the "overdoses" they bring in here.*

No one even looked at me. One after another, hospital workers raced or sauntered past me as I leaned on the column, quivering. The reality that my child could have died started to settle in. Sliding slowly down the column, I started shaking as tears furiously ran down my face.

Never had I felt such an overwhelming sense of sadness, fear, panic, confusion, and helplessness all in one crashing moment. I had no clue what to do, how to react, what to feel. I just wanted someone to hold and comfort me, tell me what to do—then what to do next. I wanted to be strong for Tracy but my heart was being ripped to pieces and the pain was crushing my chest.

After what seemed like forever, just as I pushed away the urge to curl up on the floor and cry my eyes out, someone finally attended to my daughter. "We are going to take your daughter to a different hospital, one that has a locked ward."

What!?

"This is standard procedure in an overdose so the patient can be evaluated and stabilized in a safe environment." The air seemed to be sucked out of me. My brain was trying so hard to process all of this information, but it was doing it so s-l-o-w-l-y, I didn't say much. I had no clue what to say.

My God, they are treating this as a serious suicide attempt.

"If you want to go home and bring back some of her things, you can do that. She needs to sit here awhile anyway while the charcoal works," the person in white told me.

"Okay, I'll go get her toothbrush, teddy bear and pajamas. What else?"

"That should do it. Just don't bring anything sharp or anything with a string or rope." The words were said so matter-of-factly and with so little compassion, I wondered if they'd had any training on handling distraught parents.

Driving home to get Tracy's things at 1:30 a.m. on a Saturday morning just added to my stress. All the drunks on their way home from the bars were sliding down the road, and I felt like I was in an action video, trying to avoid being hit. At least it kept me alert.

After following the ambulance across town to another hospital, I spent the better part of the night locked into the ward, filling out forms and talking with the intake people, but learning little. By 5:00 a.m., I was heading home just as the sun was coming up. I wrote my husband a note to wake me at 8:00 that morning so we could head back to the hospital to meet with Tracy's temporary therapist.

Usually I was pretty tuned in to my intuition and could easily decide what was right but all the stress had made it tough to hear my inner wisdom. As we were headed to the hospital, Bobby and I had just a few moments to make the difficult decision whether or not to still attend the dinner and Broadway show to celebrate a friend's fiftieth birthday as we had planned that evening.

At first, it seemed obvious we wouldn't attend. How could parents have fun while their daughter was locked away in a psych ward? Then we remembered what our family therapist had told us, that it was morally imperative that we take good care of ourselves, even make sure that our self-care was our number one priority. At the time the advice seemed odd since Tracy was the sick one, but she explained that if we had nothing left to give, we wouldn't be able to care for Tracy's tremendous needs. Once we understood what she was telling us about it being a marathon and not a sprint, we were able to heed the advice to put our metaphorical oxygen masks on.

As we struggled with what to do, we were reminded that the hospital had limited visiting hours and the guidance from that deep inner therapist came through and alerted me that we would go crazy sitting at home alone with our fears. We realized that laughing and being with friends would help us recharge.

Finally, we reasoned that our daughter was in the safest place she could be. So with trepidation, we decided we should follow through with our plans and enjoy ourselves as much as possible.

After visiting Tracy in the locked ward, we met with her temporary psychologist who seemed to have more answers and ideas for helping her than anyone we had met with so far. It was a long day of meetings but by late afternoon, for the first time we felt hope that she might one day recover.

Our travel bag filled with fancy clothes for the evening, we headed off to our friend's house for a half-hour nap before the birthday celebration. Too soon, my girlfriend, who knew what was going on with Tracy, woke me with a glass of wine in one hand and a cup of coffee in the other. "Drink them both," she ordered. I drank them alternately while I got dressed. She suggested that we try to enjoy the evening and share our upsetting news with our other friends at a later date. It seemed a bit odd to not say anything to our close friends, but we didn't want to ruin the party, and I knew that if I said anything I would lose it and start crying.

I was surprised to find I was actually enjoying the evening and could even remember how to laugh. Being with our regular group of old friends helped us have a lovely but rather surreal evening of fun. We enjoyed the escapism the Broadway show provided. It was clear later that this was exactly what we needed when a playwright friend told us that plays provide a willing momentary suspension of disbelief that creates poetic faith and helps the story to feel real. Becoming immersed in the story helped us be present, which suspended our misery and gave us the break we needed.

Surprisingly, our ability to enjoy the evening in the midst of such a crisis felt like we were reclaiming power over our lives.

The following week most of my energy went toward listening to Tracy, dealing with the insurance company and trying to understand the horrible illness that had caused Tracy's overdose.

About a week after the birthday gathering I managed to find the energy to tell my close friend Pamela about Tracy's latest health crisis. She became very upset that I hadn't told her about it the night of the birthday celebration. I realized her ranting boiled down to her being angry that I didn't ask for help the way *she* needed me to. I was stunned. She was so self-focused, she couldn't grasp the concept that we needed *not* to talk about Tracy that evening.

As I became more adept at setting boundaries, I let Pamela know that her reaction wasn't okay with me. She is no longer a friend as I've chosen to have only truly respectful people in my life. But one never knows the issues other people are dealing with. A few years later, I found out that Pamela had been diagnosed with narcissism, which helped explain her bizarre reaction.

Bobby and I now took the possibility that Tracy might succeed in committing suicide very seriously. On the one hand, the professionals said she was just trying to escape the pain, not necessarily attempting suicide. On the other hand, they told us it was still a very real possibility. This explanation still brought on a fear response that wasn't easy to shut off. I became a mama bear and I wanted to protect my daughter with every cell in my body. We continued to do everything we could do for her.

Every time she left in the car, it was a challenge to not go down the tunnel of "what ifs." *What if she drives into a brick wall? What if she isn't paying attention and has yet another accident? What if she loses her license? How will she have a job? She'll be dependent on us for everything . . .* my mind continued to race.

We were told to lock up all of our medications, both prescription and over-the-counter. Tracy had to take her medications a few times per day so we kept those out. It seemed pointless to me to hide our medications because she could just as easily overdose on her own prescription medications, but we did it.

Tracy had always been a deep sleeper but the addition of Trazodone, a mild anti-depressant, which toned down her anxiety and helped her to fall asleep, made her sleep even more deeply.

On mornings we needed to be somewhere early, the process of waking Tracy became an even more daunting task. I'd walk into her room and start making noise half an hour before she needed to get up. I would play music, bang dresser drawers, talk to her, tap her legs—it was quite a routine.

Bobby had already left for work one morning when, after knocking on her door, I walked loudly into her room. Even with me clunking the door against the wall and jabbering away, she didn't flinch. I thought that was odd. *Wow she's really in a deep sleep this morning,* I thought. "GOOD MORNING, TRACY!" I shouted. Nothing. Not a twitch or sound. Fear sent adrenaline rushing through me, *Oh my God, is she dead? Did she overdose?*

I made more noise, shook her legs and shouted even louder. Nothing.

Summoning all the courage I had, I crouched down next to her bed and looked carefully at her sweet 16-year-old face. She looked alive—her color was normal—but I couldn't see any up-and-down motion of her chest. *Is she breathing or not? Oh dear God, do I want to know? What if she is dead? What do I do? I have to find out. Please wake up, Tracy.*

Slowly reaching my right index finger toward her face I braced myself. *Will it be warm or cold? I cannot believe I am doing this. Who does this? What kind of sick joke is this that a parent has to touch her child's cheek to see if she is alive or dead? Parents shouldn't have to do this, should they?* Here I was in her darling pink and blue little-girl bedroom facing this grown-up sickness. The contrast highlighted how crazy this felt. So many questions raced erratically through my mind. *Why do I have to do this? Where is her dad right now? Why isn't he doing this?*

Finally my fingertip gently made contact with her soft cheek. It took a few moments for my adrenaline-soaked brain to process the information: *Her skin is warm! She is not dead! I could breathe again. Relief, confusion, tears. Why am I alone? I cannot do this.*

That's when I knew *I* needed help. I needed to talk to someone. But who? I felt I had burdened my family and friends to the point that no one really wanted to listen to me anymore. And they felt helpless too.

I couldn't talk with my mom; I was afraid it would break her heart. She had been so supportive, non-judgmental and nurturing of me through everything. She had told me how much pain it all caused her, as her own instincts told her to protect me, and yet this was her granddaughter. Her feelings of helplessness caused her to feel angry amidst the confusion of the behavior the eating disorder brought on. I knew all of this had taken a toll on her and I didn't want to hurt her anymore. The loneliness amplified my pain, as it seemed there was no one to talk with to help me sort this all out.

Two other mornings I went through this horrific routine,

wondering if she was alive or dead, before I finally sought out a therapist, just to have someone help me sort out all of the craziness.

Luckily I was directed to a therapist who specializes in counseling women who have experienced trauma. She validated my reality: "Melissa, first of all, parents shouldn't have to do what you did." Through my tears I managed to squeak out, "But am I being overly dramatic or over-reacting?"

"No, Melissa. The reality is that Tracy is still in a phase where she is at a real risk for suicide attempts or an accidental overdose—and with all the medications she takes, it's a real possibility. You are not overreacting and you are not being dramatic."

It was a relief to know I wasn't going crazy. For the first time, I felt heard, validated, understood, and comforted, which was what I needed but hadn't known how to ask for it.

I felt I had looked down the barrel of the scariest gun in the world and lived to tell about it. I now knew I could be fearless in the face of anything else life could throw at me. What else is there to fear when one has faced the possibility of her child dying? This has strengthened me to endure this long slow recovery process.

Now in her early twenties she has found some non-traditional treatments that, added to the traditional, are helping Tracy regain her health and a joyful life.

MELISSA'S TIPS FOR FEARLESSNESS:

1. Educate yourself about your child's addiction.
2. Face the fears and ask yourself: What is the worst that can happen?
3. Ask for help.
4. Get support.

5. Set clear boundaries with all people (including family and friends) in your life. Lessen or eliminate contact with unhelpful and disrespectful people.

6. Practice extreme self-care (do something enjoyable every day). Get plenty of sleep, eat well and exercise.

7. Use Mindfulness Techniques developed by Dr. Marsha Linehan—www.BehavioralTech.org.

8. Commit to having joy be present in your life no matter what the situation.

9. Have fun, even if it feels like you are faking it.

7

Mickie's Story

The Genes Load the Gun, the Environment Pulls the Trigger

Mickie found me through Eating Disorders Anonymous (EDA) where she is learning to accept what she sees as an addiction. As you read in an earlier chapter, professionals in the eating disorders world disagree on whether or not eating disorders are addictions. In the article, "Understanding the Complex Relationship Between Eating Disorders and Substance Use Disorders," in the Renfrew Perspectives, a professional journal, Bethany L. Helfman, Psy.D. and Amy Baker Dennis, Ph.D., say, "Eating disorders (ED) co-occur with substance use disorders (SUD) at an alarming rate. Prevalence data suggests that roughly 50% of individuals with an ED are also abusing drugs and/or alcohol, which is more than five times the abuse rates seen in the general population (The National Center on Addiction and Substance Abuse [CASA], 2003). Not only are there high rates of substance abuse (SA) among women with ED, women who use alcohol and drugs demonstrate high rates of disordered eating." Given these high rates, Helfman and Dennis encourage the research community to study these populations together and create formal connections between the eating disorders and substance abuse communities.

In doing all of these interviews and hearing so many stories of people having eating disorders as well as substance use disorders,

I am looking forward to more discussion in the professional community to allow for more cross-training of substance abuse/addiction specialists and eating disorders specialists. I also see a need for more research into this intriguing piece of the puzzle.

Mickie's belief is that God will let her know when she is ready for the next step in her healing. Even though Mickie still has some distorted eating behaviors, she knows she needs to take time to eat. EDA has given her the support and skills to accept where she is at, and instead of berating herself when she slips-up, she can now relax in the knowledge that when she is ready to eat healthy and exercise healthy, she will. I know "exercise healthy" may sound redundant to some of you, so I'll explain. Many people with eating disorders tend to over-exercise to the point that it becomes life threatening. They need to learn to exercise in moderation. Moderation is the key to so many things in life.

MICKIE'S STORY

Walking Murphy, my tan cocker spaniel, through my neighborhood, the stress of my home life seeped out of my body as I finally relaxed. My sweet Murphy-girl kept me company each time I walked, which was my favorite way of escaping the chaos and unpredictability of being a 12-year-old living with two alcoholic parents. Typically, I would have either the Eagles or the Grateful Dead playing on my portable CD player, because they helped me leave my worries behind as I soaked up the warm sunshine I craved. I didn't know then that soothing, calming chemicals called endorphins were washing over my stressed brain, brought on from the motion of walking.

Ours was a fairly classic dysfunctional family living with the wrecking ball of addiction. My parents tried to present a facade of "perfect parents," but it was only that, a facade. The reality was sheer mayhem that left me feeling ungrounded, stripped of everything. Counting on my parents for any predictability became a fantasy. I developed coping techniques to help myself feel safe, which was necessary because I was also sexually molested by multiple family members. It was an ideal breeding ground for an eating disorder.

Mine is a classic example of the now familiar metaphor: The genes load the gun and the environment pulls the trigger. Despite everything, I got straight A's, cleaned the house, and tried to be perfect. And being perfect included being thinner.

There was so little that I could control. The weekdays were not too bad but the weekends were scary. My parents would go out, get drunk, then come home and fight. Soon, the drive to become thinner became a control issue. Eating or not eating was something I felt I could control.

Eating disorders don't just happen overnight, they develop slowly and creep into one's life. Mine began with worrying excessively and obsessing, then over-exercising, restricting food intake and on and on. Eventually, and fortunately for me, my aunt noticed my extreme weight loss, the scars from cutting myself and other eating disorder behaviors and got me some help.

In a small town there can be few options for care providers. My primary physician diagnosed me with anorexia and I spent the summer with my first therapist—but I didn't apply myself. When she told me she wanted to talk with my dad when he picked me up, I got into his car and told him that she said I was fine and I didn't need to come back.

My dad and I didn't have the best communication in the world. At the worst, he said to me, while I was eating a sub sandwich, "I know you're purging again." I just wanted to throw the sandwich in his face. At our best, I hated to hear, "Did you eat today?" I got so sick of hearing that question, it made me want to rebel even more. Then I wouldn't eat at all. In a sick sort of way I was punishing my parents by torturing myself.

Part of my self-torture was the cutting I would do to my arms to numb the pain. I know it sounds backwards, but many of us with anxiety do this to ourselves as a way to numb our internal pain.

My next therapist, Luanne, was the only stable person in my life from age 15 to 23, when she developed cancer. Luanne was like a mom to me; she really listened and was the only consistent person who reassured me I would be okay. She not only specialized in helping people with eating disorders but she has what I refer to as, "the special brain it takes to understand the crazy shit we do." I still miss her.

I learned my most valuable lesson while working with Luanne: God will let me know when I'm ready. Perfectionist tendencies would come out and get in my way. I was such a "doer," I had trouble simply "being," so she would always say, "Just be." She helped me learn that it's all about *finding that balance.*

While I was still working with Luanne I earned my BS degree. She really helped me stay on an even keel so I could complete college—and even go on to become a Licensed Alcohol and Drug Counselor (LADC). With my LADC license, I took a job at a rehab facility; however, I left after a short time because it felt like a pretty sick environment. From what I could see, the staff was sicker than the clients. I quickly found a job in a mental health ward in a hospital doing outpatient chemical dependency treatment. To my dismay, this place was worse than the previous one. This very stressful job only increased my problems with eating and, before long, drinking.

Apparently, the stressful job, combined with my increased drinking and eating-disorder behavior, along with the "good" stress—plans to marry John, the love of my life, and buy a home—pushed me too far.

At 23, I admitted myself into a large hospital-outpatient program for eating disorders where I had to learn how to get well and do the work to make that happen. My dad did one thing that was helpful at this time: he came to a family group session. I remember telling the dietician that I was excited to tell him about how well I was following the meal plan.

Outpatient treatment in this program helped me understand what a normal diet looked like, and I learned not to be scared of food. I ate breakfast, snacks and lunch with the other patients and learned what normal portions were. I found out I could trust that my body would process the food and it would not go right to my butt and hips. They taught me to eat. At one point while I was there, I learned that using food to cope is the symptom and that I was there to learn to manage symptoms. I probably did my treatment in a way opposite the traditional treatment model. That model would have been to nourish my body, then address the emotional baggage. Even though I had a consistent and beneficial therapeutic relationship with Luanne, I was still doing what in the eating disorders recovery world is called "using symptoms" as a coping mechanism when I became stressed.

I'd been giving lectures in my profession as a chemical dependency counselor. I now realized I should be a student. After this treatment program, I impulsively quit my job at the hospital and started working at a halfway house, a much healthier environment that helped me to continue to move toward fuller recovery.

Truthfully, though, I feel God was taking care of me. I needed more experience and healing time so it worked out.

Learning to "let go and let God" brought me farther along in my recovery and also in my emotional maturity. It became clear to me that people in recovery, i.e., me, need to be more honest. I noticed that when I was honest with my mom she was compassionate; hiding things from her was counterproductive. When I was hiding my emotions, the only things she seemed to be saying were, "You need to do this; you need to do that." By this time I was working with a new therapist named Mark because Luanne had left on her medical leave.

I was 25, had a career and was married to John. In May 2007, I gave birth to our daughter, who is our pride and joy.

Unfortunately, I had a difficult labor and delivery and developed a major case of post-partum depression (PPD). I spent that Thanksgiving in the mental health wing of a hospital, where they wrongly diagnosed me as bipolar and put me on a bunch of anti-psychotic medications. After I was discharged, my outpatient psychiatrist kept putting me on different anti-psychotic medications. Because I continued to feel horrible, depressed, and over-tired, I finally told the psychiatrist, "I'm not bipolar, I just need my Lexapro" (anti-depressant medication), which I had previously taken. The psychiatrist said it would cause mania. I told them to give me the Lexapro and if it caused mania, they could diagnose me then.

Of course it didn't cause mania, but I did have to go through withdrawal from the anti-psychotics, which caused insomnia for months. I had a supportive workplace at the halfway house for chemically dependent clients, and they understood when I was too tired to work. I've been on Lexapro ever since—and will never go off it. Higher doses make me more energized and focused, not manic as they once thought.

Recovery isn't a linear path. I can still shop 'til I drop when I'm really upset, lonely, sad, bored, or happy because I just got paid. I often wonder if it's a genetic code in my brain. My biggest thing now is remembering to eat. It's not about weight; I find I get a high from not eating so I have to resist that temptation. The high I get lets me feel light, energized, and focused. When I do sit down and eat, I get bogged down and sluggish.

Right now I'm accepting where I'm at and that I have

addictions. I know I must be willing to learn to trust. My eating is still distorted but God will let me know when I'm ready. Instead of beating myself up, I accept where I'm at, and when I'm ready to eat healthy and exercise, I will.

I am still working on my daughter's baby blanket that I started while I was pregnant. She's almost two. This is a perfect example of my letting go of the black-and-white, all-or-nothing perfectionist behavior. All the colors of the rainbow can show up now, including gray. I have more acceptance of the grays in life, and the blanket will get done when it gets done. Obsessiveness still appears occasionally but now there is no need to beat myself up for it. I don't need to make obsessing or beating myself up a habit.

I have a funny mirror in my bathroom that I call my circus mirror. It is a bit distorted, which is just fine since my view of myself is usually a bit distorted. For instance, if I don't eat as much as I think I should, I think I look thinner, and when I eat too much, I think I look fatter. Intellectually I know it's ridiculous but on some distorted emotional level I've convinced myself otherwise. Our brains are super amazing in the way we can believe what we teach ourselves to believe. I mean, that whole concept of thinking we have to look a certain way is so messed up. If you deny reality enough, your brain simply adjusts.

EDA (Eating Disorders Anonymous) works wonders. I have found that a little light bulb goes on, and the realization strikes: *Oh yeah, I don't have control, but I don't need to worry about that!* This idea is all quite amazing for a control freak like me.

Prior to attending EDA, I went to Al-Anon, which helped provide tools for dealing with my mixed-up family. It backed up the work that Luanne did with me. I know she is still alive, and I'd like to let her know how much she helped me. She taught me that kids put unnecessary blame onto themselves; I needed that awareness to let go of the responsibility for things that happened.

Thanks to Luanne, I knew I no longer had to take any responsibility for my mom's actions when she appeared in my room at 3am, drunk after what I suspect was an evening out being unfaithful. It was a huge burden off my back to understand that I don't need to give any energy to the fact that my mom is still oblivious, claiming she doesn't have an addiction. I need not pay attention to her Jekyll-and-Hyde routine of "Oh, poor me," followed by anger.

I like the Alcoholics Anonymous model of dealing with addiction—we work with alcoholics who are abstaining. AA opens its arms to the drunk on the street; as long as there is a desire to stop drinking, they'll accept you. I feel like my philosophy of "Screw the food, let's deal with the real issues" is honored in EDA. When I go there I get honesty, openness and willingness (in AA we call it H.O.W.) to keep on keeping on. No longer do I just shut down; I am learning to speak up more.

Postscript from Becky: After I finished her story, I talked further with Mickie; she shared with me that after doing our first interview, she finished her daughter's baby blanket.

Before going to publication, I learned that Mickie suffered a very serious relapse. It was similar to the major depressive episode after the birth of her daughter. Mickie felt herself slipping into a depression for about six months and the anxiety increased to the point she overdosed on her medications and slit her wrists. Fortunately she survived. It has taken a few months but now she is doing much better.

MICKIE'S TIPS:

1. People with addictive behaviors might not always be receptive but I believe they'll remember what God wants them to remember.

2. We cannot control other people's behaviors but we can keep planting the seed and hope they'll listen. It's all about planting the seed.

3. Listen and be compassionate. I had people who really listened and were compassionate and it made a huge difference for me.

4. Be supportive by just having a good time. Play games, give unconditional love, and don't talk about the eating disorder all the time.

5. We need to find a better system for finding the right medications—and doctors need to trust their patients' knowledge, feelings, experience and history. After all, we as patients are our best advocates and know our bodies and minds.

6. Eating disorders hurt others; we know that. Eating disorders are family diseases. *You* can't make me better, *I* have to do that. You have to take care of yourself. We can't love another until we love ourselves.

7. I needed validation and normalcy; I needed attention, not smothering. Some ways to accomplish this would be to ask your loved one in recovery how his/her day was, then watch television or play a game together.

8. Get family therapy; the whole family system is affected.

9. It's really not all about food; it's about different issues.

10. Check out how EatingDisordersAnonymous.org can educate and help you.

8

Beth and Tom's Story

Not All Treatment Centers Are Equal

When I interviewed Beth, the mother of 17-year-old Danielle, I thought much of her story sounded like a movie script. Beth and her husband Tom were willing to try *anything* to help their daughter.

Many parents don't know *what* to do because too often the health care professionals they turn to for help don't know either. I hope, through Beth's story, you will feel less isolated if you take your own child/loved one to a treatment center. There are lessons this family learned that you too can learn to make your own path to recovery easier.

Beth's story occurred when even less was known about eating disorders than is known today. Unfortunately, not enough is known about effective methods and often parents are led to believe that the treatment available to them is the only option. As you will see in other stories, there are good treatments and good treatment centers, though the philosophy and the actual treatment regimens can differ greatly. What's most important is to find the right treatment for your loved one, which can include trying a family-based therapy (FBT) approach, finding different care providers if you're not satisfied with the ones you've been working with and exploring several treatment options. This story of failed treatment sheds light on the reality that treatment isn't one size fits all.

Much of the world puts eating disorders into only one category, and that's anorexia. To many, if the patient isn't skeletal or near death, if their bones don't show like some super model's, they do not have an eating disorder. Unfortunately, many people, including care providers, still operate from this outdated paradigm. Millions of people with eating disorders are either an "average" size or even a larger size.

Seven years ago, when Beth was living her nightmare, bulimia was thought not to have as high a mortality rate as anorexia. Some researchers today are questioning that. Research done in 2009, however, shows the mortality rates to be nearly the same.

BETH'S STORY

Tom was driving, I was the navigator, and Danielle sat in back, absorbed in her celebrity gossip and fashion magazines, as if on a family vacation. As we drove north I wondered, *Is it okay when you are transporting your child to an eating disorders treatment center to enjoy the scenery? What do you talk about? Is having a pleasant diversion allowed?*

Driving up the long tree-lined lane leading to the picturesque country manor that housed the treatment center, my husband Tom and I felt like we should be arriving at some lovely bed and breakfast for a long weekend of relaxing. The incongruence of it all made us laugh a bit. *What terrible parents we must be to laugh at a time like this,* we thought, which made us want to laugh even more.

The long curvy, wooded driveway was so romantic. Seeing the elegant white colonial building up ahead helped calm our nerves.

After walking through the beautiful, peaceful country-house setting, past the pretty horses in the yard, I felt almost serene. So it was a shock when we stepped inside—it was right out of the 1975 film, *One Flew Over The Cuckoo's Nest.* No more beautiful country manor. The place was intimidating, even scary. Grayish pink plaster walls, charts everywhere, rules posted and locked doors. The staff was locked behind glass, handing out meds.

All of the research I had done on the Internet and in speaking with others had led me to believe that this was the best place for our daughter Danielle. At the time, I couldn't find other parents to talk to, though now, thankfully, more resources are available to give parents support and the information they need. At that particular moment, though, I looked around and thought, *Uh oh, what have we done?*

⸻

Hours earlier, a perky flight attendant had asked, "How are you folks today?" Didn't she see the tears streaming down my face? I wanted to scream, "Leave people alone when they are miserable!" It was an intrusion into our little cocoon of private suffering. My husband and I were not seated near our daughter. Danielle was busily distracting her zombie self with mindless magazines. Tom and I were sad and fearful—but yet hopeful—about this crazy journey ahead of us. We just needed to hold hands and comfort one another. After all, who takes their child across the country to some strangers in an eating disorders treatment facility? At that moment, we felt very alone—like we were the only parents ever to have done this.

We had all been living in the foreign land called bulimia for some time now, perplexed by the behaviors that came along with it. Our darling, bright, lovable youngest daughter had turned into an insolent, obnoxious, uncooperative, argumentative, and very secretive stranger. Her grades dropped suddenly and her friends no longer called.

Most importantly, her normally round body began shrinking. Her previously gorgeous thick and shiny hair fell out in massive quantities, and what was left was pulled into a scrawny ponytail. We couldn't seem to get to the source of Danielle's many aches, pains and physical ailments that she had recently experienced. We didn't understand the swelling of her lower jaw that appeared even as she lost weight. At that time we didn't know that salivary glands swell due to the recurrent purging, which gives many people with bulimia a very rounded chin line.

Frequent trips to doctors to find the cause of Danielle's constant stomach pains and intestinal issues had not helped. We finally got the bulimia diagnosis and spent several months trying local hospital programs and meeting with individual therapists and nutritionists. We were told not to talk about the obvious troubling issues, including food, to back off and let them care for our daughter—that was all the information we got. She got worse.

Bulimia was now part of our lives, living in our home, inside our daughter—an eating disorder we sometimes called "Bully." This bully was powerful and mean—and daily created so much disruption in our household it was wearing us out and slowly eroding our previously sound marriage.

Tom and I, and our son, needed a break, a respite from this nightmare. We reached a level of desperation after we tried everything our community could throw at this all-consuming illness. Instinctively, we knew we could no longer accept being told to stand by and watch as she grew sicker by the month.

At the time she was finally diagnosed there was no transitional housing, no safe place for Danielle to go where she could work on her issues on her own. She needed to manage her depression, anxiety, and obsessive compulsive disorder (OCD), and learn new skills for coping with the stress of it all. Months of acting out and blaming us for everything, wasn't creating a healthy life for any of us. There were no respite care programs available for us. As much as we didn't want Danielle hundreds of miles away, we thought that this residential treatment was one way we could hope for her recovery to begin and, at the same time, give us a chance to catch our breath.

We were willing to risk a lot to take her so far away—we were grasping at anything we thought could help. Nothing had helped so far. Her suicide attempts had unraveled us; we were living in constant fear that the next time she would succeed. We desperately needed a lifeline to save our daughter and our sanity.

Inside the treatment center we wondered if we had somehow been transported into our very own horror movie. "Surreal" is the only way to describe it. I felt like I was having an out-of-body experience, except the feeling that I had a terrible gaping hole in my chest reminded me it was all too real. The strange numbness, fuzziness and my lack of ability to make sense of anything all combined to make me feel like I'd left reality and ended up in some strange Oz-like place where I had to go through the motions. I now knew the true meaning of the term "raw fear." Today, I know that I was experiencing "trauma haze."

My daily life had been a "haze" for months. I will never forget the looks on the faces of my mom, sister and friends when I would forget the simplest things. I had no idea that I was not able to remember (that's how out of it I was) until I saw the shock, confusion and concern on their faces.

Normally a very competent, highly functioning (as one psychiatrist put it) adult, dealing with this illness had turned me into a bumbling idiot who couldn't remember simple things like bringing groceries into the house. I can still hear my sister's voice echo in my head—the questioning, almost irritated drawn-out version of my name, "Bethhh?" Hearing that, I knew I'd done it again, totally forgotten something I should have known or should have done. When I read about Post-Traumatic Stress Disorder (PTSD), I realized I had many of the same symptoms. The brain shutting down is a protective mechanism that the body puts into action to preserve itself. There is a technical biochemical description of what was going on, but all I know is that my body was protecting my brain from all the stress—and at that point it was basically stopping any non-essential functions. Or at least they seemed to be non-essential to life, but when you burn up one teapot after another, you start to wonder if maybe memory *is* essential to life.

I also wondered if this would be my new permanent state of mind . . . or lack thereof. *Oh, it's December, I guess that means I should buy Christmas gifts. Who cares about Christmas gifts when you are expecting another shoe to drop out of the sky? Can't we just skip it this year? It's just more things to take care of.* My "lack of affect" (as the shrinks call it) was quite apparent. My mom said I seemed like I was dead. I was so numbed by all of the shock, loss, stress, and trauma that even this didn't faze me (except I felt bad that we were causing my own dear mom such despair).

‿〜

We three sat on the little skinny bench, trying to laugh at the fact that even these experts didn't seem to understand that not everyone with an eating disorder has anorexia; our backsides just didn't fit on the bench. We looked at each other and laughed that sickening kind of laugh you do inside when you feel trapped.

On my lap was a two-pound white three-ring binder bulging with papers. Sticky notes marked the most important pages with labels like "Insurance," "Doctors," "Therapists," "Invoices,"

"Dates," and "Timelines." Keeping this book was a great idea from the care coordinator at our insurance company. It became my "brain" when my organic one was too stressed.

Actually, now, ten years since we started dealing with Danielle's health issues, I am on my second binder. This book was my "memory" when my own wasn't working fully—or not at all. It held all the information my head didn't, especially when my brain had shut down. Each time we spoke with a care provider, the insurance company or anyone who gave us information, I collected it in the binder: name, date, phone number, comments, referrals, advice, events, etc. That way when the next care provider asked what the previous one had said, I had it down. My philosophy was that this would aid them in treating her. Some were grateful and found it useful.

Many times our insurance company decided they could get out of paying a claim (yes, I am cynical but it's reality) because we were scared out of our wits that our child was going to die. Sadly, we parents are so pre-occupied that we won't argue or maybe even notice when the big insurance company doesn't pay the claim. When this happened to us, I went right to my notes and looked up the date, time, the name of the person I'd spoken with and my notes on the conversation with the insurance company.

⤳

"Here is your schedule," a faceless person now said, handing me a sheet of paper. Then nothing. More sitting on the skinny bench, staring at the glassed-in nurse's station and trying not to cry. When someone finally noticed us, she seemed angry that we were just sitting there. We were hustled down the hall past the bony girls confined to their beds, girls who were not allowed to even shower or visit the toilet alone. These girls symbolized the near-death type of anorexia that many people stereotype as "the only true eating disorder."

Digesting all of this was overwhelming. I asked, "You mean these girls are confined to their beds 24 hours a day?"

"No, they can have supervised visits to the restroom. If we let them go by themselves they'll do deep knee bends in the shower and put batteries in their bras before weighing time. They aren't even allowed to hang their limbs over the sides of the bed as that burns off calories."

I flashed on the Nazi concentration camp films from high school. It took all I had in me not to run screaming out of there. I felt like throwing up—how ironic is that?

When dealing with various staff members we were frequently and rudely reminded that our daughter wasn't *that* sick (meaning she was far from even being considered "thin") and we should feel fortunate. She would be able to participate in all the activities, socialize with the other girls, and wouldn't be confined to a bed in constant full view of the secured nurses.

We became aware that the staff's attitude in this center was that to be deserving of their help, you had to look a certain way. And they were the "trained" people.

As we toured the rest of the place, it looked like a college dorm with girls lounging around, watching TV and chatting. But there were posters everywhere of the "art" they had created to remind themselves of how they really are good people, not the monsters they have convinced themselves they are.

Danielle was taken away, to where we didn't know, and we were directed to another waiting area. Finally, after what seemed like an eternity, Tom and I were led into a room to meet with the psychiatrist. By this time we were exhausted, overwhelmed and totally unprepared for the psychiatrist who was a slightly younger version of *One Flew Over The Cuckoo's Nest's* "Nurse Ratched,"— stern, businesslike, and most certainly, unfriendly.

It was quite apparent that she was not trained to calm frightened parents, and she seemed burned out from dealing with eating disorders and the people associated with them.

I was wondering why she wasn't saying something like: "I'm so sorry that you are in this sad situation." As Tom and I sat on the proverbial couch, she proceeded to clearly convey the message that we were damn lucky to be there. Oh yeah, lucky. Sad but true—we did have to know someone who knew someone to get in as quickly as we did.

I pulled out my three-ring companion (my white paper brain) and was immediately reprimanded.

"I need you to put that down!"

I thought, *What is she talking about? Put what down? She can't be serious. She doesn't want me to take notes? She obviously doesn't know how traumatized my brain is, and that the second I walk out this door, I won't remember a thing she said.*

"Excuse me," I explained, "I'll never remember what you say, so I have to take notes."

"No! Please now, put that down so we can get started. I need your full attention!"

Eeek! Am I back in junior high? I reluctantly set it down, and thus have no idea what she told us—something about her seeing our daughter while she was there for the month-long treatment, as well as monitoring her medication.

I think it took about ten minutes for me to resume breathing normally. Again, I felt like vomiting, crying, and running out of there, screaming. *And this is a top-notch, well-known treatment center? Very highly regarded? If true, then what are the other centers like?*

At that point, *WHO is it that needs to be committed?* was going through my head. The total lack of acknowledgment (and outright disregard) for the overwhelming pain, panic, fear, sadness, hopelessness, confusion, and despair we were feeling just made the hole in my chest feel even larger and more raw. Writing everything down in the three-ring binder was my only way of having a thread of hope of keeping all the details straight.

The experience was so physically painful that it was one of those times I actually looked down and felt my chest to see if the hole really was all the way through the skin. This event enlarged the hole, which was now about the size of a cereal bowl. This woman, and all the other providers, didn't know or didn't have time to care that our hearts were breaking right there in front of them, causing us great physical pain. I later heard this is sometimes called a "broken heart" because it actually hurts just like when you have a surgical incision, only no one gives you anything for the pain.

Dark humor saved us again once Tom and I finally got out of that place and could laugh about feeling like throwing up. "We can never tell anyone we laughed about that!" we joked, sort of. No one would ever get it and people would think we were terrible parents—something we had already been told—but not in so many words. We laughed about that, too. "Let *them* do it better," we said as we left without our daughter. We didn't like leaving her in that scary place but we were out of options.

A torrent of conflicting emotions filled us as we flew home without Danielle. But we also went home without ED, "The Bully." It was bittersweet like nothing else. We breathed a cautious sigh of relief.

Help. She was finally getting help and was safe for a while: she couldn't harm herself there. We went home depleted.

It felt good to not have the eating disorder around our home. We could enjoy a meal and relax for the first time in as long as we could remember. We enjoyed a sabbatical from drama for four weeks. Mostly. We made two trips to the center for therapy appointments. As the day drew near to go back to bring Danielle home, my fear level escalated again and reached an all-time high.

BLESSED WITH A SUPPORTIVE LIFE COACH

I was fortunate to be working with a life coach, Goldie, during this time. I'm quite certain that without her I would have succumbed to the fear. On the couple of days that I couldn't get out of bed, I remember thinking that it seemed extremely appealing to just go into the corner of my room, sit on the floor facing the wall, curl into the fetal position, and silently rock, rock, rock forever. One of the exercises my coach did with me was to deal with my fears.

A few days before going back to retrieve Danielle, Goldie took me right into the heart of each fear, not just stating them but also making me feel them to my core. These fears were of losing: my daughter, my marriage, my mind, and my health, home, friends, career, family, money—everything. This was as close to (if not) hysteria as I have ever been. The fear: the monster (ED) would try to take my life away. Destroy my life.

Amazingly, by the end of that exhausting hour, I was calm and realistic. I knew there was no way I would let any of that happen. Goldie helped me gain the gift of a new perspective; her expertise allowed me to begin to have peace and joy where fear and panic had lived.

Beginning to embrace the concept that worrying about Danielle hadn't helped her and would only continue to wear me down helped me to embrace this new way of coping.

I slowly began to accept the fact that Danielle might die, while at the same time I realized that worrying about her would do her no good and could take me down with her.

I became, for the most part, able to live the title of one of Doris Day's most popular songs: "Que Sera Sera—Whatever will be, will be." The peace and calm were amazing. They still are for the most part.

How do I continue to embrace this perspective when yet

another unexpected shoe drops out of nowhere (and they still do)? I keep breathing, using the tools I've been taught and try to always remember: *I get to choose how I react.*

This was a turning point for me, really for my entire life—to learn that *I get to choose* how I react to things. We all know that bad things happen in life. It is how we react to them that makes the difference. Stating that—and really believing it, and acting on it are very different.

That day I was able to realize my inner strength and see how I had been giving away my power. Before, whenever someone's life was in turmoil I let myself get pulled right into it.

I didn't instantly master this new way of choosing how I react—that took me another four years. Yes, it took some practice (I did not do it perfectly) to remember that I had a choice about how I would react every time another stressful or unexpected situation occurred.

When we made the trip to bring Danielle back home, I was able to do so fearlessly. None of my fears had come true and that made me stronger—I was healthier, my marriage was intact, and we could still pay the mortgage. My new-found strength helped me convince the insurance company to pay for the entire stay, therefore assuaging my financial fears even though our travel and other costs were significant.

When we brought Danielle home she was no healthier; the eating disorder was just as powerful as before. The only differences were that she was worn down and her spirit was slightly broken and she was now afraid. What she had seen at the treatment center was quite frightening. She learned firsthand that people indeed die from these diseases.

None of us had any resolution. No treatment outcomes were outlined for us. I asked, "What do we do now?" "Will you coordinate with the treatment team back home?" "Where do we go from here?" They offered no real answers, just told us to go back to what we were doing before. We felt hopeless.

My concern was that any slight progress she had made would be lost without a coordinated effort between the treatment center and her health care team at home. Just recently I learned that this type of coordination is finally being put into practice. Some cities are even creating transitional housing for people with eating disorders, thanks to generous people who care deeply about this cause.

Danielle went back to her previous treatment providers and continued on and on and on. Truly intense, brain-rattling, regular shoe downpours continued until Danielle was 18, when her treatment slowly transitioned into a routine of recovery. Unfortunately, but as is typical, her eating disorder morphed into other addictions such as drinking, drug use and excessive shopping. Every medication change was a test for us all. It still is.

"We see a light at the end of the tunnel, but unfortunately it looks like an oncoming train." was our rehearsed response for so long. Finally, as she began to recover, we could say, "The light at the end of the tunnel no longer looks like a train." With either one of these responses, the expressions on people's faces were priceless, giving us another opportunity to be amused—instead of horrified. Often now, we use an answer we learned from another parent: "Well, if you charted her progress, you would see improvement." That usually satisfies people, and we don't need to go into the complex details that can be tiring to share, and to hear.

Sometimes I still react unconsciously instead of choosing how I want to react to something very challenging. But the difference now is that I notice—and then I get to choose to change to a healthier way of reacting to, or approaching, a crisis or challenge. It is hard to describe how incredibly freeing it is to not feel like I have to take on someone else's pain and suffering. Regardless of what is happening with my daughter, I can choose to smell the roses, smile and have joy in my husband, my son, my career as a veterinarian and many other parts of my life.

It was definitely a transformational time that has forever changed me. And this is a gift that I now say was almost worth all my suffering (here I need to recognize the irony that I caused much of my own suffering).

My ability to choose my reaction was reinforced at an Al-Anon meeting a friend took me to. "In Al-Anon we learn not to suffer because of the actions or reactions of other people." This comes directly from the official Al-Anon Family Group Headquarters, Inc., literature labeled "Detachment." It's certainly not easy but I now believe it is essential.

Being coached around my worst fears was truly a pivotal moment for me; it was my own "emotional CPR." I really had to totally trust Goldie to allow myself to be so vulnerable during the exercise she did with me. But I think one benefit of being so utterly drained is that you let go of any previous pretense, because you just don't have the energy for it.

Goldie also made a request (as coaches do with clients to move them forward), that I view my daughter Danielle standing tall and successful, that I give her respect, trust, love, and compassion—and that I honor her. This was a huge challenge at the time considering I was not only the "enemy" in Danielle's mind, I was also still treading water and barely keeping my head above the swells.

Deep sigh. Wow, seven years ago . . . it looks so different from this vantage point. Rereading those requests from my coach, I think, *Of course that is the view of Danielle I needed to have if I was going to believe that she would improve, and show her I believed it.* It's so obvious now. But even with the stress haze affecting my memory, I do remember thinking that was crazy. When it was a constant cycle of crisis, drama, pain, fear, and daily disasters, it all seemed like a delusional lie.

But I had to believe she would recover, stand tall and be successful. I had seen my children grow from completely dependent babies to independent, competent kids. I knew I had to use that same blind faith. The other choices weren't good. I will always feel a debt of gratitude to Goldie for so lovingly, gently, patiently, and firmly guiding me to a healthy perspective.

Danielle is still doing her recovery her way, and that's okay. We maintain hope for full recovery.

BETH'S TIPS:

1. Learn to face your fears, understand and then challenge them so you are in charge.

2. Know that you always have the choice how you react.

3. Have a sense of humor—even if it is "dark humor." It might be what saves you that day.

4. Recognize and acknowledge to yourself and others when you are in a "stress haze."

5. Remember, you are never the only person dealing with this particular problem—it just feels like it a lot of the time.

6. Develop ready answers to insensitive comments or questions—because they will come. If you know who will make those comments, consider not spending time around them.

7. Keep a good eye on the medical bills and on the insurance company. If, due to stress, you are unable to do it, see if your spouse or a friend will help you keep everything organized.

8. Just because a treatment center has a good, or even excellent, reputation does not mean it can or will help your child. Find the right place for her care.

9. Practice the "What will be, will be" attitude because worrying about something all the time does not help *anyone*.

9

Meredith and Lilly's Story

No One Can Do It Alone

As I sit in this frozen tundra called Minnesota, watching the chickadees seize the brief moment of afternoon sunshine to sip water from the tip of an icicle, I see a portrait of self-sufficiency. The chickadees don't ask for help but, in essence, they are receiving help from the sunshine. It reminds me of Meredith, whose story is next.

As a mother of a daughter recovering from an eating disorder, I can speak to being hesitant about asking for help. There is so much exhaustion, confusion, blaming, shaming, and hopelessness present when you are living in the dark forest of an eating disorder, it is hard to know what to ask for. Others may see you need help, but don't know what to offer.

What does support look like? When everything is so confusing and there are no good answers, it seems pointless to ask for something that seems impossible to get—help.

Friends and family can help transport other children to lessons/games/events, do laundry or yardwork, take you out for a day or an evening, or bring over some meals (though that could be fraught with peril). Sometimes the best a friend can do is offer an ear for listening. These are extremely difficult situations that take an enormous amount of compassion and listening. What isn't helpful to hear is what Meredith heard: "Can't you just tell her to stop?"

Someone suffering from an eating disorder cannot simply stop.

It would be much more helpful to ask family and friends to understand the gravity of an eating disorder, listen when you want to talk, and acknowledge what you are going through. Making a list of tasks that need doing will make it easier to ask for help with research or sorting out the insurance mess. When you are fighting for your child's life and you don't have much energy left for anything else, allow others to help ease your burden.

For many, faith is a big part of recapturing hope and being able to maintain sanity. Being able to hand over the ill child to a higher power gives peace to many parents. One of the best things anyone did for me was to give me a CD of some spiritual songs. I didn't listen to it a lot, but seeing it always reminded me of my friend's concern. Sending a card of encouragement or flowers can be such a gift of support.

So much shame is involved in this illness, along with a stigma that isolates people; any act of support and kindness will help to lessen that isolation.

Sadly, like so many others, Meredith's situation is complicated by alcoholism. My hope is that in their sadness you will feel your own acknowledged and thus have your feelings of isolation lessened. In addition, I hope seeing the mistakes they made will help you with the decisions you need to make.

MEREDITH'S STORY

Looking back about 20 years, I can see that the taco-eating contests my husband Ted had with my step-daughter Lilly probably helped to feed Lilly's eating disorder. Ted would eat all day long; his life centered on eating. He especially loved the all-you-can-eat buffets.

Taco-eating contests were just the beginning. The eating disorder insidiously crept into our lives with subtle telltale signs that we chalked up to normal adolescent behavior—secrecy, sullenness, defiance, and often-peculiar eating patterns. Sometimes Lilly would have a fit if her food was not carefully arranged on her plate so the different foods didn't touch one other. At other times we would watch her stomp out of the room if the texture or color didn't agree with her at that moment.

After being a pudgy 12-year-old, Lilly suddenly started losing weight. I squirm uncomfortably now, wanting to slap myself because at one point I even said, "You look like America's poster child for anorexia." Even with my background in mental health, it hadn't yet occurred to me that she really could have an eating disorder. Luckily, I was able to apologize to Lilly years later for that damaging comment.

Midway through high school Lilly's best friend was killed in a car accident. Lilly retreated to a corner and sobbed for hours. Trying to console and comfort her, I rubbed her back as she mumbled somewhat defiantly through her tears, "I can do this alone." I told her, "You cannot do this alone; I will not abandon you."

Staying under the radar was always her goal, and in her attempts to avoid attracting the wrath of her alcoholic father, she didn't want to draw attention to herself. I now realize she had a love/hate relationship with her father, and eating was part of her attempt to please him. That a child loves her dad is easy to understand, but it gets complicated when alcoholism is involved and the child doesn't understand her father's behavior when he's drinking. It was so painful to watch as Ted complimented her when she gave him a run for his money in their taco-eating contests.

The constant fear of getting her dad riled up kept teenage Lilly clinging to my side at the kitchen sink. This is where we talked, speaking softly. Our relationship strengthened while she

told me her problems as we stood on the three squares of lino-
leum doing the nightly dishes. One evening, she quietly shared
with me that the night her best friend died was when the purging began.

There were symptoms and I hadn't paid enough attention. Her
sad, sad eyes, total lack of interest in being social, the increased
time she slept, and her disinterest in life had grown by the day.
When I grasped how seriously she was grieving and that she was
depressed, I finally realized how isolated she felt.

Now I knew we needed professional help. By this time Lilly
was almost finished with high school. I called a colleague in the
mental health unit at our hospital who agreed to see Lilly.

It is important to be as empowering as possible with any teen,
but especially so when his/her self-esteem has hit rock bottom. In
an effort to show Lilly how capable we saw her, we encouraged
her to drive to the appointment herself. I trusted Lilly to keep the
appointment; however, a week later we learned the truth when
my colleague called and said Lilly never showed. It didn't make
sense to me. It wasn't until years later that I learned that the shame
brought on by the eating disorder leads to secrecy and lying. The
self-loathing combined with the brain dysfunction, often keeps
people from obtaining help and moving toward recovery.

I didn't know what to do next. I loved Lilly with all my heart
and hated the fact that I didn't know how to help her. Sometimes
I felt like I didn't even know her. I eventually learned to separate
Lilly from the eating disorder, which helped me to react more
calmly to her irrational behaviors. In the early days I didn't grasp
this concept and found my patience being tested regularly.

My fear was elevated because I knew I was alone in my quest
to get her help. Her father wouldn't help her and probably would
do more harm than good. Because of his alcoholism, he had
many problems of his own and was in no shape to help. He just

added to the problems with his disrespectful comments and obvious lack of interest in her life. In fact, during one of Lilly's more belligerent moments Ted threw her against a wall and warned, "Don't you pull any of that stuff here with me!"

I realized that this was the beginning of the end of my marriage, yet it took time to acknowledge and take action. I still didn't ask for or accept any help.

I was afraid Lilly would die. Lots and lots of prayers were the only things that worked for me. I would go down to our lakeshore and pray. Begging for her healing and for my peace, I told Satan that even though he wanted our daughter, he couldn't have her. Fighting for her life was what I was doing—and many a day it felt like a losing battle.

The times by the lake made me understand the power of prayer. Prayer made me realize that I had to keep pursuing help for Lilly. I couldn't give up!

It wasn't easy, as Ted never had any understanding of the counseling process. He thought they were all "a bunch of crazies" and, "What good did it do to tell a stranger your problems anyhow?" He understood the eating disorder even less than I did. His was such a narrow-minded view. He was more interested in drinking anyway. Despite the lack of support, this greater-than-me power gave me the strength to not give up on her, even if I had to do it alone. I kept encouraging her to get help.

I knew worrying didn't work. Worrying didn't help. Worrying didn't solve any problems—it sure didn't help Lilly. But as loneliness crept in slowly in the wee hours of the night, I lay sleepless, worrying. Loneliness also became my companion during the quiet middle of the day when I was home alone.

Again, the power of prayer saved me. I would hand over my loneliness and ask for comfort, companionship, and peace in return. Serenity would spread over me and calm me, if only momentarily at first. My prayers alternated between being for Lilly's recovery and my own sanity.

The eating disorder disrupted every part of our lives. It spread into every aspect of life like smoke in a house fire. Between the stressful meals, the lying, secrecy, ever-present sadness, even during "fun" trips to the beach, we were constantly aware of the eating disorder's presence. Daily, I was struck by the irony of trying so hard to save Lilly's life and, at the same time, feeling so angry with her behaviors and everything that the eating disorder was taking from each of us.

The behaviors of an eating disorder can be impossible to understand and very aggravating for family members who don't understand what is causing them. Even once you understand that it is the eating disorder—not the person—that is causing irrational and disrespectful behavior, it is still difficult to be patient with him or her.

We had a breather for a little while, as things appeared to settle down when Lilly went off to college. We saw her for short visits, but soon they became infrequent. At winter break, she hid herself in bulky sweaters, thus I was able to avoid thinking about the eating disorder. Then one day we went to the health club together because Lilly said she was concerned about the "freshman 15," the 15-lb. gain that often accompanies the first year of college. After our workout, we went to the hot tub. Seeing her in her swimsuit, my shock was so extreme I blurted out, "My God, Lilly, what have you done to yourself?" Her reply was, "Mom, I'm just really fit." I had been so hopeful that she was doing better, but seeing how incredibly thin she was, I knew that her eating disorder still controlled her life.

Lilly didn't come home for spring break that first year. Soon afterward, though, she called, saying, "The campus nurse practitioner wants to talk to you."

"What's wrong?" I pleaded.

"Something about my liver," she muttered.

The nurse took the phone from Lilly and said, "You need to get down here now and take your daughter to the hospital! She is going to the gym three times a day! Other students are reporting that she eats only vegetables. Her skin has turned orange from all of the carrots she has been eating. She has what is called carotenemia.

"When we weighed her, she removed her rings and spit out her gum first."

Panicked, I raced to campus as quickly as possible and found out she'd seen the nurse practitioner a couple of times and had been told to call me but hadn't. The resident assistant had thought about calling me but wasn't sure if it was respectful of Lilly's rights. I sat in her dorm wringing my hands until she returned from yet another trip to the gym. She was so ashamed that when she saw me, she wouldn't even look at me and barely spoke. It took my breath away to see her now skeletal form.

The nurse had told me not to let her drive a car, as her electrolytes were so low she could have a heart attack, but Lilly didn't want to leave. She had a dinner date and told me, "Mom, I'm so confused. I'm trying to figure out whether I should go and not eat—or go and eat and then come back and throw it up."

I told her neither was an option. I firmly told her, "Lilly, I'm going to drive you home now."

Lilly insisted she could drive. Not wanting to upset her even more, I reluctantly agreed to let her drive and I rode along. She talked the whole way, which was good, but it was clear that she was still in denial that she was ill.

Lilly had been through one hospital program for eating disorders during high school, which was a dismal failure. When I brought her home from that first experience, she sat in her bedroom and cried for hours. I didn't want to put her through that same program.

I found a new hospital with a program that treated people with eating disorders within a unit for all types of adolescent mental health issues. Enough kids in the unit had eating disorders that they were able to have a nightly eating disorders group. It was a good fit for Lilly.

One boy in the unit with bipolar disorder inspired her. "Mom, if he can work on his issues, I can work on mine, too." I was so hopeful that this second hospitalization would do the trick for her.

However, the mental health intake was a horrible experience for her. The nurses confronted Lilly about many of her lies. They stripped her down to her underwear and took photos. She was so bony that, to be comfortable, she had to sit on a cushion when she was at the table to eat.

Back home, Lilly asked me for a garbage bag. When she threw out all of her diuretics and laxatives, I felt she had turned a corner. We all went to bed and these thoughts rambled around in my head: *Is this what "normal" families do? I feel like I'm running a mental health ward here with my alcoholic husband, and a daughter with an eating disorder. I have to give the suffering away, take in the serenity. I need to pray some more. What else is there to do? I guess this is a way of asking for help.* I reasoned that even the birds let the sunshine help them out from time to time. Even though I never asked anyone for help, I did ask God, and He gave me peace.

Family therapy was offered and this time Ted agreed to go. Talking about feelings was not something that happened in our home. He just wanted to make jokes during the sessions. He was obnoxious and embarrassing, on top of being incredibly insensitive.

I tried to make it seem as if life was okay even though Ted was a walking disaster. The facilitator knew from experience that everything wasn't fine, but that we were the kind of family who pretended it was. When Lilly began to cry, I asked her why. The psychologist came over, put her arms around Lilly and said, "I can see that this is too difficult for you in this setting. I can set up an appointment for just your family." It was then that Ted made his most outrageous comment, saying, "I think we should just hook her up to a vacuum cleaner hose and mainline roast beef sandwiches."

On the way home I told Ted and Lilly, "I need to make an appointment for our family for tomorrow." They both told me they didn't hear anyone say we should do that. *Am I going crazy? Why did I hear that and they didn't?* The pattern of avoiding issues had gone from bad to worse in our family.

When I talked to the psychologist the next day, she confirmed that, indeed, she had suggested we have a family appointment. Because of the craziness and denial of our family, that appointment never happened.

The next year Lilly went to a new college where she met the man who would become her husband. I'd like to say they lived happily ever after ... but you already know this isn't a fairy tale. However, she did get better, for a while.

Lilly still had lingering body image issues, and I understand this is common, sometimes even lifelong for some people with eating disorders. Visiting their home one day after they were married, I saw roses on the table and commented, "Oh how sweet; he gave you roses. What a wonderful husband you have, Lilly."

"Mom, when he wanted to hold me and be intimate I freaked because I just couldn't handle it. I feel so fat and ugly. He felt so bad he sent me two dozen roses."

Soon after, she found a group recovery program for eating disorders in her small town and also received acupuncture, which helped her anxiety and improved her diminished fertility.

THE NOT-SO-HAPPILY-EVER-AFTER

The happily-ever-after part is that she was able to get pregnant, has had three children and is still married. The not-so-happily-ever-after is that Lilly still has relationship issues with many people in her life to this day, including me. She won't speak to me—I am the safe one, and it's easiest to blame the people who are safe. Knowing she is still working on her "issues" helps me accept this, but it is still incredibly painful. I do not see my daughter nor my grandchildren.

I am respecting her need for privacy to finish healing her wounds, and I try not to take it personally. I began taking better care of myself, which helps me to cope with this loss, and part of improving my self-care was the courage to end my unhealthy marriage.

I intellectually know that it is very common for people with addictions (including eating disorders) to blame others, especially those who feel the safest. I have heard people with addictions say that they take out their anger on those who they know can take it and, more important, those who won't hold it against them. Lilly knows that I'm safe, and I know that I am safe, but it still hurts ... a lot. I comfort myself in the belief that when she is ready to claim responsibility for saying good-bye to her eating disorder, she'll stop blaming me. For the most part, I have peace. And that is a huge accomplishment.

TIPS FROM LILLY'S MOTHER, MEREDITH:

1. Pay attention, as an eating disorder diagnosis can be easy to miss. I work in the mental health field and missed it.
2. Educate yourself about eating disorders.
3. Find lists of care providers and get referrals for therapists and nutritionists.

4. Investigate eating disorder programs before signing up. It doesn't matter if they are well known; it has to be a good fit.

5. Good resources may include: a pastor, therapist, or a care coordinator at an insurance company.

6. Be willing to ask for help from friends, family, and professionals.

7. If you don't know how to ask for help, find someone who has been through a medical or mental health crisis and learn how he or she asked for help.

8. Be aware of other possible pre-existing issues such as physical abuse, domestic violence, sexual abuse/incest, date rape, etc. If you suspect anything, get help. One resource is the Abuse Wheel—The Duluth Intervention Project—http://www. theduluthmodel.org/wheelgallery.php.

9. Know that other mental health issues can mask the eating disorder. Be open to dual diagnoses, such as depression, anxiety, substance abuse, etc.

10. Find ways to keep a sense of humor, even if it is a bit dark.

10

Dexter's Story

Dad: Blissfully Ignorant in His Man-Cave

"Can you help me find treatment options for my daughter?"

Mothers are usually the ones looking for treatment for their daughters. However, this email message was from Dexter, the father of a daughter with an eating disorder.

Hearing from this dad who was sitting atop his motor home in southern California, I immediately sensed he wasn't a typical dad. Dexter was stepping outside his comfort zone, literally and figuratively. He was doing maintenance on the roof of the RV he calls home when I called him.

I can count on one hand the number of dads who have contacted me for treatment information. It's almost always the mom, friend, sister, or even the person with the illness who calls or emails me looking for treatment options.

Though most of us tend to be at a loss when it comes to living with and treating eating disorders, Dexter flat-out says, "I was clueless!" Many parents, especially dads, remain in denial for quite a long time, and prefer it that way. For many men, all the emotions involved and talking about feelings sends them running for cover. Dexter was no different. He admits his first impulse was to say, "Can't I just go into my cave and hide out until it's over?"

This ability of so many fathers to remain emotionally detached to the point of being uninvolved quite amazes me. Talking to mothers for this book and in my day-to-day coaching, I've learned it's quite common for fathers to ignore or even deny there is a problem. Many do not participate in the treatment or help to find resources, and they avoid the gripping fear that many of the mothers feel. There must be some middle ground between what often is under-involvement by dads, such as Dexter and often over-involvement by moms to the point that the rest of their lives come to a screeching halt—but that is another book.

Some of us moms living with eating disorders could learn from the opposite sex to achieve a *middle ground of being healthy caregivers.* A healthy middle ground is a goal for a lot of people, and most certainly for people living with eating disorders in their families. A wonderful resource is a book by Margery Pabst and Rita Goldhammer called *Enrich Your Caregiving Journey.* More information about the book is in the Resources section.

Caring for someone with a life-threatening illness is exhausting and keeping yourself healthy in the process is essential. Finding out what that looks like for you will be a process and I hope Dexter's experiences will help you see how it looked for him when he wasn't engaged and how different it was when he participated in his daughter's recovery.

DEXTER'S STORY

"Blissfully ignorant" could closely describe my awareness of my daughter's situation until one crucial moment. I'm not even really sure when it all started, or how old she was when it all began. Chelsea's mother and I were separated and she lived with her mom. I traveled a lot. As a result, I saw Chelsea only every couple of months during her last years of high school and early college years. That may sound extreme but with the hectic lives all of us led, and Chelsea being in her late teens to early twenties with a very busy schedule, it was tricky to find times we were both available.

I knew she had lost a lot of weight and that her mom and our older, married daughter had talked about eating disorders and what to do to help Chelsea. I know now that I wasn't taking it seriously. When I saw a photo of her on a boat in California, taken over the Fourth of July holiday, she was clothed from head to foot in long pants and long sleeves. I thought, *That is really odd; it was so hot out.* Her face never looked emaciated so it was easy to stay comfortably in denial because I, like many, thought you must be emaciated to have an eating disorder. Since she had started wearing long sleeves, bulky sweatshirts and loose pants quite a while back, it became "normal" to see her dressed that way. Even after seeing that photo, I didn't think much about that. Like most dads, I'm quite clueless and, frankly, pretty insensitive and unaware of how my kids are dressed. I was focused on making money for our family.

Having practiced law for about ten years, I call myself a recovering attorney. I went on to do other things but my background helped prepare me for my daughter's legal troubles. One night Chelsea was stopped for driving under the influence, but since she was quite close to our house the officer decided not to arrest her. I was shocked and enraged. Chelsea knew she shouldn't drink and drive. Our kids were raised knowing it was a family value that they not drink, but if they decided to, they should have a designated driver. It seemed really odd to me that she would do this. I gave her my best "Dad lecture" to which she had some story, followed by, "I'm sorry, I'm sorry, I'm sorry." I figured that was the end of it.

Yet sometime later (I have no idea of the timeframe), she got into a single-car accident very close to our local grocery store.

She was *really* drunk. The store manager came to the scene and told the officer that Chelsea had been shoplifting—and it wasn't the first time. She was handcuffed and jailed. I went with her to her court hearings, where she was assigned community service.

The whole thing totally shocked me, and I was completely confused by the shoplifting. When we were told her blood alcohol level I knew, from my law days, that it was so high an average person would have passed out. I also knew that only a person who drinks constantly would be functioning at all at that level. Reality slapped me in the face and opened my eyes to the fact that something very serious was going on with my younger daughter.

Part of Chelsea's sentence was to attend AA meetings, and since her license was suspended, I drove her to the meetings and her community service commitments. This gave us a lot of time to talk. Again I heard a litany of "I'm sorry, Dad," excuses, etc. Her mother was mainly concerned about Chelsea's eating disorder, but I was absolutely convinced the drinking problem was more important. I said, "She could die today from the drinking; let's focus on that." My state of denial allowed me to ignore the eating disorder. I talked and talked to my daughter, realizing later that most of it came out as a lecture. Chelsea's response varied slightly this time. She kept saying, "Yes, yes, yes . . . I promise, I promise, I promise."

Had I known then what I know now about why people with eating disorders wear sweatshirts year round, the seriousness of eating disorders, and that drinking can be a factor, I would have done everything entirely different. When Chelsea's mother convinced her to see a therapist about the eating disorder I still said, "She should see someone about the drinking—that could kill her today!" I had no clue the eating disorder could be just as deadly as drinking and driving, maybe even deadlier.

Both her mom and sister attended group therapy with Chelsea, but I didn't know they were going. They also found her a nutritionist. When I returned from a business trip Chelsea asked me to attend group therapy with them. While I was sitting there with other families whose daughters were dealing with eating disorders, my daughter told me for the first time that she had anorexia nervosa. I immediately said to the therapist, "What can I do?"

She suggested the book *Talking to Eating Disorders*. I bought it that night. I read the entire book the next day and found it very enlightening. I began to understand a little about eating disorders. I learned some things to talk about and, more importantly, things *not* to talk about. For example: Don't ask your daughter every day what she weighs. It seems so basic now, but back then I just thought, *Whoa, how do I do that?* But if you see your loved one wearing sweatshirts and long pants on hot days, it is okay to ask, "What's up with that?" I had no clue she was trying to hide her frighteningly thin body and that she was freezing most of the time due to her dangerously low body weight. I encouraged Chelsea's mom and sister to read the book, too.

Looking back with clearer eyes, an enlightened brain, and current knowledge, I know now that I just plain ignored many important red flags. I'm not beating myself up here; I'm just mentioning these things for the benefit of other families.

Excessive drinking and eating disorders often go hand in hand. I had no idea that they had anything to do with one another. I wondered, *How could it be so common for people fighting eating disorders to have a drinking problem?* Now I am getting the picture of how much pain Chelsea was in, and that drinking helped to lessen her pain.

Unless you're educated about eating disorders, it is tough to know how incredibly dangerous and life threatening they really are. It is very confusing, and it makes little sense to those of us who don't have addictive personalities and who aren't in horrifying emotional and physical pain. Early on I thought she was doing this to herself. Now I know she didn't choose to have this disease.

As I drove Chelsea to her many appointments, we had more time to discuss how she was doing with her recovery. I never pried for information about her sessions with her individual therapist. She would just tell me she was gaining weight and doing well. During the month of group therapy, we made a commitment to go out to dinner once a week when I was in town. We realized we hadn't spent time alone since she'd gone to college. Those weekly dinners became an important time for us to reconnect and for me to check on her progress. Soon I began to suspect I was being "fed a line," along with my meal.

Every week she claimed to be doing well and having good sessions with her nutritionist, therapist and other treatment providers. Then came the moment I remember very specifically. I asked my usual, "How are you doing?" I got the typical, "Oh, I gained another two pounds this week" in return. I gently confronted her, saying, "Chelsea, if you'd gained all the weight you've been telling me you've gained, you would weigh about 150 pounds now." She couldn't answer.

I knew something more was wrong but I was afraid to push her. *She's going through enough right now,* I told myself. I just kept trying to encourage her to be truthful and continue her therapies.

A few months later we attended a family wedding. Chelsea wasn't covered from head to foot for the first time in years and as soon as I saw her bony arms I felt like crying.

I had no idea what to say or do. It was the most helpless moment I've felt as a father to stand there and see my daughter's body disappearing before my eyes and not be able to save her. I was scared saying something would do more damage than good. I told myself, *She's seeing a professional therapist, a nutritionist, several doctors; I must be doing everything I can to help my daughter. I will just keep quiet and keep going to the weekly family therapy meetings.* I knew she'd keep telling me the same old story, though.

Chelsea was to be a bridesmaid a few weeks later. Two months before the wedding she had said, "I want to be the prettiest bridesmaid at the wedding. I'm going to gain weight." But when she attended the bachelorette party in Las Vegas, which included tanning by the pool, she didn't feel comfortable in a swimsuit. She appeared in her long pants and sweatshirt and felt like everyone was talking behind her back.

After the pool experience the bride became nervous and concerned whether Chelsea would be able to wear the backless bridesmaid dress. She went to Chelsea and kindly said, "I know you don't feel comfortable having people see your body. I'm not asking you to stand up there and wear that dress if you don't want to. I understand. You'll still be a bridesmaid, we can find a different dress." Chelsea was relieved. The day of the wedding however, she couldn't even stand up there. She drank so much at the reception, she spent most of the time in the bathroom throwing up.

A few days before Christmas we met with a doctor who requested to speak with our entire family: my ex-wife, our older daughter, Chelsea, and me. As the four of us sat in the tiny exam room, the doctor walked in and announced, "I'm very concerned about Chelsea. Her electrolytes and potassium are so low she is going to die soon if she doesn't get intensive inpatient treatment immediately."

"What do you mean by inpatient treatment? A hospital?" I asked.

The doctor replied, "If she doesn't get into a 24-hour inpatient eating disorders program immediately, then get her to a hospital to get medical care to save her life. Talk to her dietician and her therapist about where she can go. They know of some good facilities."

My mind was racing. "We need to find a treatment center, talk with our insurance company, and deal with so many details, it will take a few days. You are saying this has to happen immediately—but it can't happen immediately. Tell us what happens in these few days. What do we do to keep her alive until then? Is the ER the answer?"

"No, the emergency room isn't the answer. I will administer electrolytes now, prescribe potassium, and you should give her Gatorade every day."

This was the moment the light bulb in my tiny brain started to turn on. Up until then, there had been a little flicker but it wasn't totally bright until this doctor said right to my face, "She's going to die if you guys don't do something." Now I had something I could fix! It was almost a relief to me.

My task-oriented mind was in full force. I immediately went into logistics mode, trying to find a place for her. No longer "checked-out dad," I became obsessed with helping her get well—no middle ground of healthy support for me.

I started trying to figure out where to call and what to do. I was compelled to take some of the first positive action during this four-to-five-year span but I still had no idea of exactly what to do. I didn't want to go with my ex-wife's instinct to send her to the UCLA Medical Center's eating disorders program. I said, "I know nothing about their program except that we all went to school there. We don't know if that is the best choice and it should be Chelsea's choice about where she will go. If we try to force her, it will backfire. She's got to decide and quickly."

Because I am in front of a computer all day every day, I took on the job of researching treatment facilities. I sent the information to Chelsea to check out and make the decision about which to enroll in. In the meantime I checked out the insurance, quite certain that these places couldn't be cheap. That turned out to be the one thing I was right about.

Though we had little time and it was the holiday, I did all the tedious research of finding places, calling them, asking what they do, how they do it, what their success rates are (or what they claim their success rates are) and whether or not they were in our insurance network.

During these few frantic days Chelsea had a third drunk-driving incident, sideswiping a parked car. Even though there was no blood alcohol problem by the time they found her, she was back in court with DUI and hit-and-run charges. The judge gave her the choice of going to jail or doing hard labor, picking up trash on the sides of the roads. Chelsea's nutritionist was beside herself, saying, "She cannot do that! I'll write a letter to the judge. In her compromised state of health it is too dangerous for her to be in the hot sun." My daughter wanted to lose more weight and the roadside work was perfect for that, so she chose community service. We tried to contact the doctor who had told us to get her into treatment immediately, but we were not able to get a hold of him and only got the incompetent young woman they had answering the phone who impatiently told us she would give him a message. Without a letter from him there was no hope of getting her a medical exception. Fortunately she entered treatment before sentencing and community service was postponed.

When I gave the list of treatment centers to Chelsea I told her that I'd heard really good things about two places in Arizona, but she was concerned about staying close to home so people could visit her. I told her that wasn't really a smart way to look at it. I said, "Forget about anyone visiting you and how far away it is.

You need to do what's best for you and your recovery. We need to get you in somewhere now."

Since I live in my motor home, I told her that if it made her more comfortable and helped her make an intelligent decision, wherever she chose to go for treatment I would work from there. She chose Remuda Ranch and on January 1 we drove to Wickenburg, Arizona.

For the next three months I lived about a mile from Remuda Ranch in my motor home and kept my routine. I worked, as usual, using my phone and computer. I played tennis with the few people who were willing to play when it was only 30 degrees outside. I also attended the weekly family sessions, which I found very helpful and eye-opening. I learned that dads and daughters often don't speak the same language. Improving my communication skills with my daughter was invaluable.

It was at Remuda I discovered how difficult recovery is for both the person in recovery, as well as the family. All of this gave me more patience, empathy and understanding. I heard other parents share their frustrations with the often long and challenging process of recovery. They spoke what I'd been thinking, "How do we look forward with positive enthusiasm and hope when there's also skepticism?"

Chelsea had experienced traumas I knew nothing about. I also learned that other things that I thought were no big deal, like breaking up with a boyfriend, were *really big deals* to her. The intensity in which she had perceived them shocked me and I began to realize that I hadn't known how to respond to her when she shared her difficulties with me. Even with the best intentions, if we don't know how to respond and relate it's very difficult to be helpful, especially when we don't understand that what our daughters are sharing may be deeply upsetting to them.

At first I didn't understand what this had to do with eating disorders. What I learned was that many people who develop eating disorders feel unseen, unworthy and uncared about. If we can listen and help them know we understand what they are feeling, they are more likely to feel our love and concern for them, which may help prevent one contributing factor that can feed their eating disorders. I found that effective communication isn't that hard if you can be open-minded and take it seriously.

The group counseling program the previous year had helped me reach the point where I could let go of trying to fix this for her but I could still be a supportive partner in her journey toward recovery. Counseling made me realize that Chelsea is an adult so what I can do to help her is limited. Unlike when she was little, this was something daddy couldn't make "all better." Prior to the family therapy in California, the only time I had ever talked to a psychologist was on the tennis courts. I am so glad I agreed to go to counseling; I went only four times, but right away realized this eating disorder was something beyond my comprehension, something I hadn't accepted, didn't grasp, or even take seriously. The counseling at Remuda further helped me take the eating disorder seriously. I also learned that I had to understand eating disorders so I wouldn't become aggravated by Chelsea's behaviors or succumb to worry.

I'm a rational guy and know that worrying about something I cannot fix is going to cause me stress, so there is no point in worrying about it. I know that sounds pretty simplistic, but I had to be realistic, just like when I play tennis. I go into each match planning to win but I know it isn't realistic that I will win every match, and if I am not realistic, I could get really down on myself when I do lose.

Chelsea worked hard with the treatment providers during her three months at Remuda Ranch. It was early spring when I brought her home, and though I was hopeful, it's been an emotional seesaw. I took her to her mom's house on a Friday and spoke with her the next day. She felt great and told me everything was great being out of what she called "confinement." Her mom was concerned on Friday night when she went out with friends right away because that meant going to bars. I asked Chelsea if she had any temptations to eat or drink in ways that were not in her best interest. Her answer was, "No, it was fine." I wondered if I could believe her.

She went out apartment hunting and out with friends again Saturday night. When I called her twice on Sunday and she didn't call back, I became concerned that she was getting herself into situations she couldn't handle (it's a fine line between being supportive and involved but not worrying.) She finally called on Monday and apologized for not calling me. I asked if she could tell me what she did over the weekend. We went over her whole weekend schedule and agreed that she would call me every day. I asked her to call me any time she felt tempted to restrict, binge, purge, or drink. She agreed she would.

Chelsea found an apartment and we spent a day moving her in. She seemed happy and more confident than she had in years. I was pleasantly surprised to see she was wearing shorts and a tank top. Clearly she gained a lot of weight from the tube feeding and work she did at Remuda Ranch. She seemed to be doing great.

Within a week of arriving home she got another DUI.

Our journey continues with me providing support while my daughter finds her way, her addictions hovering close by.

DEXTER'S TIPS:

1. Learn all you can about eating disorders. You can start with my website: http://dad-eds.com/blog/.

2. Improve your communication skills and use them with your children. Talk with your daughters and sons—actually communicate using a magic concept called dialogue. Your role as dad in this dialogue starts and ends with listening and being interested, without judgment or criticism about any feelings your son or daughter might express. Open the door to any subject. It is your absolute responsibility to teach your daughters how to deal emotionally with the media, the diet industry, the Barbie doll image, their friends, their enemies, and the world.

3. Go to the family classes/groups that are offered to you. Take advantage of counseling and learn new skills to interact with your daughter or son and also with the eating disorder.

4. Find ways to take care of yourself so you can be the most effective support possible for your son or daughter.

5. Take the eating disorder seriously. These are life-threatening illnesses that require complicated treatments.

6. There is no place in your daughter's eating disorder for bullying, badgering, or waving "Dad's magic fix-it wand." It takes patience, tenacity, understanding and a lot of courage to support your child through whichever treatment method is chosen.

7. No single cause exists for anyone's eating disorder. Eating disorders are complex and very complicated. Just as there is no single cause or blame, there is also no single magic cure. And we (parents) are not to blame. None of us should feel even an ounce of guilt. I don't.

8. If your daughter comes home upset because someone said she was fat, please avoid doing what I probably did when my daughters were growing up. Most likely I would have said

something like, "Who cares? She's an idiot . . ." None of that will matter to her. She doesn't want you to discount her feelings or tell her she's wrong to feel hurt. She just wants you to validate her and her emotions. She wants to know you care about how she feels. Tell her you know she's upset and you care and you're sorry. Ask her what you can do to help make her feel better, to comfort her.

9. When your child starts making comments about what a pretty body is, be innovative and creative. Use teachable moments such as television programs that objectify women. Talk about it. Listen. See if he or she is developing body image issues. Self-confidence issues. Self-esteem issues. These are keys in the development of eating disorders. Listen not in judgment, but in love.

11

Kitty Westin's Story

ED Doesn't Win When We Choose Joy

Kitty Westin has been doing advocacy work for families with eating disorders since her daughter, Anna, lost her battle with anorexia on February 17, 2000. Thanks to Kitty, many more families are able to get treatment for eating disorders paid for by their insurance companies. Kitty is a role model for all parents living with the nightmare of eating disorders. Her advocacy work has also helped to reduce the "blame-the-parents" game.

Kitty and I first met in 2004 at the National Eating Disorders Association (NEDA) Conference in Chicago. I briefly introduced myself and thanked Kitty for the outreach and advocacy work she'd been doing. Even though we are both from the western suburbs of Minneapolis, Minnesota, and we had both recently parented a child with an eating disorder, we hadn't met, though I certainly knew of her work.

Writing Kitty and Anna's story was painful but I am grateful that Kitty and I have continued our conversation. In my most difficult days I didn't know any other parents to talk with who had been down this awful road. Getting to know Kitty better and talking about our many similar challenges has helped us both.

Children and adults *die* from eating disorders that have

destroyed their physical ability to live properly. Poor nutrition can damage their organs and sadly, the heart is an organ that is only so strong and can fight for life just so much. Children and adults also die by their own hand from the pursuant depression that often accompanies an eating disorder.

After five long years of pain, Anna silenced the eating disorder. Unfortunately, in doing so, she ended her own life. She said goodbye to this place that felt so unfriendly, unhappy, where she felt worthless and felt no one was listening to her . . . though, in reality, many people were listening and trying to help.

KITTY'S STORY

On the pristine north shore of Lake Superior there co-exists wild violence, beauty and peace. This dichotomy is similar to the striking differences that simultaneously reflect the joy and peace that co-exist in me, alongside my broken heart.

My husband, Mark, and I owned our north-shore property when our daughter Anna was still alive. Although the cabin wasn't built yet, she loved it there. Anna spent hours walking and sitting on the rocks. She used to tell me that it was the only place the eating disorder couldn't follow her. Of course, I still saw struggles and symptoms, but she felt more in control and calmer when we were there. I would have moved up there if the eating disorder really couldn't have followed us.

Anyone who has been to the north shore knows it holds a special energy that draws people to its rugged rocky landscape. Today, we truly have fun, joy, peace and happiness in our lives on the lake, as well as in our daily lives back in the Twin Cities.

Conscious choice and sheer determination that the eating disorder couldn't take this, too, makes it possible for my husband and me to enjoy being at our cabin in northern Minnesota.

Our lives had been rugged and rocky for a long time. Mark

and I had spent years helping Anna fight her battle with the eating disorder. The day Anna died we felt we had two choices: we could crawl away, lick our wounds and say, "We never have to have eating disorders in our lives again." Or we could say, "Yes, Anna lost her battle, but is there any way we can help others not lose *their* battles?"

Mark and I chose number two—educating and advocating— to help others and heal ourselves.

ANNA'S DEATH ISN'T THE END OF MY STORY— IT'S THE BEGINNING

Although the media has always wanted the sad story of her life, and how our lives were affected, I feel it is important to be clear that Anna's death was the beginning.

I've often told the story of our lives up to when Anna died. But now that we've accomplished so much in Minnesota and nationally, I want to share the *whole* story, including the good anger and our motivation to change the outcomes for other families impacted by eating disorders.

That very first day after Anna died, I brought my family together and we made a conscious decision that we would somehow find a way to get through the horror of Anna's death and the horror of the eating disorder—without it taking us down. It tried—oh, how it tried.

The eating disorder wanted to tear apart our marriage and freeze us forever in sadness and pain. It was trying to find a way to eat us alive. There was a powerful feeling, even after Anna was gone, that the eating disorder was still in our family. We were all determined to not let the eating disorder win. It took time but slowly we gained the upper hand.

I tell other parents, "Get angry!" then use that anger to do something about it. My anger could have turned into bitterness, but I felt Anna's spirit and wanted my anger to work for good. I wanted to use the energy of that anger to honor Anna's spirit by not letting the eating disorder destroy us, and by preventing others from being destroyed.

Anna's presence is still with me; her spirit has helped me be her voice and a catalyst for change, which has, in turn, helped in our quest to keep the eating disorder from winning.

As a psychologist, I was trained to believe that feeling the spirit or presence of a deceased loved one was nothing more than a mechanism mourners use to feel good. But Anna's presence was so strong, and I felt so clearly that she wanted me to be her voice, that I had trouble denying it. I read Dr. Janis Amatuzio's book, *Beyond Knowing,* which validated these new feelings as well as the experiences we were having. Now I know I'm not crazy, in denial or using defense mechanisms to cope. I am able to say that this is who I am, someone who can sense the presence of a loved one who has passed on.

I completely agree with author Mitch Albom who, in *Tuesdays with Morrie,* says that death ends a life, not a relationship. I am Anna's voice. It took me years but I have gone through volumes of Anna's journals, discovering a wealth of information. Some of it is instructional as to what I'm supposed to do. She talked about never letting your voice die. Reading her words, I was impressed at her wisdom and understanding.

Her body was damaged and worn out and she couldn't live with so much pain anymore, but I think she knew her voice would carry on through me and others.

ED hasn't won. Many, many lives have been saved because of Anna's death.

If someone gave me the choice—I could have Anna back or do this work—I would, of course, want her back. I still miss her, and my heart remains broken, I long to touch her and smell her.

I can't do that, but I do have the choice to live a joyful, fulfilling life, and I *am* doing that.

My long, slow climb out of the depression that followed Anna's death included a phone call to Dr. Walter Kaye, a well-known researcher in the eating disorders field. I asked him, "How do you go from being a healthy spirit to being dead?" I needed some answers.

He helped me to process some of the noise rattling around in my head. My two other daughters, who grew up in the same house and heard the same messages, hadn't developed eating disorders. When I expressed fear that they might, he reminded me that eating disorders aren't simply "behavior problems." They are serious illnesses. He told me to trust my gut; if I suspected any issues with food I should listen to the instinctive voice in my head. It wouldn't necessarily indicate an eating disorder but I should explore it and educate myself so I would understand what I was dealing with and would know the questions to ask.

WHAT I WISH I HAD KNOWN

I am abundantly aware that going back and doing the "what if" game is completely useless, but for the sake of learning everything I can to help all the others just beginning or in the midst of this unchosen journey, I want to share what I would have found helpful and what was not helpful.

PARENTS ARE *NOT* THE CAUSE!

The message I want to share, first and foremost, is that parents *do not* cause eating disorders and I will go nose to nose with anyone who disagrees. I didn't do everything perfectly, no parent does, but I didn't cause the eating disorder. Dr. Cheryl Dellasega in her book, *The Starving Family,* states it clearly: "Unfortunately, as treatment begins, both mothers and fathers often find themselves in a double-bind situation, negatively labeled by health care professionals and a source of anger and resentment from a child who irrationally views them as the enemy. Even families who may have contributed to the eating problem don't benefit from being judged or blamed because parenting does not stop when a child develops an eating disorder. If anything, it intensifies."

From my experience, many therapists and other care providers are as desperate as we are to find a source of these deadly disorders—something that may lead us to a cure—and because they haven't, they have blamed the families. I agree with Dr. James Lock of Stanford University who says, ". . . Clinicians have blamed families, excluded them from treatment, and instead focused on the individual relationship of patient and therapist as the incubus for recovery."

There are lots of myths and misunderstandings that somehow parenting styles cause eating disorders. I have refused all along to take on that guilt, and I don't believe it was better for Anna to exclude us, her parents, from her recovery. I've heard it called a "parentectomy," the "parent-blame" and "controlling-mom" belief that has been so prevalent in eating disorders treatment.

Certainly some parents and families have made some egregious parenting mistakes. Occasionally, evil people do horrible things; however, this is a very small percentage. In those rare cases, they should be separated during the treatment.

I have gone on record stating I firmly believe that parents and families should be part of the team and be treated with utmost respect and dignity. Care providers need to be astute as to whether or not a patient is being honest. As a practicing psychologist, it is essential that I gain my client's trust. Then I must ask myself, "When do I question what the patient is saying? When do I bring the family in?" When I hear things that sound judgmental or blaming of the family, I will suggest, "Let's bring your family in and talk about how you are seeing this very differently so they can support you." I then reassure the family that they didn't cause this.

Other things I wish I had known:

Watching my words: I had no idea that the power of words, my own words about my size and shape, were something that could have an enormous impact on contributing to a child's body satisfaction. I grew up in this culture that clearly promotes that I, as a woman have to be a perfect size and shape to be worthwhile.

I wish I had known the types of statements to avoid making around my young girls regarding my own body, unintentional comments that could potentially lead to life-altering and deadly disorders. Don't comment on your own body shape to others.

First reference to dieting: When Anna was 14, she said she wanted to go on a diet. I didn't say much. I remember thinking, "That little thing doesn't need to be on a diet." Had someone said, "Kitty, this could be a fatal decision," I would have done things differently. I would have been more curious and questioned my daughter's statement by initiating some open-ended dialogue such as: "Anna, tell me more about that. What's driving that?" If she answered, "Because I want to be healthy, I'm going to become a vegetarian," I would now know that this could lead to restricting behaviors. I would have been more alarmed and taken a firmer parenting stance by stating, "If that is a choice you want to make, tell me how you are going to get more protein and some of the iron and minerals you would get from meat." I definitely would have been more authoritarian about this.

I realize I couldn't make her stop. But because I was confused and really didn't have enough information, I feel I kind of rolled over on that and didn't explore it enough.

Health class curriculum messages: Now I know parents need more information. Is this "diet" something your son or daughter is choosing for moral reasons? Did they, like my daughter, get messages in health class about low-fat, low-calorie diets being healthy? Or, like Anna, were they shown gross films about how cattle are treated at slaughter time?

Had I known that beginning to eliminate a major source of protein from one's diet can be a fatal decision, I would have talked to the health teacher. I've always been outspoken, and I would have confronted the school about giving students the message that they shouldn't eat meat. I just didn't connect the dots. I don't think the people designing the curriculum see the potential for damage in people prone to these disorders.

We don't realize how dangerous some of these messages can be. Everyone's biology is different and there are multiple contributing factors to eating disorders. The more parents, educators, the medical community and the general public understands about eating disorders, the better chance we have of preventing eating disorders in the next generation.

Our child's care providers: We are all responsible for helping to prevent these life-destroying disorders, and one thing care providers can do is educate ourselves as much as possible. Learn enough about these confounding, confusing illnesses to understand that they are always morphing into something else. These diseases are smarter than we are, so we need to have a strong knowledge base.

Expressing your opinions: As a parent, you may wonder, "What can I say to the treatment team to help them be more effective?" Care providers need to hear from parents: "I am confident that I am a good parent. I cherish my child and I will do anything to help her fight and recover from this illness."

When they say to us, "You have to stop being the food police," we need to say to our son or daughter's health care team, "I will stop being the food police, but please tell me what I can do to help her. Food is her medicine."

Giving parents tools: I wish I had had the courage and confidence to say: "We need to be armed with the right tools to support our child. We are on the front lines—we're the ones at the dinner table."

The care providers aren't there when we've just prepared a meal that was a chunk of our grocery budget, only to see our child throw up that precious food right after she eats it. The health professionals aren't there showing us what to say to prevent that or how to react when it happens.

I needed to be told more about what to do, instead of what *not* to do. It isn't enough to tell families to not be involved. It's not like a drug addiction where you can keep the drugs out of the house. Food *has* to be in the house and our loved ones in recovery have to be in the house with it. We need the confidence and support that comes from hearing that other families living with these devastating disorders have succeeded. We need to know we have the right to ask questions and ask what might work for our individual needs. We need to feel like we are part of the treatment team.

A great resource for learning what to ask and how to get your needs met is The Academy for Eating Disorders, which created a Worldwide Charter on Action for Eating Disorders (see it at http://www.aedweb.org/source/Charter/). Every family should be handed the charter when they go in for treatment. "The Charter was created by the AED to ensure that eating disorders—serious mental illnesses with often severe physical consequences—are treated as such, and that patients and their families are afforded every opportunity to receive high quality, affordable care," said

Lynn Grefe, NEDA CEO. The Charter states, "The core value underlying this document is that a partnership among patients, their families, and the treating team, with rights and responsibilities for all sides, is imperative for any quality eating disorder service or individual health care encounter." We need to have the language and skills to cope with the overwhelming hopelessness that shows up full force many times a day.

Separating your child from the illness: Being able to distinguish Anna from the eating disorder was an essential skill that we developed as time went along. There were days when Anna was resistant and angry—not herself at all. We tried to maintain the perspective that the eating disorder was fighting for its life as Anna was gaining strength and recovering.

We refused to acknowledge that this behavior was okay. Before she was 18 we could force her to go into treatment. Once she was in inpatient treatment and getting 24-hour support and help from the professionals, she would pretty quickly become agreeable. The treatment team and secure environment could give her the support she needed to fight the symptoms. But there were many obstacles when we tried to get inpatient treatment, the biggest one was our insurance company. The story about how we handled the insurance company's refusal to keep Anna in the hospital, the decision that led to Anna's fatal outcome, is detailed on the Anna Westin Foundation website, www.AnnaWestin-Foundation.org).

The eating disorder is very wily and can convince you that your child is doing well. I had to recognize when the eating disorder was present instead of Anna. It reminded me of a two-year-old's tantrums. You can't take it personally. When words got ugly, I knew it was the eating disorder.

If it happens to you, you don't have to sit and listen. You can hold them, if that works for them or you, or you can walk out of the room. I would literally say, "I'm not having this conversation with the eating disorder; I will talk with Anna when she is here." Then I would leave the room. I looked at it as a setup and I would refuse to engage. Engaging is a setup and is as futile as talking to a drunk alcoholic.

Choose times when you can have a discussion. I learned to recognize when anorexia was there and Anna wasn't. She told me this gave her the strength to fight the eating disorder. We would write notes back and forth. I would write, "Anna, have a fabulous day! Anorexia, have a sucky day." Anna told me, "Mom, thank you. You know I'm not my eating disorder."

Comments from friends and family: As confounded as we, as parents/caretakers, are by this illness, our friends and family usually are completely unable to grasp the complexities and don't understand it at all. Why should they? These are logic-less illnesses that have not been studied enough to determine exact causes and effective treatments. Unless you spend months studying eating disorders, it is tough to be able to comprehend what is going on. Some families have told me that their friends have said to them, "Why don't you just tell her to stop?" Unless you have the proper background and training you could think that is possible.

This book's title is meant to really drive home the understanding that it is *not* possible to tell someone with an eating disorder to simply stop. If that worked we would have all done it. Not only does it *not* work, it just adds more pain and frustration to the lives of families who are living with these deadly disorders in their homes. One thing you could say to these well-meaning friends and family members is, "Thank you for your concern. We want to fix it too, but there is no quick fix for this. Just know we're going through a very difficult time and could use your good thoughts and understanding."

In our society there seems to be a belief that somehow eating disorders are just a behavior problem.

This "just tell them to stop" attitude doesn't work and doesn't help anyone. If necessary, one thing you could say to people who continue to treat it as willful behavior is simply, "Please think before you speak. It's an illness. If she had cancer you wouldn't say, "Just tell her to stop having cancer."

Another challenge is when family and friends make comments about your child's appearance. The immediate family usually understands fairly quickly that it is detrimental to make comments about the appearance of their loved one. It is the extended family and friends who have a more difficult time embracing this new rule. Comments about appearance can cause major setbacks. For example, an out-of-town friend could visit, see your child looking better, and say, "Oh you look so good, you look much healthier!" Such a comment might seem innocent and safe, but what the person with the eating disorder hears is, "You look fat, you've gained way too much weight and you are gross and ugly." It's hard to believe that such a well-intended comment could be interpreted this way, but it often is.

You really have no way to educate all your friends and extended family. If an old family friend who sees your child has achieved a healthier weight says, "Wow, you look great!" you can take your child aside and ask, "This person was well meaning, but what did your eating disorder hear?" She may likely say, "I'm so fat, I'm disgusting." You can do some damage control and address this directly by then asking, "What do you know is true?" Remind your son, daughter, spouse, sibling, etc., that the eating disorder hears one thing, but he or she can have the strength to not hear those negative messages.

I spoke with a parent of a daughter recovering from bulimia and binge eating disorder who had this experience. Her daughter had been overweight and had worked diligently to slowly and healthily lose the needed weight. When she arrived home from college for the holidays, a close family friend said, "Wow, you look great!" This parent cringed and thought, "Oh no, that could reinforce the need to lose more weight and she could and lose too much." Health providers need to understand this and watch the words they use too.

This mother wished she had had the tool I just mentioned to combat the negative messages the eating disorder most likely sent to her daughter. She would have added, "Let's put this in perspective. She said the wrong thing and the eating disorder got more ammunition. Your stronger voice needs to be heard." You can remind your loved one in recovery that it is a cultural and societal thing to judge and comment on appearance. They have been ingrained to hear these comments a certain way and being reminded of their own strong voice can help them combat the negative messages the eating disorder sends.

Relapse possibilities: When Anna was first diagnosed I wish I had known that with all eating disorders, including anorexia, the likelihood of relapse is very high. I would have done some things differently; I would have been more diligent and watched more closely to recognize early signs of relapse. Anna relapsed in September 1999 and the eating disorder took her less than six months later. Research and time made me smarter and gave me more accurate information to use as the years went on.

My philosophy on recovery: People don't need to die of this illness. I believe that improved education and prevention, as well as access to the right care, will help more people survive. Many doctors in the eating disorders arena agree with this.

There seem to be two camps: one camp believes there can be complete recovery; the other camp thinks that there will always be a risk of relapse. The risk-of-relapse group believes you must always be vigilant. I often get the question, "Can a person be cured?" I really see no point in arguing about the definition. Does it really matter what you call it? If your loved one is working on recovery and defines it as cured, that is fine. If it is more helpful to say your loved one is in recovery, that is great too. What works for your loved one is what I feel is the way to define recovery.

Choosing a treatment center: If you decide to use a treatment center, keep shopping until you find one where you, the parent, feel validated. Some will still treat parents or family as part of the problem. Ask questions and if you feel unsupported, go elsewhere. One of the places Anna got treatment gave us the impression that they were thinking, "You've done enough damage—now get out of the way." Parents need to be a part of the recovery process even though it requires enormous patience and some standing back.

A much better and more helpful message would be, "We know you've been through hell and now we're giving you permission to stand back and take care of you for a while. Your daughter has work to do by herself; we'll keep you informed. In the meantime, here are some resources for you." In my opinion, parents need about three months at a California spa at a very minimum. This may sound too flip, but it is important to take care of your own needs too.

ACKNOWLEDGING THE LOSSES

Many people are curious about how we have "successfully" grieved the loss of our daughter, especially those who are grieving their own losses. So very many losses accompany eating disorders. The list is almost endless, beginning with the loss of joy, loss of dreams (yours and theirs) and the loss of experiences you will never share. These can range from big things (no wedding, no grandchildren) to the ordinary things most of us take for granted, such as enjoying meals together.

We all have so many dreams—for our children, especially— but also for our sibling, spouse or other loved one who may be missing out on life due to an eating disorder. It is essential to allow yourself the opportunities to spend time acknowledging these many losses, one by one, so you can move forward with your lives.

There is a sort of "magical thinking" part of the grief process. Taking time to accept the reality lets you strategize and ruminate. But thinking, *What if I could find that right moment and change the outcome?* keeps you stuck.

I had to get through the judging and guilt about past mistakes. I needed to beat myself up. I needed to experience the pain. I beat myself up for a comment I made when Anna was five years old. This did not move me forward; it didn't do any good—and it didn't keep her alive. Though it is very, very challenging to stop doing that, we must.

I don't know how I realized one day that this is really not help- ful, but somehow I was able to see that in order to survive, I must really let go and leave the past behind. I cannot change the past.

A Family Disease: I really encourage families to get their own counseling and help during this family illness. Not only does the patient need support, the entire family does, since these illnesses take a toll on all who are touched by them.

Parents need to be as healthy as possible to survive and help their loved one. Eating disorders are excruciatingly painful ill- nesses. I'm really proud of Anna, especially that she fought for five long years—from the age of 16. I feel that there were a lot of other options we could have tried. Suicide was not my decision, I was angry with the eating disorder, the insurance company and many other things but I have never been angry with her. Never give up—never stop loving your child. That is where it's important to differentiate the person from the illness.

I learned how essential it is to never give up hope and never stop loving the person fighting one of these illnesses. I remember vividly calling the doctor, saying, "Anna is in a heap on the bathroom floor crying. What do I do?" It's overwhelming and such a helpless feeling when your loved one is so distraught and in so much pain—and you can't do anything. When the doctor told me to get down there and hold her, that's what I did and it calmed her down. She needed me to sit there, hold her and let her sob. Sometimes all you can do is comfort them. I would tell Anna, "I am here and I love you so much." Always be there with that open heart and love. I know it can be challenging when the behavior that is directed at you is unpleasant, to say the least.

Some people who have recovered have said that having people who didn't let them off the hook, who pushed them—and who also loved them unconditionally—helped them get better.

KITTY'S TIPS:

1. Educate yourself as much as you can about eating disorders. Join other families so you are not alone.

2. Trust your gut in all facets of living with and treating this illness.

3. Separate the person from the eating disorder.

4. Ask for what you and your loved one need from the care team.

5. When you are thinking of making comments about appearance, yours or others, don't.

6. Get support and counseling for your family.

7. Allow yourself to grieve your losses.

8. Don't take on blame—you didn't cause this illness.

9. Know that you have a conscious choice to make about whether or not this disease will take you down.

10. Never give up hope and never stop loving.

11. Most importantly, learn how to listen effectively. It is an art and must be practiced.

12. In 2007 the Eating Disorders Coalition presented an extensive list of policy recommendations that would significantly improve the lives of people suffering from eating disorders to Congressman Patrick Kennedy and asked him to take the lead on this issue. He agreed. In February 2009, Congressman Kennedy introduced the first bill in the history of Congress to comprehensively address eating disorders, the Federal Response to Eliminate Eating Disorders (FREED) Act. In April 2010, Senator Tom Harkin introduced the companion Senate bill. The FREED Act:

- Expands research on the prevention of and effective treatment of eating disorders: Coordinates research on eating disorders at the National Institutes of Health and across the federal government, and creates research consortia to examine the causes and consequences of eating disorders, and develops effective prevention and intervention programs.

- Improves the training and education of health care providers and educators: Authorizes grants to medical, nursing, social work and other health-profession schools to train health care providers in the identification and treatment of eating disorders, and grants to train teachers and other educators in effective eating disorder prevention, detection and assistance strategies.

- Improves surveillance and data collection systems for tracking the prevalence and severity of eating disorders: Tasks CDC with addressing the lack of accurate information on the incidence and severity of eating disorders. Requires the development of new methods to accurately collect, analyze and report epidemiological data to ensure that the incidence of eating disorders and related fatalities are better understood.

- Prevents eating disorders: Authorizes grants to develop evidence-based prevention programs and promote healthy eating behaviors in schools, recreational sports programs and athletic training programs.

- Builds on existing reform efforts to ensure that treatment is available and affordable: Creates a patient advocacy program to aid people suffering from these diseases and their families to negotiate the health care system. Incentivizes states to ensure that adolescents covered by Medicaid are diagnosed and treated.

As this book goes to print in late 2010, the FREED Act has support in both the House and Senate. The Eating Disorders Coalition and its advocates will continue to work towards passing this bill. To enlist your own legislators to support the FREED Act, please go to: http://www.eatingdisorderscoalition.org and write a letter to your Members of Congress!

12

Stacy's Story

Perfectionism; Not All It's Cracked Up To Be

When Stacy was 13, during her month-long August visit to her father's, anorexia got a strong hold on her and took over completely. As soon as she arrived back home, just before school began, her mother knew right away that something was terribly wrong. In spite of getting medical help immediately, anorexia took away the next ten years of Stacy's life.

Here is the story of a girl who could at times be the smartest, sweetest, prettiest and most popular girl in school, and at other times would make herself and those around her exasperated by her difficult behaviors. It was a pleasure to interview a healthy Stacy and to tell her story. Now 33 and recovered, Stacy wants to make sure you hear what *didn't* work because she feels it is much more useful than the clinical information found in textbooks.

STACY'S STORY

Gazing out over the azure-colored sea in Mexico should have been calming and enjoyable. With the rhythmic blue ripples of water gently breaking against the shore, relaxing seemed to be the order of the day on a tropical vacation with my mom and siblings. I could see my family beginning to unwind and thaw out from our freezing Maine winter as we sat in our comfy lounge chairs by the pool overlooking the sea. But all I could think about or, I should say, all my eating disorder would let me think about, was food. I hadn't escaped—the anorexia had followed me on our vacation and would steal any precious relaxing moments from me.

Worrying about the next meal, I kept thinking, *Oh no, I have to face food again. I cannot control this anxiety, but I can control what I put into my mouth. I hope they don't say anything to me as I push the food around on my plate. Maybe they will be busy enjoying themselves and won't notice. Part of me hopes they will confront me so I can get rid of these cruel best friends, "Ed" and "Bully."*

Out of the six kids in our family, I was the perfect little girl—I gave my parents the least amount of trouble. I got good grades, had lots of friends and kept trying to be the perfect child in an imperfect family.

I knew better than to say anything about the unspoken tension in the house as my parents' marriage began deteriorating. I just kept doing everything really well—perfectly, actually. In reality, I was a normal preteen girl who had an emotional issue I needed to deal with, which was the result of never hearing that my parents' marriage problems were not *my* fault. I found myself wondering why my parents seemed so busy, but yet so quiet. Every time they passed one another in a room and did not speak, I felt I'd done something wrong. Watching them, I began to formulate the story in my head that it was my fault that they didn't like each other anymore.

Sitting on the living room floor watching our favorite Friday night show, I was happy to be hanging out with my siblings as our parents busied themselves in the periphery. All I wanted was to sit on my dad's lap and snuggle, but I knew I had lots of competition for his attention. I wanted to be perfect, so I kept still and quiet.

The self-blame led to a need to feel control and power. Since I was only 11, there wasn't much I could control but one thing I could control was what I ate. That's when Ed came into my life and I began to abuse food as a way of coping.

After the divorce I spent a month each summer with my dad in Myrtle Beach. The summer I was 13 I was so relieved to be going to Dad's for the month of August.

Sitting with him at breakfast that first day, the morning sunshine streaming across the kitchen, I got to fix my own breakfast. I knew as I slowly picked at the few pieces of fruit, his typical oblivion was going to serve me well. He wouldn't notice I had basically *stopped eating*. I carefully straightened the silverware, the salt-and-pepper shakers, the napkins, and the coffee cups— everything on the table had to be in order. Keeping order was essential: it helped keep my life from spinning out of control. He didn't notice.

After carefully washing the dishes, each one cleaner and drier than the one before, I neatly arranged them in the cupboard. *Keep busy, keep order, don't eat, do exercises, do anything to avoid discomfort* was the mantra I repeated as I felt my growing body changing.

Later that week, I went out to mow the grass for the second time. Being busy, I could avoid acknowledging the strange feelings I still had about the divorce. This new living arrangement served to only increase both my anxiety and the loss of control over my life. Each day, before showering, I had to drink more water, do some sit-ups and go for a long bike ride. I was always very secretive with my rituals. It wasn't hard.

When I returned home to Mom's in September, she immediately knew something very bad was going on. My weight loss was dramatic, just like my behavior. The anorexia had taken over and had spiraled out of control. She contacted a therapist.

I continued on—my grades kept improving, I joined cheer-leading, track, choir, the science team, and on and on. The daily quest to keep moving and avoid eating continued.

I went downhill so quickly that by December Mom knew she needed to get me more than the therapy we were trying—I needed more intense medical help. I was slowly killing myself.

In mid-December I was admitted to an outpatient facility, then later admitted to the inpatient program. I dealt with it by pretending I was a "secret agent," watching everyone from the inside, seemingly going along with everything they said, and always, always being the perfect patient. I knew their approach wasn't going to take my Ed away from me. Each day they would give me food and medicine, then check my heart rate, take blood and continue to treat the medical aspects of the eating disorder, but no one pushed me to address the reasons I was an emotional wreck. I didn't understand the theory of first nourishing the brain (called refeeding) before beginning the psychological work. I kept wondering, *When will someone ask me what is making me do this to myself? They are so concerned with how much I weigh, what my blood pressure is—what my numbers are. Doesn't anyone get it that I need to address some of these emotional issues and learn new skills to feel I have some control over my life?*

I had only one inpatient therapy session during that hospitalization, which my dad flew home for. Nothing came of it. The only other therapy was in outpatient and, ironically, no one seemed to care about that. My head felt so clear: I could see that I needed to address the underlying reasons for my irrational behaviors. How could I be the only one who saw that?

Today, I find it interesting that my psychiatrist and many psychologists would still say that my body had to be nourished *before* the Cognitive Behavioral Therapy (CBT) would work. My experience is that most people with anorexia are sharp as a tack. It seems to me that CBT and refeeding (the medically supervised re-introduction of calories) should happen concurrently. I can almost guarantee that there would be extreme push-back from the patient, but that isn't a reason not to do it. People (parents, pastors, teachers, friends, and medical care providers) all stopped pushing me too early.

These questions need to be asked:

Do you have body image issues? What are they? Why do you think that?

If you don't have self-love and self-respect, do you know why?

Though this is a biological brain illness I feel that there are emotional issues that must be addressed; however, it is different for every person. I can admit now that I would have been very resistant to any attempts to push me and am quite sure I would have made it a very miserable experience for anyone who dared to try.

The eating disorder specialists kept saying that I couldn't process the therapy until I was medically stable. I don't know what they were thinking—my brain felt perfectly clear. It seemed such a lost opportunity. I know the medical community stance is much different; however, this is my perspective as a patient.

Becky told me that research is showing that re-nourishing the brain is a necessary first step before the brain can process the therapy. Lucky for Ed, they didn't encourage the emotional work, and Ed got to live inside me a bit longer and manipulate me, my thoughts, my family, and ultimately, take over our lives.

Despite all the positive feedback I got for being so thin, Ed continued to help me create a great deal of drama in my life. Everything was always a bigger deal than it needed to be and often became a crisis. Halfway through high school, Ed took a backseat to Bully as the eating disorder morphed into bulimia.

I had just moved to a new school and hadn't made new friends yet. Sitting at the dinner table, Bully and I made a great team. As the potatoes were passed they smelled so good we would take some and load up on all the rest of the delicious dinner my mother had prepared. Gobbling it all up quickly, and feeling extremely full, we took seconds and sometimes a third helping. Bully and I tricked my family into believing I was better. It *looked* like I had conquered my demons. Bully and I knew what they didn't—I was sneaking off four to five times a day to throw up, purging everything I had eaten.

I'd gained weight and was medically stable; that seemed to be all anyone was concerned with. Yet, I knew I still hadn't dealt with my issues, and I was by no means healthy. Ed and Bully were thrilled because they'd outfoxed the experts. I was really torn. I loved my best friends, Ed and Bully, but deep down I knew they were evil best friends—destructive and dangerous. I knew it—but I couldn't stop.

The high I got from bingeing and purging kept me from feeling too much pain. Besides, no one approached me about what I was doing to myself. I kept thinking: *Someone will challenge me to stop.* I sometimes got the impression that my mother and siblings thought if they "ruined" my good-girl image it might do more damage than good. At this point, I really, really needed family to push me, to "be in my face."

From the vantage point of many years later, I think it would have made a difference if someone had simply asked, "What is making you do this to yourself?" I might have answered, "I have a serious emotional issue." I was very willing to admit I needed help. I knew something was wrong, but I didn't have the tools to say *what* was wrong. It's so embarrassing to admit something is wrong, let alone know whom to trust.

Bully really kicked it into high gear when I went away to

college. Even though most college students experiment with substance abuse, I couldn't because "good girls" don't do that.

Hogging the bathroom as I purged yet another meal, I could hardly stand to think how rude I was being to my roommate. Bully didn't care about respect, for me or anyone else. Bully and I would spend hours in there together, getting our little high from purging meal after hideous meal. We left such a mess behind, I don't know how my roommate tolerated it. She never addressed it and neither did I. She just started staying away from our room.

Part way through college, I ended up in the hospital. I was exhausted, my body worn out. Someone finally realized how depressed I was and put me on anti-depressants. My poor ravaged body rejected one medicine after another that the psychiatrist tried. The depression, or the reason for it, hadn't been addressed up until this point.

My constant zombie-like state caused by three kinds of medications prescribed within two months didn't seem to faze the psychiatrist. He just kept changing medications, never giving them a chance to work.

I left school after my freshman year when my scholarship ran out. I lived at home and worked for a year. During that time I know I was more of a burden for both my mom and younger sister, Amy. Amy had no idea how to deal with a sister who was such a pain in the butt. Mom was equally bewildered. Every once in a while, she would say, "You are eating so much food, and it costs so much money."

Eventually, I enrolled in a school close to home and lived on campus. Over the next two to three years, I realized I couldn't keep living this way. I started to address the emotional issues (not the body image for a change), the little-girl issues about the divorce and my dad moving out during the divorce. With the help of a therapist I faced how painful it was that I didn't see him very often.

Things began to change. I stopped bingeing and I developed normal relationships. I had a romantic relationship with a guy who wouldn't tolerate any type of eating-disorder behavior. He had no patience for it. He would confront me with questions, such as, "What are you doing to yourself?" and "What is up with these behaviors?" Then he would push me to look deeper by saying, "Let's talk about what's really bothering you," and "Let's talk about how this is affecting your health."

I was finally emotionally mature enough to realize I could say to myself, *Do you know how this is hurting your heart, your fertility, your teeth? Your skin looks horrible, you look tired all the time, your hair is dry and brittle, and your fingernails are all broken and dry.* I was finally really ready to say, "I look and feel horrible and I can't do this anymore." I had to get to that point to ask myself, *What is my problem?* I finally addressed my emotional issues. I still can feel the same emotions, but now I can address them in a much more productive way.

Finally, I want you to realize there is hope! Eating disorders controlled my life for 10 years, but for the last 12 years, *I* have been in control of my life!

BECKY'S COMMENTS ON STACY TODAY

Stacy, who is 33, feels very lucky to have been able to put her eating disorder behind her. It pains her to say that she feels like one of the lucky ones because so many people spend most of their lives as slaves to their eating disorders. In Stacy's case it was a 10-year process before she started to live a really healthy life.

Occasionally, Stacy's mind will start working in that old familiar way, but now it is easy to nip it in the bud. She gives herself what she calls, "an emotional smack on the head" and asks herself some tough questions such as, *Why am I doing this?*

Having a supportive husband helps, too. When Stacy pulls

the typical female question on him, "Does this make me look fat?" he'll ask, "What makes you do that? Why don't you ask me, instead, 'What do you think of this?'" She says he is good at calling her on things and will be very inquisitive in a non-judgmental way. She says, "He treats me the way I wish I had been treated all those years."

When I probed Stacy for more details about her turning point toward recovering, she immediately said during college she hit rock bottom and slowly began to have some self-respect. Her behaviors were so destructive that she started to think: *What will my future be like? What's after college? What will happen if I continue to let Ed rule my life? Will I have good strong relationships and friendships? Will I be able to have children?* She found herself at a crossroads and, fortunately for her, was exposed to people who didn't tolerate the behaviors.

A number of small things also happened in a short timeframe that led to her recovery. She became a restaurant manager and people looked up to her (even though she didn't feel she was someone people should look up to). Stacy had to act like she deserved being looked up to; she had to be a role model. She started to recognize that she needed to be a person who actually took care of herself, a person with some self-worth. Most important, Stacy realized that she hadn't liked herself for a very long time. She wanted to like herself again.

Stacy told me she didn't know how to stop doing what she knew wasn't good for her, the behaviors that caused pain for others as well as the economic issues, until she got to the point that she was ready to take responsibility for herself and move on. She still feels guilty that her eating disorders affected her family, especially her mother and younger sister, and wants the reader to know that she now understands how much eating disorders impact family members.

STACY'S HINTS:

1. I needed to be challenged with my emotional issues—not in a blaming way, but in a protective, supportive way, with a simple question like, "What is driving you to do this to yourself?"

2. To create trust, don't make assumptions about what your loved one in recovery is doing. Instead, ask them to explain what is going on.

3. Avoid labeling someone as an anorexic or bulimic. I needed to hear positive affirmations about who I was and I needed to feel appreciated for being me.

4. Challenge the professionals when things aren't working. Suggest trying things differently, or trying new approaches. Don't be intimidated by their credentials. Insist that the family be included in the treatment plan.

5. If insurance runs out, push for coverage. See Kitty and Diane's chapters for more on insurance.

6. In general, it's embarrassing to say your child or sibling has a problem. A lot of people think it's just an eating issue. It's like drug addiction/alcoholism—you become addicted to the behaviors. Part of it can be perfectionism—if you're going to do it, you're going to do it perfectly. You get addicted to sticking to it. People don't understand that it's a disease, not just a behavioral issue.

7. If you do push your loved one and get a negative response, know they may not be able to control their behavior and they do need you to push them.

8. Try not using a scale as a health gauge. Communicate that total and overall health are what matter. I feel that if, earlier on, health care professionals had assured me that this was the right approach, I might have had a healthier self-image.

9. It is possible to have a new frame of mind and feel better about yourself. There isn't a cookie-cutter process, so each person has to find out what works for her or him.

10. Keep in mind that people in recovery hear things differently than what is actually being said.

13

Dar's Story

Letting Go with Love Is Possible

Dar was so worn down by worry and taking care of her daughter, she didn't have the time or energy to do things that filled her up. As much as she needed the parent group at the eating disorder treatment program Nancy was enrolled in, she couldn't get there. The one time she attended only one other parent showed up. *Why?* Dar wondered. *Was it that parents found it hard to confide in others or maybe didn't like discussing their child's eating disorders in person? Or,* Dar thought, *maybe the other parents are just as tired and worn down as I am.*

Dar was painfully aware of her own feelings of shame, guilt and failure. Her expectations tripped her up when she saw her child not succeeding, and she was concerned that somehow it was her fault.

Dead ends had greeted Dar everywhere she looked for help in understanding her daughter Nancy's eating disorder. She felt that reading books probably did her more harm than good as reading people's stories of living with eating disorders added to her fears. It terrified her to hear how horrible these disorders are when what she needed was hope and encouragement. Most of her friends had little knowledge of eating disorders and certainly didn't understand what she was going through so Dar found it most helpful to talk with parents who *did* understand. She says our support group telephone calls helped her keep her sanity.

One of the concepts we talked about in those groups was "letting go with love." Most people are confused by the term and think it means that parents are not involved except for driving to appointments or paying the bills and listening. In reality, "letting go" is choosing not to take on or join their loved one in their fears and anxieties. It means continuing to participate and engage without needing the loved one to like it, being active in seeking and following through on treatment without being overbearing, and accepting the ups and downs of the process.

Listening to Dar tell her story, I heard about the many different emotions she experienced at one time or another during her nine-year journey with her daughter and the eating disorder that moved in with them—emotions other parents have also expressed: extreme frustration, terror, concern, empathy, anger, suspicion, resentful, overwhelmed, protective, love, calm, acceptance, sadness, panic, and grief. Some of the emotions she alternately felt were opposites, such as lonely/supported, hopeless/hopeful, helpless/helpful.

Dar became so emotionally and physically drained that she found it very challenging to simply care for herself. As a single parent, bearing the whole load of parenting, Dar wasn't even aware of her own needs. I finally had to ask the question, "If you get sick, who will take care of your daughter?" Over time, she not only learned how to care for herself, but also learned how to let go of control and live in relative peace, even with the constant knowledge that there might be nothing she could do to save her only child.

Working with Dar in the parent group coaching calls, I witnessed some of their painful journey as it unfolded. Seeing the progress that Nancy has made, and continues to make, is encouraging, as it looked quite bleak for a long time.

DAR'S STORY

Sleep finally found me that night. It hadn't been easy to sleep during this latest resurgence of Nancy's eating disorder but I was deeply asleep. I never heard my 20-year-old daughter come into my room. I woke to see Nancy standing above me, saying, "Mom, I think I am dying."

Looking back, I can hardly believe I had the wherewithal to simply say to her, "Come and lie down with me." As I hugged her I told her everything would be okay. "No, Mom, it won't be," was her response.

I felt so helpless. It seemed there was nothing I could do to help my daughter feel better, much less get well. This was by far the hardest, scariest time Nancy and I had experienced since her father died years earlier. I feared she might be right: she could be dying. She had voiced it; she was terrified. So was I.

I had seen the torture the eating disorder had inflicted on her and couldn't stand the idea of this thing destroying her any longer. As we lay there hugging in my bed, I told her, "I wish I could take this eating disorder and have it be mine instead." My words scared Nancy, who said, "Don't you ever say or wish that!" She told me she felt there was an out-of-her-control evil dark force living within her. That's when I realized she felt as helpless as I did.

That night, lying in bed holding Nancy, smelling her hair, took me back to when she was a little girl. Suddenly I thought, *My God, I'm going to lose her. What if she can't take the pain anymore and harms herself?* Then, just as suddenly, I realized I had to be strong and remain calm so she would come to me when she needed to. I knew I was going to fight with all my strength to not lose my daughter, even if it felt like a futile fight.

It was so quiet in the house, total silence, except for Nancy's breathing. Knowing she was breathing was consoling and allowed me to have a rational conversation with myself. *She's okay right now, lying next to me. She'll confide in me if it gets to be too much. I've got to be here for her. But I'm so tired I need more strength, and more energy. I've let myself get too run-down with all my worries. Becky's right; I have to take better care of myself so I can help her . . . I need to plug the emotional drain and fill myself back up so I can be here for her.*

When Nancy finally fell asleep, I silently allowed the tears to flow down my cheeks. When the mini pity party ended, questions began racing through my mind. *Something has got to be done about this, but what? She's seeing a doctor, a therapist, and a nutritionist—what else can be done? I'm going to call her counselor tomorrow and explain how serious this is.*

When I called Kelley, Nancy's counselor, we talked about having Nancy committed, but she didn't want to do that. Kelley was very concerned, but felt it would break her trust to try to get Nancy committed. I called the county but they wouldn't help commit her either, saying they cannot commit without proof of someone posing harm to themselves or others. My mother's intuition that harming herself was a real possibility was not enough evidence. Learning to accept that no one would commit her for her own good was a tough lesson.

The frustration and fear were absolutely overwhelming—I didn't know where to turn for help. I felt trapped, and so alone. My every instinct was to save my daughter and I couldn't find a soul to help me. All I could do was hold on to the hope that someday she would get better. The only thing that seemed to help me was knowing I would be there for her. Somehow I knew that I just had to hold on until she got older, got something new in her life, and wanted to do something about the eating disorder. My little piece of hope was that as she got older she would decide enough was enough.

At the same time I began the slow, painful process of letting go with love that Becky talks about. I knew I couldn't force Nancy to get better and, after exhausting all other options, I didn't know what else I could do. I knew that by letting go I was not giving up. I also knew it would be the best way to support Nancy. And I knew it wouldn't be easy.

The enormous shame that is part of eating disorders kept Nancy from sharing much with me. But after that scary night in my bedroom, Nancy had a different attitude. She opened up to me a little bit more. It was both a blessing and a curse. The blessing was that now she would tell me if she was considering harming herself, something that wasn't as certain before. The curse was that now I heard more about her horrifying pain—which broke my heart.

"Mom, anytime I eat, bad things happen," was hard to hear but at least she was talking to me. I finally learned how it all began. In fifth grade, Nancy's class was given the assignment to write down everything they ate that week. Doing this made Nancy aware of the number of calories she was consuming. Tracking calories became a monitoring game: How few calories could she consume each day? This turned out to be a trigger for Nancy, who then began keeping a food journal.

The pattern soon evolved into a binge-purge cycle—in fifth grade. She was grossed out by the bingeing and purging and eventually asked me to send her to treatment, which I did, and the long journey of trying different treatments began. Traditionally, it often takes many tries at treatment and sometimes years of trying different therapists and treatments. That was certainly true for us.

In spite of getting treatment, Nancy gradually took in fewer and fewer calories until days in a row would go by without her eating any food. Finally honest with me, and herself, Nancy admitted the bulimia had morphed into anorexia. I immediately made an appointment with a local treatment facility and invited Nancy's best friend, Mary, to accompany us.

I know it seems impossible that, as her mother, I didn't know what was happening, but I didn't. I worked multiple jobs, nights and days, and by this time Nancy was old enough to have a job at our local grocery store. When I questioned her about eating, she told me she had eaten at work and I believed her.

Though she had been willing to receive treatment for her bulimia, Nancy was totally uncooperative about treating the anorexia. She didn't really want to get rid of it. I have heard this is more common with anorexia than it is with bulimia. She was afraid to eat and afraid of what would happen when she ate.

When she learned of the treatment center appointment, Nancy lost it. "You stupid people," she shouted at Mary and me. Mary still came with us to the appointment and I encouraged her to keep going to future appointments. Total patience, tenacity and understanding were necessary. Mary and I had to remind ourselves often that Nancy wasn't saying the hurtful things to us; it was the vile eating disorder speaking.

When I learned the reason she felt that she couldn't eat was because I "constantly hounded" her to eat, I was crushed. However, at the same time, I knew it wasn't Nancy's will to "use her symptoms," as they say in treatment to describe the behaviors such as restricting food, over-exercising, bingeing, purging, etc. The eating disorder was in her conscience when she ate. I felt I was in a cage watching some invisible beast devour her.

In the throes of her self-loathing, she didn't care about herself—she didn't care if she lived or died. The thing that always stopped her from harming herself was how much she knew it would hurt Mary and me. It took a long, long time to get to that point.

Nancy tells me now that a big part of her slow climb to recovery was her love for other people. She saw our worry and tears and even though she couldn't help what she was doing, hurting Mary and me bothered her tremendously. Seeing what she was doing to the people she loved only served to deepen her sense of shame that she was a bad person, which of course empowered the eating disorder and drove her to not eat at times.

It is part of Nancy's personality to put other people first, as she is a very giving, caring person. When I see her putting herself last, I call her on it. It's so odd and such a juxtaposition, because in the midst of the eating disorder, she was incredibly selfish.

Sometimes I wanted to yell at her but knowing that it was the disease causing the selfish behavior helped me do what I needed to do, and that was to express my love for her. When there was nothing else I could do to help her, loving her and expressing that love were the only tangible things I could contribute to her healing.

The eating disorder put Nancy through hell. As she began to recover, she made herself eat every day. Once she consciously shifted to wanting to get well, she worked extra hard with her care team, even though she was still afraid of eating and what would happen when she ate.

The challenges were constant. Getting fat was her main fear. One day she called me from the grocery store and said, "Mom I can feel the fat growing on me."

I replied, "No, Nancy, you cannot feel fat growing on you this minute." I was just glad she called and was feeling safe enough to tell me about her fears.

She found ways to trick herself into eating. She would typically eat late at night and have a couple of beers afterward, which made her sleepy. Then she would sleep and not have to think about the food she had just eaten. This seemed to work for her but it is, of course, the opposite of what many people are told they need to do to maintain healthy weight. I'm realizing that we each need to do what is best for our own individual bodies. Learning to respect that in myself and in others has been a huge lesson in this journey.

Continuing to be tenacious was as important as being my daughter's advocate. Even though the program she attended was a good one and the counselor was theoretically a good one, at one point we had to switch to a different therapist, one with whom Nancy "clicked." It's incredibly essential to have a trusting relationship with, and a good connection to, the therapist in order for the treatment to be successful.

We have come so far, both Nancy and I. Life no longer seems like being in a Stephen King novel. This fall, Nancy is going to attend chef's school, which has to be the definition of ironic, yet I understand a food-focused career is very common for those who have recovered. She is also engaged and planning her wedding; they don't plan to invite the eating disorder to the wedding or into their lives.

I knew from experience that people who haven't experienced living with someone with a mental illness just don't get it, and can be judgmental. But once I became comfortable with the people in Becky's support group and knew no one was going to judge me, I looked forward to talking with others who understood this craziness. It gave me a stronghold during the violent storm we were enduring. I am so glad to have had the help learning to let go with love and not give up on Nancy.

As Nancy and I were talking about this interview, she finally told me what she had been doing that night when she came to my room crying, saying she thought she was dying.

She had been in the garage with the car running, intent on ending her pain by killing herself. She said my simple act of love, holding her that night, motivated her to keep fighting the battle against her eating disorder.

DAR'S TIPS:

1. Find what works for you to be able to take care of yourself. Find an outlet, whether it is confiding in a friend, participating in a support group or going for a walk.

2. Allow sadness and then find joyful, fulfilling activities, including exercise.

3. Notice when you are being controlling.

4. Recognize that the eating disorder isn't your loved one's fault.

5. Learn to know when you are emotionally drained by the eating disorder and choose to set clear boundaries with it, so you can fill your own cup.

6. Remember to respect yourself and be a good role model.

7. Pay attention to judging yourself and others. This will free you from expectations that cause pain and suffering.

8. Get support from the healthy people around you—if you can find any. There are healthy people out there, but you may need to find new people in your life.

14

Heather Henderson's Story

Eating Disorders Do Kill

Ironically, the young woman in this family's story worked for a wonderful organization that promotes healthy self-image and body image for young women. Heather Henderson worked for Nancy Gruver at *New Moon Girls*, a wonderful magazine for young girls, and then for Nancy's husband, Joe Kelly, whose work I have admired for years—he founded and grew the Dads and Daughters organization, and continues his work as "The Dad Man" (www.theDadMan.com).

Joe and I have crossed paths several times. He is striving to help fathers take an active role in encouraging healthy self-concepts that many people feel are helpful in preventing the very illness that cut short Heather's important work when it ended her life.

We talk about what a small world it is, but when my editor told me that her neighbors were the parents of a daughter who had lost her battle with an eating disorder, I wondered if I would meet them and be able to interview them for one of these stories about families coping and finding hope.

When I did meet Kris, I realized that she was the mother of the brave young woman I had read about. Heather's work as Joe

Kelly's right-hand woman was integral to the success of the Dads and Daughters organization.

Once a strong athlete, Heather's heart was weakened from more than eleven years of malnutrition due to her eating disorder. One day her heart simply stopped working.

As you have read in some of the other stories, eating disorders impact so very many people, and all who know a person caught in its grasp feel the damaging effects. Many people were impacted by Heather's death.

Much was written about Heather's accomplishments and her illness in the first year after her death. Her hometown newspaper, the *Paynesville Press* (Minn.), won state and national journalism awards for its series about Heather.

Heather's parents, Bill and Kris Henderson, continue to advocate for better health care for people with eating disorders. Since day one, sharing Heather's story has been their way of continuing the work about which Heather was so passionate.

On the first anniversary of her death a memorial hike celebrating Heather's life was held. Heather's mom, Kris, shared these powerful words that day.

"I speak as a mother who carried Heather for nine months, nursed her and, with her father, loved her and her sisters. We exposed them to as many experiences as we could—books; art; music; sports of many kind, as participants and observers; family traditions; vacations; and so on.

"I hoped they would grow up to be independent, strong, assertive young women in today's world and would defend their convictions by speaking out. I hoped, also, that they would have a sense of humor, and be kind, caring, and loving toward others— as they all did beyond my expectations.

"I wished for health and happiness. For Heather, that changed when she started on a roller coaster of an eating disorder. Her family rode with her for eleven-and-a-half years, along with friends and co-workers. The roller coaster ended for Heather, as I often feared it would, with her death.

"I feel the rest of us are still on the roller coaster, missing her greatly. Life for me is not the same, as part of me died with her. As her mother, I miss so many things, especially our friendship that was growing as a mother and adult daughter.

"I loved our mother-and-daughter talks, her ability to discuss an issue passionately—my father encouraged her to do this—and to question the world in which she lived. I also remember going to garage sales with her for just the right find at a great price, seeing her red car drive in at home for special occasions, or just because she wanted to come home, and be greeted by her "I'm home!" and a big hug. I also remember working on sewing projects for her or her friends, watching *ER* and *The Practice* every week and then comparing notes.

"There is also the future that she won't have—happy with family, friends, and a successful career.

"I am proud to have had Heather as a daughter, and also Heidi and Karen. Heather left the world a better place by having been here."

In interviewing Kris about the eating disorder's impact on their lives, she shared many insights about their journey and about Heather's struggles. I have written their story from Kris's viewpoint, which shows this mother's unconditional love, a love that transcends death.

HEATHER'S STORY

A vigil was held at American University in Washington, D.C., in the fall of 2001, a year after Heather's heart gave out. Students at American University, concerned about eating disorders, shared powerful remarks about three brave young women. They held the vigil to educate about the dangers of eating disorders, share the hope that there is help available with more effective treatment—and honor the lives of these amazing young women whose lives were cut short by eating disorders.

Our middle daughter, Heather, was one of the women spoken about and honored that night. It was an opportunity for Paul Yandura from the National Mental Health Awareness Campaign to speak about this non-profit organization dedicated to combating the stigma, fear, and shame associated with mental illness. It is my hope that sharing Heather's story will further reduce the stigma and make treatment a reality for millions who are not getting help.

As family members, we have all continued, in our own ways, to do outreach and try to make a difference in education, treatment, and outcomes for others facing these devastating disorders. Our family finds it hard to comprehend that it has been over nine years since Heather died. We will never be the same; there are holes in our hearts and our lives. Accepting that she will never be with us again is still a challenge. It is especially confounding because this illness is something that should be curable and preventable.

Heather wanted to get better—she wanted to live. Occasionally, I feel that in some ways it was a slow suicide, yet she wanted so badly to get better. Our minds, bodies, and spirits were nearly as beaten down as was Heather's heart muscle from eleven-and-a-half years of the struggle against her eating disorder.

Prom should be a fun right of passage. But an off-handed, albeit insensitive, statement about fitting into her prom dress started this unstoppable downward spiral. Heather wrote these words in the July/August 1999 issue of *New Moon Network:*

"My boyfriend and I were discussing the prom. I held my

prom dress up against my chest and turned from side to side, saying, 'See? Do you like it?' to which he replied, 'Yeah, you'll look
good. But you know, you'd look great if you lost ten pounds.'"

She continues with the turn her life took as a result of that
statement: "The responses that flew through my startled mind
were so chaotic and numerous that, despite remembering the
incident clearly, I can't exactly recall my response. I only know
that within a few minutes I had risen to his challenge, thinking:
'All right, I'll show you. I will lose ten pounds by prom.' And
with that, I embarked on the first diet of my life—me, a three-
sport athlete who had always taken for granted that my body was
just fine. Now I worried that I'd been fat my whole life and no
one had bothered to tell me until now. I was so ashamed."

It is still shocking to me that such a confident, intelligent,
successful, and outgoing athletic teenager could be so dramatically affected by this boy's comment. As insensitive as this comment sounds, I feel he was a victim of our cultural stereotypes
of how girls and women should look, what they should weigh
and what is beauty. Heather quickly lost that ten pounds—then
the dieting and purging spiraled out of her control. Soon, she
was picking at her food and forcing herself to throw up after
meals. Heidi noticed this and she and Heather's friends at
school told us what was going on because Heather hid it so well
from us. We had no idea.

All these years later I still remember the discussions we had
while she was in high school about eating and keeping up her
energy for all of her sports. Heather knew she needed to eat for
her body and brain, but more than once she couldn't keep up
with her teammates during practices due to a lack of strength.
We talked about eating adequate amounts of a balanced diet to
keep up her energy for track and gymnastics. Her sense of failure
was terrible when she didn't meet her expectations in sports.

So few resources existed then; there was almost nothing available to read. Bill and I desperately wanted more knowledge about what was happening but learned very little. We were all frightened, and finally let the coaches know what was going on with Heather. Occasionally the gymnastics coach wouldn't let her participate in certain activities in order to prevent injury. We learned from our family doctor that the body will deplete other organs first to preserve the heart muscle. This helped us to understand the trouble she was having with running.

This whole thing was so totally unexpected; we didn't know what to do. When we first contacted our family doctor, we learned that because we lived in a rural area, the only thing available was a support group with other people with eating disorders. Unfortunately, they had all been sick a lot longer and were older, so our 16-year-old wouldn't fit in well because she had only been ill a couple of months.

As we visited the first mental health professionals with Heather we heard the unbelievably frustrating news that she didn't fit all of the diagnostic criteria to enable her to receive treatment:

1. She hadn't had the eating disorder long enough.
2. Her menstrual periods hadn't stopped.
3. She hadn't lost enough weight.

Because she didn't fit into the rigid diagnostic boxes, no one took her illness seriously. We felt so helpless. All they could suggest was the support group that wasn't a good fit, so we went to a regional mental health clinic where Heather could receive individual counseling and we could get family counseling as needed.

The sense of helplessness was overwhelming at times and I cautiously confided to only a couple of close friends, which I really needed to do to keep my sanity. Otherwise, to protect

Heather's privacy, we didn't share what was going on with many people until after she died.

How do you avoid noticing when your daughter's eating habits have changed? Heather didn't want either herself or food to be the focus of our meals but the situation was so unusual for us; we were unprepared as to how to address it.

Typically, after dinner she would dash off to do homework, school activities or get on the phone. We hoped she really did what she told us.

Heather's illness couldn't be our total focus as we had two other daughters and we needed to find time for ourselves as a couple. My husband, Bill, and I were working full-time and we wanted to attend college events with Heidi, our eldest daughter. Karen, our youngest, was still in high school, busy with sporting and music events that we enjoyed attending as well.

Karen was upset with the turmoil the eating disorder brought into our family. Fortunately, some of her high school friends were helpful and understood what she was going through as a sibling of someone who was very ill. Heidi had been away at college and working so she had experienced this difficult time differently than Karen did at home. One Christmas I remember Heidi coming home from college to what had become our "new normal"—and she could hardly wait to get back to school. From one day to the next, the girls never knew what their sister was going to be like.

As a senior in high school Heather got involved with a fundamentalist church youth group—I called it the almost-"record-burning" type. The way they pulled kids in from other churches felt so seductive. On the one hand it seemed like a good thing for Heather, but on the other hand, she had such an addictive personality, was so vulnerable and yet so defiant, we were concerned about what she was being exposed to. Bill and I had many discussions with her about the safety of what she was being exposed to but she didn't care to listen to our concerns. This defiance was our on-and-off companion during the roller coaster ride that was our lives for the next several years.

Cooking for Heather became very hard as she became fussier about what she would or would not eat. After she left home, she became a vegetarian, which was even more challenging when trying to figure out what to fix that she would eat and also keep down.

No one gave us help on how to handle any of this. Role-playing with the counselor, to know what to say and what not to say, would have been helpful but we didn't know about role-playing then.

Soon Heather was off to college. Although we looked forward to her visits home, they were bittersweet. The dread of what foods to fix overshadowed the joy of having her home. What had once been joyous holiday celebrations became a source of tension. It was really hard to know how to act with so much food around. My dad would be with us for the holidays and he, of course, understood less about eating-disorder behaviors than we did, which added to the stress. The whole idea was foreign to him.

Even when she was really sick, Heather still loved making and helping with the evening meals. She especially loved the traditional oyster stew for our Christmas Eve meal and so enjoyed making it, along with the lefse and our Scandinavian salad called gifta (pronounced yiffka). These were foods that the eating disorder couldn't stop her from eating. What a relief to see her still be able to enjoy those traditional foods.

We didn't want to stop having our traditional Christmas morning coffee rolls we call tea rings. Heather and her two sisters learned to make them in home economics class, and they had become our Christmas stocking-opening snack. Our family still enjoyed them, and yet we didn't know how to talk with Heather about how strange it felt to have her there but not partaking. Often conversations were strained when she was home.

When Heather started college in the Twin Cities, she began seeing a counselor and dietician on campus. It didn't help much, and moving into her boyfriend's family home over the summer break didn't improve things. Sophomore year she started going downhill quickly, and when she moved into her own apartment for a short time, she hit a real low. The nurse at the student center suggested she get into a nearby treatment program. During her time in college and after graduation, Heather ended up in the emergency room a number of times, and we suspect it was during this time the initial heart damage symptoms began.

While Heather was home over the summer she traveled to the Twin Cities for eight weeks of outpatient treatment. During the weekly medical appointments the head doctor was very condescending and treated us like idiots from rural Minnesota. Heather was able to "con" everyone there, which made us wonder how smart *they* were. The whole program she was in felt like nothing more than a bandage—a very expensive bandage. We attended the family session only once and didn't find it very helpful either.

This was 1993 and the group health insurance where Bill worked wouldn't pay for her treatment, as they considered it mental health, so we had to pay it all out of pocket. Getting both positive and negative results in treatment and needing a change, Heather transferred to the University of Minnesota at Morris for her junior and senior years. We made sure she saw a counselor and nutritionist regularly, and she found a therapy group there that was a good fit for her. We would regularly visit and make sure things were on track. Heather started helping coach the girl's gymnastics team, and the head coach took her under her wing. They even shared housing.

That next summer at home went much better. At times, when the symptoms weren't being so controlling of her, we could more easily talk about what to do to support her. She talked about how well she was doing.

By her senior year, though, she spent more time with other students with eating disorders and Heather started sliding downhill fast. She no longer wanted to talk with us much, and when we did talk, she often yelled at us. Being on the receiving end of Heather's angry outbursts was so hard on me. I was told in counseling that Heather felt safe to lash out at me with her anger because she knew I loved her and would love her no matter what. It helped to know that I "caught it" because she felt so safe with me.

Another difficult time was when Karen was participating in a local queen pageant. When Heather called to say she wouldn't be with us to support her sister, Karen was upset that her big sister wasn't coming home. Bill and I were so disappointed and angry, we had a heated discussion about it. We were struggling with the whole tough-love philosophy—do we give into what she is trying to pull or not?

As in many families, one parent believed that "tough love" was the way to go, and the other just didn't want to make any waves. Bill didn't want to hurt Heather, and possibly even push her away. This is not uncommon. I have heard other moms say that their husbands were frustrated because they couldn't "fix" their daughters' illnesses. (When I was preparing for my interview for Becky's book, I discovered that my husband really doesn't remember much about that time—and doesn't want to even think about that terrible time.)

It was at that point we had to make the decision about the strain the eating disorder was putting on our marriage. It was so draining, and the highs and lows were so huge. We were constantly walking on eggshells, afraid to confront Heather for fear of an outburst.

We had to decide what our priorities were. We chose to focus on keeping our marriage and family healthy instead of letting the eating disorder control us. This didn't mean we stopped loving Heather or stopped wanting her to be healthy.

Sadly, after college graduation she became estranged for sixteen months. Her younger sister, Karen, who was now in college, was caught in the middle as Heather drew closer to her and communicated with her but not us or Heidi, her older sister, with whom she had previously been close.

My husband and I felt a constant sense of dread that Heather would die at a young age. Fear was ever present, and it was hard not to let that color our lives. We were so grateful she had a great boyfriend at the time who kept us updated on her condition.

During this estrangement Heather still wanted to get well. She tried to get into research studies for help with her illness, but was either "not sick enough" or "too sick" to be accepted, causing more frustration for everyone.

This estrangement was so very, very hard for us. That first Christmas when Heather wasn't talking with us was especially hard. Christmases had been such happy times for our family. Finally, we went to Duluth to visit Bill's sister and family because it was too painful to be at home. Our level of coping wasn't great at times, but we were always thinking about her, even when she wasn't with us. We tried not to worry and felt so sad for the frustration Heather must have endured. Even then, we were afraid that she would die while not being a part of the family—or one of us would die without being reconciled. If she had died before we reconciled, I don't know how we could have survived. I think it would have somehow been even harder than it was.

The protective mother instinct in me came out; I kept talking to Heather's boyfriend and, through him, would invite her to family events. It was a rude awakening to us when they moved in together, and for him to be living with the eating disorder 24/7. But knowing that she was living with her boyfriend was a source of comfort to us.

Through yet another communication with her boyfriend, I invited her to her grandpa's ninetieth birthday, and she agreed to attend. It was scary at first because we didn't know how she would act or how we should act toward her, but it was the breakthrough we needed and, slowly, we became a family again for four years.

Heather moved to Duluth and began working in marketing for New Moon Publishing and then she fulfilled her dream of being the editor of their young women's magazine, *HUES*. In Duluth she continued her recovery work with her dietician and counselor. After *HUES* ceased publishing, Joe Kelly asked her to help him launch DADS, a non-profit organization that strengthened father-daughter relationships. Together they accomplished great things working for gender justice. Heather really enjoyed living and working there and this was a happy time for all of us.

Both Heidi and Heather became engaged and we were all looking forward to the weddings. Heidi's wedding was scheduled first and Heather was to be the maid of honor. Just days before the wedding, on a sunny day in September, Heather's boss, Joe Kelly, went to her home because she hadn't come to work. He found her, dead of a heart attack, on the kitchen floor with her dogs on either side of her.

Bill got the call at work, then brought his heavy heart home to tell me our middle daughter and her body had lost the fight against the power and control of her eating disorder.

We gathered as a family that evening and decided together that going ahead with the wedding was what Heather would have wanted. All of us just tried to get through it. We were all numb; what emotions we felt were a mix of happiness because of the wedding, and sadness that Heather wasn't there as maid of honor. As we look back at the wedding we can say that we had "fun," grateful for so many hugs.

Later that week our family attended the first memorial in Duluth, where Heather lived and worked. A second memorial at our family church was held a week later. In between, we had to gather Heather's belongings from her house; her fiancé was as grief-stricken as we were and didn't want them around to remind him of her.

After her death, we received hundreds of cards, as did her employer. That is when we learned how many lives Heather had impacted and how highly people thought of her. We knew she was special, and we now learned that so many others knew it too.

As we approach the tenth anniversary of Heather's death, there are still times when our family has difficulty talking to each other about Heather due to the circumstances of her death. Working on this chapter has helped our family start to communicate better and to heal.

We hope that by telling our story, others might seek help sooner, and families will understand that *even when* the affected person wants to get well—to be free from the eating disorder—sometimes it has too strong a hold, and sometimes the damage to vital organs has already been done, as in Heather's case.

Feeling a responsibility to "fix" this sometimes-unfixable disease is yet another item on the list of things for loved ones to let go of to regain peace and remove feelings of guilt for the "what-if's."

Since Heather's death, I have spoken at schools and churches, telling our stories and getting the word out about how deadly eating disorders are. I'm always willing to talk with groups; I can be reached through Becky.

I use the seashell analogy, showing how each shell is unique, sometimes pretty, sometimes rough, on the outside but beautiful on the inside—like people. Sadly, Heather found other people beautiful, but never really believed herself to be beautiful.

On the first anniversary of Heather's death, at the memorial walk in her memory, Karen recalled that "Heather was always the first person to tell others how beautiful and wonderful they were—even though she couldn't believe it about herself. I know I've learned from her in that respect: we all should try to tell our friends and family that they are beautiful, and that we're proud of all that they are and will become."

My husband Bill expressed our family's hope that something positive will come out of this tragedy of our daughter dying at age 27 1/2. As part of his talk, he said, "Almost every day I hear of someone who, after hearing Heather's story, has either taken a step toward getting the help that they need or are reaching out to help someone else."

We want to keep Heather's story alive so that, like the ripples on the lake where we live, the message spreads to others. As we look up high into the sky and see a bald eagle, I think of Heather's spirit floating freely above us, watching over and reminding us that she is always with us.

KRIS' TIPS:

1. Plan what to say during challenging dinnertimes.

2. Cooking for your loved one with an eating disorder can be frustrating. Try to find ways to reduce the dinner-table tension.

3. Push for early aggressive treatment if you suspect someone has an eating disorder. Research now shows that early treatment equals better outcomes. Do everything you can to get her or him help.

4. When trying to gain insurance payments, don't take no for an answer. Be persistent.

5. With the death of a child, you have to hold onto positive memories.

6. Spreading the word about how dangerous eating disorders can be is very important—it has reached epidemic proportions in some rural and metro areas among high school and middle-school age girls. Body image and eating disorder issues are starting earlier all the time. I've read about elementary-age girls and younger who are preoccupied with their body image.

7. If you become estranged, do everything in your power to end that estrangement—but if you can't, find other ways to find out how she is doing.

8. Always try to tell your friends and family that they are beautiful—and that you are proud of all that they are and will become.

9. Realize that one insensitive comment about weight, diet, body image or general appearance might launch an eating disorder.

10. Research is showing that genetics may be related to having a highly addictive personality, which with a combination of factors, may lead to an eating disorder.

11. Remember that you have to make time for your other children, your spouse, and yourself as this child's illness cannot always have priority.

12. Get counseling for your family, as needed, to help cope with your loved one's behavior and the disease.

15

Jayne and Ashley's Mother-Daughter Story

Denial Is Dangerous

This mother and daughter each wanted to share her perspective to demonstrate how different the parent's experience can be from that of the child in recovery. Some excellent mother-daughter books on eating disorders are available, should you find this format helpful to you. I am grateful to both Jayne and Ashley for willingly sharing their stories with me for this book. Their differing viewpoints of the same eating disorder provide useful insights into what began as a sports injury and quickly became something much more serious.

ASHLEY'S STORY (THE DAUGHTER)

When I looked at the girls around me in the hospital, I thought, *These girls belong here but I don't.* My body image and thinking were so distorted I thought saltine crackers were too enormous to consume. At the same time, I couldn't see that was the reason I belonged there.

I was 20 years old. Six months earlier I injured my ankle playing college basketball during my sophomore year. Basketball had been my dream, and now I couldn't play for three months. I was devastated.

I had always been an athlete so I never had to worry about my weight. When I got injured and couldn't get any exercise at all, it seemed logical to me to cut back on eating because I was scared I would gain weight.

When I was able to move about again, I still feared gaining weight. I added exercise to the restricted eating. Sadly, I got positive reinforcement as I began losing muscle mass. People made comments, such as, "Wow, you look good . . . are you losing weight?" As an athletically built girl, when I started to lose my muscle, people saw it first as losing weight. The compliments, coupled with my perfectionist tendencies, quickly fed my desire to lose more weight. I wasn't getting the usual positive feedback for playing basketball, so when I got it for weight loss, it spurred me on.

In January 2004 my coach told me that because I had lost weight so fast I had to quit the team unless I attended an outpatient eating disorders treatment program. Shortly after I began the program I was sent to the hospital for evaluation. They admitted me right away because my heart rate was dangerously low, 38 beats per minute (bpm). A healthy person's resting heart rate is between 50–100 bpm.

After two weeks I was sent back to the local eating disorders treatment program. Once discharged, I went back to the same behaviors and kept losing weight. Later, upon returning to college, the weight loss continued. I was admitted to the hospital for the second time in August. I did whatever they wanted me to do and knew what I had to say to get out of there. The eating disorder and I knew we would be reunited as soon as I was discharged.

My family became so irritated with me that after awhile they stopped visiting me in the hospital. This hurt me, but now I see that it was a good thing to push me and not feed into my need for attention. I think they were trying to use tough love in order to get me better.

My fiancé at the time called off our wedding, saying, "You need to choose me or the eating disorder." As I gave him back the ring, I calmly said, "I guess I choose the eating disorder. You make it too hard to live with my eating disorder—you always ask me about how I'm eating. So I'm going to just let you go." When I told Becky this story I found out mine wasn't the only wedding ruined by an eating disorder. She was told about a young woman who began a "diet" to lose weight for her wedding. Combined with her genetic makeup and personality traits, the dieting spiraled out of control and quickly evolved into an eating disorder. The young woman collapsed at the altar and had to be rushed to the hospital.

The third time I was hospitalized they kept me for four weeks until there was a bed open at Remuda Ranch, a treatment center in Arizona. By this time I decided if I wanted to live I had to find a different way as the hospital thing wasn't working. I knew I was going to die if things didn't change, and I wanted to give "surviving" my best shot. Going somewhere else seemed my only option.

My mom and I flew from Minnesota to Arizona right after I was released from the hospital. It was a good decision, but we had to fight with the insurance company to get coverage for my stay. My mom was willing to put her house up for sale or take out a second mortgage to pay for my care.

"Why are you doing this to Mom?" my upset siblings asked. They weren't greedy; they just weren't quite sure how to handle it all. It was so stressful for them to watch Mom go through this when she has always worked very hard to keep financially above water by herself.

My siblings were angry, thinking I was being selfish—craving attention and wanting people to focus on me. "Are you really sick?" asked my brother, with whom I had always been really close. "Are you lying to me?" He took it the hardest; he knew I lied to him. Our relationship is still strained. They finally told me they wouldn't be coming to visit me. When I was in Arizona they seemed relieved; I was less of a burden there.

Mom had so much on her plate at the time. Her mother was dying at the same time I was sick, and she went through stages, alternately thinking, *She can get better* and *She's not going to fix this.*

During the two months at the treatment center in Arizona, my grandma passed away. I was released for the funeral but I missed saying goodbye to my grandma in person like my siblings were able to do. When I flew home for the funeral, things were very strained between my family and me. What did they expect? That I'd be 60 pounds heavier? The way my brother looked at me, I guessed he was thinking, *You're down there in Arizona wasting Mom's money—you had better get better.* I missed spending Thanksgiving and Christmas with my family that year; I'm not sure they missed me.

It's very difficult for families to know what to say or do. In family therapy, they hear that any number of things can trigger destructive behaviors, so they are afraid to say anything, and yet they don't want to enhance the depression by not saying anything. Nothing seems right.

Family week occurred two weeks before my release from Remuda. It was a time to learn tools and meet a number of other families in varied situations with eating disorders. I invited my mom, dad (my parents are divorced), brother and ex-fiancé. I told them, "I've lost control. I need your help to get better, and need you to understand how hard this is for me." Only my mom came. That hurt—it felt like a dagger to the heart.

I was working really hard and needed their support. It seemed like they just didn't care. I talked with my ex-fiancé during the end of my stay at Remuda and told him I needed him as a friend. We had been together since junior high. When I told him, "I need you here for me," he picked me up from the airport, and we talked every night. We regained our relationship. If I hadn't had the support of my mom, who was always there for me, and my fiancé, who was there for the most part, I would have felt that no one really cared if I lived or died.

If I were to identify a "breaking point" that shifted me toward recovering, it would be that Remuda, a Christian-based facility, helped me to find God and let Him—not the eating disorder—rule my life.

When I was released, follow-up care was going to be essential, so I moved in with a girlfriend and resumed treatment at the local eating disorders program. I lost a little bit of weight but have been able to maintain since. I lived in a small town, so people would call my mom or my fiancé and tell on me if I was running too much. To this day, people still watch me to make sure I'm not overdoing it with the exercise.

I married my fiancé and had a baby after trying to get pregnant for two years. An eating disorder does so much damage to the entire system; fertility is often impacted. I was so happy to finally be pregnant but the postpartum body changes have been hard. I look at pictures of how I used to look and think I know how to get back there using my old tricks. Then I look at my husband, my baby and my parents, and I know I can't do that to them, but every day is still a challenge for me.

Currently, I don't go to any support programs; I stopped the last treatment program in 2006 and haven't restricted or over-exercised since. I still have triggers but am able to manage them now. Looking at my son, who is my main source of inspiration and motivation, I remind myself how much it would affect him if I went back to my old ways. I can appreciate my current life as a mother, wife, daughter, sister and teacher. I get positive reinforcements from these external sources all the time. These people are a big part of my life and are what keep me from relapsing.

Although I am still very conscious of calories and fat intake, I try to watch my consumption in a healthy way. When I say, "How much fat does this have in it?" my hubby will say, "Do we need to worry about that?" And I often remind him, "You know what to look for; you'll know if I have a problem."

Although my husband, son and I sit down to meals together, I typically eat a frozen weight-loss meal but I feel I'm doing what normal people do. I couldn't put into my body what my husband does at each meal. He's a big guy who eats a lot and it's not the healthiest, so it's hard for me to be around when he's eating. I didn't eat out for about five years. Now I am trying to do what normal people do, like sitting down to eat the same dinner as my husband and son—that's something I would like to be able to do someday.

Four years out of Remuda, I have a life. I gained experience and knowledge from being there; I didn't gain anything from being 83 pounds. Life is better than it was before. In the midst of it all, it didn't seem possible that life could be this good, ever.

Postscript: Since doing the initial interview, I am happy to report that I am getting a lot better at eating what my family eats, and just prior to publication of this book, I gave birth to my second child!

JAYNE'S STORY (THE MOM)

College basketball was her dream and Ashley got to play. When Ashley hurt her ankle during her sophomore year of college, it never occurred to me that this could be the impetus for an eating disorder. She had always been an athlete and I just figured that when her ankle allowed activity, she would be back into sports, regain her fitness level, and would play many more games. It wasn't my habit to watch her eat, and it never occurred to me to observe her eating after she was injured.

John, Ashley's 24-year-old brother, first brought it to my attention one night as he and I were taking out the recycling after dinner. "Mom, when Ashley was home for the weekend I noticed that she has lost a lot of weight. I think she has a serious problem, an eating disorder, and we need to keep an eye on her."

My reply was, "John, you don't know what you are talking about. That's ridiculous; Ashley wouldn't intentionally do that to herself."

I was in complete denial. I didn't want to face it—or deal with it. Ashley had always been in sports, and I had heard that girls in sports typically don't have low self-esteem with its often-serious implications.

As time went by, John's concerns were in the back of my mind, but I didn't know anything about eating disorders. I thought you could just stop anytime if you wanted to. I couldn't imagine why anyone would willingly let something like an eating disorder demolish the dream to play college ball, not to mention destroy her overall health. As you can see, I had no idea how powerless people can be over these devastating illnesses, and had absolutely no concept that they are biologically based illnesses and are not a choice.

Sports had always given Ashley a good feeling about herself and her capabilities. A perfectionist, she always excelled in school. I assumed she wouldn't compromise her scholastic achievements—and she didn't. Somehow she was able to earn all A's throughout the duration of her illness. The perfectionist in her would allow no less.

I was glad she had her fiancé, Doug, a long-time friend of the family, in her life. So I was doubly shocked when he later confirmed what John had told me earlier. Then I remembered grocery shopping with Ashley and thinking it was odd that she would look at the ingredients on food packages to see the amount of calories and fat. She had never done this before. I didn't understand at the time that she was reading food labels to restrict calories, sugar and fat. I later found out that, ironically, these same food labels were intended to aid those with heart disease. I'm sure no one at the American Heart Association ever dreamed how dangerous these labels would become in the hands of so many with eating disorders.

The first time I found myself in a hospital with Ashley and Doug, I couldn't believe how bad it was. That is when it really hit me that this was really serious.

Ashley was smart about some aspects of negotiating this illness, or perhaps it was the eating disorder that was so smart. I was totally fooled. As a mom, I thought the hospitalization would change her. I was so proud of her and how dedicated she appeared to be in her recovery, thinking, *Wow, good, she's doing exactly what she needs to be doing to get well.* Boy, was I wrong.

She was doing just what she knew the hospital staff wanted her to do so she could be released and begin all over again. I now believe that very structured follow-up is necessary to prevent the kind of recurrence that we experienced.

Since Ashley was so compliant, I felt it was safe to leave her to go to my dying mother's bedside across the state. Frankly, at that time, I had too much to handle physically and emotionally to stay on top of everything. I was worrying about Ashley, making sure that insurance was covering her treatments, and hoping she was getting well, while at the same time my mother was in the final stages of a terminal illness.

Sometimes I hear rumblings from care providers, the media, or acquaintances about the family of a person with an eating disorder not doing enough—and sometimes, for doing too much. I've learned that life doesn't stop; there can be many simultaneous drains on our attention, energy and time and a parent can never do too much to help a sick child.

Ashley was so physically and emotionally weak; she simply did what the monster, the eating disorder, told her to do. One time she went to Doug's apartment and the act of walking up the stairs was so strenuous that she passed out. Another time she fainted she hit a wall, smashing her face and severely injuring herself.

I remember Ashley telling me about being in her college classes on a hot fall day in southern Wisconsin. She wore a lot of layers so people wouldn't see how thin and sickly she looked. One day, walking across campus, she became very hot and thirsty. She remembers thinking *When I get to school, I'll get a drink of water.* But the eating disorder's voice was stronger, telling her, "Don't you dare drink water—that's water weight." She walked past the faucet.

That was when I realized the ED monster had taken over her life, it was controlling her—there was no way she could get better on her own.

Ashley's siblings were getting angry. They saw how much she was putting us all through and watched me use up my life savings. I was even considering getting a second mortgage on the house to help pay for the treatments.

When Ashley was at school, we worried because we didn't know whether she was okay. But when she'd come home for the weekend to get some rest, seeing her so very sick, we gained a whole new set of worries.

Those weekends brought us relief because we could see how she was doing, yet they also brought home a very crabby, nasty daughter. She was so nasty at times that we knew it wasn't the "real" Ashley talking, but at first it was difficult to understand that it was the evil eating disorder, which we could not see or hear, creating the awful behaviors. We felt the monster was eating her alive.

When Ashley didn't want my help, in the back of my mind, through all of the ugliness, I knew it wasn't Ashley. Ashley didn't behave like that. I simply figured she was starving her brain. So many of her behaviors were not consistent with the daughter I knew. I would tell myself, *This isn't Ashley and we'll do whatever we have to do to get the old Ashley back. Down deep, she has to still be in there. Deal with it, and don't yell at her—that will make things worse.*

As her mother, I couldn't seem to do anything right. I tried so hard to love her and not do anything to upset her. It was so exhausting that by Sunday afternoon, when she headed back to school, I was so relieved, then felt guilty that I was relieved.

On Monday mornings my co-workers were surprised when I told them that work was my "vacation," a good distraction from the worry and suffering. They were also amazed that I never missed work during this whole time; they knew how drained and stressed I was. They were a large part of my support system throughout Ashley's illness.

During the summers, Ashley worked with me at the school as a custodian. One of our jobs was to wash trashcans and distribute them to the classrooms. The school had a four-wheeled cart that could carry thirty garbage cans, so we could quickly transport four to each room. One day I noticed Ashley taking just one garbage can at a time, walking all the way across the school, then repeating the exercise for all thirty cans. It drove me crazy watching her create constant movement, simply to burn off more calories. This realization brought deep sobs out of me, and I recall crying out to a co-worker, "I can't do this anymore!"

At lunch break, Ashley wouldn't eat with us. She would find some excuse to leave the building, then would run around the park. She even found computer programs that helped her know how much exercise it would take to burn off the calories for each food item she ingested.

As Ashley and I were discussing our part in this book, she told me that during this time, at home whenever she saw me go outside to hang the laundry she would seize the opportunity to run up and down the stairs—anything to burn off more calories. I had no idea. Who would ever dream of such a thing? An aside to readers who may be in recovery themselves: please don't let your eating disorder see that as an idea for you to try—it almost killed Ashley.

My good friends at work helped me get through the ongoing crisis of Ashley's eating disorder by encouraging me and giving me hugs. They would often ask me how things were or if there was anything they could do. They knew my money situation was bad, and organized a fundraiser at school when my mom first had cancer surgery. The money went for gas to visit my mom 120 miles away and my daughter, 100 miles the other direction. Knowing I had people to help me out, including caring neighbors who asked how I was doing, all kept me going. The support I received from all of these people helped get me through this nightmare.

Though initially I wasn't knowledgeable at all about eating disorders, I had to make sure she would survive. I told her I would try in any way I could to help her get better. I was determined not to lose her.

One of the things I *could* do was fight non-stop for insurance coverage for her hospital stays. The last time she was in the hospital, she was kicked off our insurance because she was no longer a full-time student. This was a "Catch-22," as she couldn't be in school because she was in the hospital. My tenacity paid off with the help of one very kind-hearted employee at the insurance company who went out of her way to help.

When I found a photo today of Ashley at her lowest weight, with her sunken eyes, looking like an old woman, I was grateful that we are where we are today. Prior to learning about the genetic factors that can set up a person for an eating disorder, I asked Ashley what she thought causes eating disorders. She said that large contributing factors are the messages we get from TV, magazines, and the media in general that "this is how you are supposed to look."

Until researchers agree on the causes and prevention, we must face the facts that this can happen to anyone. Ashley was on the "A" honor roll, active in sports, close to her family—we didn't believe this could happen to her or to us.

Now a 26-year-old schoolteacher and married, Ashley has made it through the worst of it. She was even able to have a son, which she calls a miracle since she was told that the damage the eating disorder did to her body would most likely prevent her from having children. Her heart sustained damage and she developed Polycystic Ovarian Syndrome (PCOS) from the anorexia. I continue to worry, as I know she still finds it hard not to use her old behaviors but she will usually eat with us during family events. Ashley has been trying to help a fellow teacher at school whose daughter is dealing with an eating disorder. I get very frustrated that this parent doesn't grasp how really sick her daughter is. However, from our experiences, I do understand the urge to bury your head—but I'd like her to know that denial isn't going to help.

JAYNE'S AND ASHLEY'S TIPS:

1. Allow the pain you see the eating disorder causing your family to motivate you to stick with your treatment program. —A.

2. Find something more important than the eating disorder and let that also be a motivator to recovery. God did it for me. —A.

3. Learn as a family what phrases are "safe" to say to support the person in recovery. —J.

4. Be a smart shopper when it comes to treatment options— learn what works for the person in recovery and what doesn't. Some people find a hospital situation helpful but others do not. —J.

5. Set clear boundaries with your loved one in recovery— healthy boundaries equal healthy relationships. —J./A.

6. Be aware that the thinking of someone with an eating disorder is distorted, not just about body image but also the reality of how seriously her health is being impacted. —J./A.

7. Family members need to ask for and accept help from others. —J./A.

8. Fight for insurance coverage; even though our American system is changing, we will most likely have to continue to fight for mental health coverage. Be persistent. —J./A.

9. Learn as much as you can about eating disorders. —J./A.

10. Know that burying your head in the sand when you see red flags, such as sweatpants, long sleeves, and layers of clothing in the summer, is not going to help anyone. —J./A.

11. Let people hug you. This is good for both the family and the person in recovery. —J./A.

16

Diane's Story

Do Not Let the Insurance Company Push You Around

Networking is one thing I truly enjoy. I'm an extrovert so it's easy and fun for me. Meeting new people and discovering the gems inside each of them satisfies my curious nature. In the process, I get to meet many inspiring people such as Diane. After being introduced to her as someone I needed to talk with, I soon found out we are both mothers of daughters with eating disorders and we share the desire to educate other parents on navigating the financial waters of paying for treatment, including the insurance issues. The costs are outrageous and many families go into debt paying for treatment.

As of this writing, according to the South Carolina Department of Mental Health website, http://www.state.sc.us/dmh/anorexia/statistics.htm, "Treatment of an eating disorder in the U.S. ranges from $500 per day to $2,000 per day. The average cost for a month of inpatient treatment is $30,000. It is estimated that individuals with eating disorders need anywhere from 3–6 months of inpatient care. Health insurance companies, for several reasons, do not typically cover the cost of treating eating disorders."

The cost of outpatient treatment, including therapy and medical monitoring, can extend to $100,000 or more.

Tireless advocates are working to make sure eating disorders treatment is paid for by insurance companies, just like any other illness. The Eating Disorders Coalition is one such example. Check out their website: www.eatingdisorderscoalition.org/ to see the progress they are making.

While interviewing Diane, she told me that the privacy laws made it difficult for her to assist her daughter as effectively as possible. She asked that, in her story, rather than share the details of her daughter's illness, I stress the importance of communication with care providers and the need to change privacy laws to better enable families to help their loved ones in recovery.

It can be a huge surprise for parents to learn that after taking care of their child's health and health care for 18 years, the morning of their child's 18th birthday parents no longer have access to their child's health information.

Even when the child is still living at home, or parents are paying tuition and all living expenses for their child away at college, overnight, access to all health care information ceases.

It's especially frustrating when the child is being treated for an illness. Without the child giving his or her written permission, no doctor, therapist, clinic or hospital can legally release any information to parents.

But they all will still accept the parents' checks.

DIANE'S STORY

I usually don't share personal details such as the scrapes on my daughter Connie's fingers from purging or how I sit and hold her while she cries when the waves of depression sweep over her. We both want so very badly for her to be well and some days it seems so far off. Connie and I both live with the eating disorder that inhabits her, as well as the constant challenges, misinterpretations, dishonesty and chaos that accompany this illness. When people ask me why it's so hard when a child has an eating disorder, I tell them about a typical day in my life.

For example, one morning Connie called, saying her wallet was stolen and she had lost her cell phone. She was calling from a gas station, pleading, "Will you bring me some money for gas?" A mother would usually be quite sympathetic to such a story, but the new "normal," since the eating disorder entered our lives, has made me distrustful of the truth of the story and skeptical about how responsible she had been.

Describing the off-the-charts self-centeredness, lying, sense of entitlement, and full-bore selfishness that coexist with these disorders is futile. Unless someone has experienced living with someone with a serious addiction or an eating disorder (the jury is still out on whether or not eating disorders are addictions), they usually think you are making this stuff up. When you have lived or worked with it, you get it.

The many accompanying conditions and underlying traits, including depression, anxiety, control, perfectionism, and fear, make eating disorders incredibly complex and difficult to understand and treat. Sometimes it can look like normal teen behavior that is taken to the extreme. As a parent I find that keeping my emotions in check and taking care of the details keeps me from feeling too sad about what is happening to my daughter. Differentiating between the eating disorder and obnoxious teenage antics isn't easy some days.

It has become "normal" for teens and women to feel bad about their bodies. Having poor body image does not mean a person has an eating disorder, but it is part of an eating disorder.

I knew too late about the "How low can you go" game so many young girls play when they are together. Connie had a sleepover when she was about 12 and the girls all went shopping. When they returned and were trying on clothes, I overheard comments that shocked me. One of the very small girls, wearing skin-tight jeans, was being taunted with, "You don't wear a zero; you wear a one!"

"No I don't, I wear a zero."

A larger girl had left her tags on that said, "Size—Large" and the girls all chimed, "Taylor, you wear a Large!!!"

The poor girl felt bad and quickly replied, "Oh, no I don't; I guess I got the wrong size."

When I questioned Connie later about why she bought a small when she usually wears a medium, she answered, "Mom, you just don't understand how important size is."

Later, I found out that the treatment center was very aware of this size issue and told me that at back-to-school time they see it a lot. It's crazy-making behavior.

As a mother, I thought I was doing all I could to help prevent an eating disorder from developing by making sure we had family dinners, encouraging a positive body image, and not allowing dieting in our home. I have learned a great deal from other parents that has helped to combat my guilt. I was so relieved to hear the following from Laura Collins, author of *Eating with Your Anorexic: How My Child Recovered Through Family-Based Treatment and Yours Can Too:* "Parents can prevent a certain amount of disordered eating, but some young people seem to be so deeply predisposed toward this illness that they will develop it no matter what their environment is."

In the process of helping my daughter I began to become consumed with getting her healthy and my health began to suffer. Other parents have asked me, "What helped you?" A major turning point for me was regularly attending Al-Anon meetings. It's very easy to understand what is crazy when you can see it in yourself. That is one of the lessons I have learned during my time in Al-Anon.

Al-Anon has taught me healthy behaviors, such as cleaning up your own side of the street or, in other words, I can only fix my own issues and I need to let others take care of their problems. "Twelve-step kung-fu," where we are taught by example, is what I call it. Al-Anon has helped me feel safe and supported to the point I don't need the therapy piece anymore. In addition, it's free and that is so important when there are enormous medical bills to be paid. One of the best gifts of Al-Anon meetings is that they help you laugh, which is so welcome after so much suffering with our sick loved ones.

Al-Anon absolutely saved my life, and supported me in "letting go." I know that my being terrified, obsessing, feeling down and having my life go to hell is not going to help Connie at all. It feels like the act of letting her go may actually cause her to die. But in letting go, you aren't dropping them to certain death. Let them go and let them swim. You have to let go eventually anyhow.

I learned that it was essential to my health that I accept that holding in my own anger was probably bad for me. The things that Connie would demand of me were things I would never agree to do for my other kids. Regular requests such as, "Could you run this over to me so I don't have to use up my gas?" became opportunities to set clear boundaries, even though she was so sick.

"Tough love with velvet gloves" became my motto, and the image in my mind gives it the right tone. Here's one example: No longer do I say, "You are cut off financially." Instead, Connie will hear, "This is how much money there is and until you are a certain age and still a full-time student, that is what I will pay." I created a contract that says she is not to ask for any more money for anything that is not listed in the contract.

One time Connie called me and was very angry, made mean comments and cried. While in her angry tirade, she hit every one of my buttons, comparing me to her father, my ex-husband, saying, "You want to tell me I'm a spoiled brat!" Within an hour, she called, apologizing to me and accepted the idea of the contract. Previously, I would have called her to say, "I'm sorry," even though I didn't have anything to be sorry for.

Before Connie called back to apologize, I called my sponsor, who helped me remain calm. I'm not yet to the point where I don't feel shaken by these angry outbursts, but I have tools now. I read the *One Step at a Time In Al Anon* book every day. Baby steps. These tools help me—and Connie. I'm not miraculously better instantly; it's slow. We're both improving, together but apart.

I didn't realize my worry was fertilizer that fed Connie's illness. Our therapist suggested I read *Distorted* by Lorri Antosz Benson and Taryn Leigh Benson. *Distorted* is a raw, brutally honest account from a mother and daughter who have lived through the nightmare of the daughter's eating disorder. Until I read this, I had no clue the thrill my daughter was getting from my reactions; this book exposed some of the lying, manipulating, and childish behaviors Connie's eating disorder was subjecting me to that I hadn't recognized at the time.

Learning to cope with these behaviors was vital. However, at the same time, I had to learn quickly how to work with our medical system and the financial issues. Connie had recently begun attending a local treatment program, and I attended the newly formed parent's group. Finding out what I could do to help and getting information on the do's and don'ts was a priority for me. Connie had already attended a different program that didn't go well. She was ready to drop out of school and get serious help.

Getting to this moment was tough for all of us. Connie was living in her own apartment and I had given her the option to attend school full-time or attend the program full-time. I was contemplating cutting off all financial support as part of the motivation for her to stick with the program.

Looking for expert feedback on this loving, but difficult, decision led me to call the treatment program. Reaching a teenaged receptionist and the therapist's voicemail for three straight weeks was exasperating. This was my first lesson in the level of tenacity I would need to receive the insurance benefits.

The fourth week, when I finally heard from the therapist, she gave me one of the most valuable pieces of information I ever received: "You might want to ask Connie to sign a Release of Information form to allow you access to her billing, insurance, appointment information, and treatment progress updates."

I did and, miraculously, Connie agreed. I had to go in person with her to sign the papers, assuring her that this wasn't for me to know the details of her therapy sessions. Privacy is essential, as is complete trust in the therapist, and I promised not to pry into their sessions. But it was necessary to have the legal means to navigate the paperwork required for insurance companies.

Shortly after this turning point, I attended a parent-support group. After listening to 15 parents in agony, crying, not having any idea where their daughters were in their recovery, I spoke up. "I know how hard it is to not even know if your child is going to her appointments, but you can ask your child to sign a partial release." This was the first time any of them had heard of this option and I am certain it would not have occurred to either of the therapists, who were donating their time, to volunteer this vital information. They are so consumed with trying to save the lives of their patients that it doesn't seem to cross their radar that supporting the parents creates more support for their patients.

We all have to take baby steps in this process, and this is one of the first steps a parent can take to ease some of the suffering. We are so afraid of our children dying at the hands of this powerful disease that just knowing they are at least attending appointments can give anxious parents hope that they are in the hands of people who might be able to help them. It's also essential to set boundaries with your child, as insurance companies won't pay for missed sessions—missed appointments need to be paid for out of pocket.

Another important aspect of treatment that many insurance companies are hesitant to pay for is family therapy. One of the most valuable tools we learned came from our family therapist who is also a nurse. She told us that the action of rocking, walking or gliding calms our brains and that we should do one of those activities with our daughter when we need to have a delicate conversation with her. It made a huge difference in her ability to handle the stress. Some treatment programs won't even tell you that family therapy can greatly enhance the individual work being done. Be the squeaky wheel—that's the one that gets the grease.

Making financial decisions became more challenging as more of our budget went to pay for eating disorders treatment. One of the things I wasn't willing to give up was the bi-weekly help we hired to clean the house. With our busy lives it freed-up more time to support Connie and refill my own well (in my case by attending Al Anon meetings) so I could stay healthy. Our cleaning ladies had known my kids since they were little and were quite concerned about what was happening to Connie. They were mystified when I tried to explain it to them one day. While in Russia, these women had lived for years with barely enough food to survive on—there were days their family of six had one potato to share. They could not comprehend why an American with plenty of food available would willingly starve herself and even more incomprehensible—why she would throw it up. It broke my heart trying to explain this to them.

College funds were eaten up by the eating disorder as fast as my heart was breaking. After Connie missed five appointments at her second treatment program, I insisted on setting the boundary that she had to pay for any missed appointments since insurance wouldn't cover them.

When she dropped classes part way through a semester, Connie thought that the fees would be refunded, but she hadn't dropped them in time to receive the refund. Since she has the emotional maturity of a 14-year-old, she couldn't manage such things or comprehend the consequences. When I told her that I didn't have the money for college since the school hadn't refunded the $2,500, she cried, but I still said no. My heart broke right along with hers, but I don't cry like I used to do. Now my heart is separated enough from hers so I am able to get through times like these without tears.

The treatment program suggested inpatient treatment at one point, but I had to tell Connie that all I could afford to pay for was the outpatient program. Letting her know that she had no other options was essential as I was not going to spend $100,000 not knowing if it would help or not. I told Connie I was saying no because I loved her and felt this was the best decision.

Through hours on the phone with the insurance company, I learned what I could expect them to pay. The care coordinator at the insurance company gave me some very good advice: "Take copious notes each time you speak with someone about Connie's case." She suggested I keep a notebook with the date, time, and name of each customer service person I spoke with when I called about a claim. This advice became invaluable when we needed to appeal a claim decision.

Keeping detailed insurance records, as well as copies of all the statements we received, paid off when we needed to enlist the help of our state attorney general's office to deal with both the hospital's haphazard billing system and the attempts by the insurance company to avoid fulfilling their contractual obligations to us.

Changing the financial responsibility for the medical expenses into Connie's name helped reduce our liability. I wish I had known that much earlier, but no one tells you this is an option when the patient turns 18.

Another piece of the paying-for-treatment puzzle is the Health Insurance Portability and Accountability Act (HIPAA), enacted by the U.S. Congress in 1996. You can look up the details of this act, which is meant to protect the privacy of the patient's medical information.

One of the challenges for parents is that HIPAA makes it difficult to advocate for your child's medical care. I truly believe *this law needs to be changed and that people are dying as a result of the HIPAA laws.* Because the law is so strict, care providers can be afraid to say anything to anyone about a patient's care. Parents can't find out what is going on, leaving them out of the treatment loop. When there is so much shame and secrecy, along with lying on the part of the person with the eating disorder, it is imperative that the care providers and family are in communication to best support recovery.

Postscript from Becky: It's been several months since I first interviewed Diane. I recently ran into her and she gave me the following update:

Both Connie and I are doing really well. Physically, she's much better though it may take years to raise her iron level to normal to regain her previous high energy. Now that she is no longer malnourished, her mind and body are healing and functioning much better. I recently bought her all new clothes as a reward for taking more responsibility for her bills and I asked her to dispose of all of her older clothes as another way to leave ED behind her.

She started going to Al-Anon after she saw how much it

helped me. She has a sponsor and really loves it. At her first meeting she was asked why she was there. She responded, "My mom's been coming for two years and I've seen what it's done for her [boundaries and peace] and I want what she has!"

I do credit Al-Anon and its teachings about "letting go" with helping me disengage from Connie's illness. I think this disengagement saved her life and I know it saved my sanity. I feel very, very fortunate.

DIANE'S TIPS:

1. Eating disorders stunt emotional development, but I believe with proper treatment and time, people can catch up.

2. Keep meticulous records of billing statements and payments so you know you are being charged correctly for treatment.

3. Make notes in one place of all phone calls with your insurance company, including date, time, and the name of the person you talked to.

4. Prepare for a marathon, not a sprint.

5. Fill yourself up so that you have reserves. For example: get massages, watch movies, lose yourself in reading.

6. Become familiar with what your insurance covers and know your rights. There is now national mental health parity in the United States. Insist on coverage for all aspects of treatment, including a nutritionist.

7. Learn how to set clear boundaries with your child. This is essential, even when, or especially when, a child is very ill. Don't fall into the pity trap.

8. Understand your rights as parents. Learn about HIPAA's restrictions. http://www.hhs.gov/ocr/privacy/hipaa/understanding/index.html.

9. *Do not* let the insurance company push you around.

10. Be aware of what your girls are doing and talking about—and try to encourage them to have a strong, positive body image.

11. Get your child to sign the Release of Information form.

12. Put the financial aspects of your child's care in your child's name, once she is 18.

17

Margie, Cathy, and Jennifer's Stories

Sisters Speak From Their Hearts

Three women, ages 45, 30 and 20, were willing to answer questions about their sisters who have struggled, or are still struggling, with eating disorders. At three different stages in life, their perspectives give a broad picture of the effects eating disorders can have on families. Their varied reactions to what they experienced, and at times are still encountering, give insights to the vast ripple effect of eating disorders. These siblings are a small representation of the unseen recipients of an eating disorder's ruthless destruction in our society. I am so grateful to the women, represented by the names Margie, Cathy and Jennifer, for sharing their private experiences so the world can have these intimate insights about eating disorders and their impact on family members

Not all questions pertained to each sister so some are answered by one or two of them, and some by all three.

1. Have you ever felt neglected because of your sister's illness?
Margie, age 45: My 30-year-old sister, Judy, didn't show any signs of an eating disorder until she was an adult. She's always been a perfectionist, which served her well through law school and in her legal practice, yet I never saw this as a sign. We both received plenty of attention as children and I never felt neglected.

However, our family dynamics are very strained at the moment as Judy "borrowed" a lot of money from my partner and me for her treatment—and now won't respond to my phone calls, and even refused a registered letter. The eating disorder is isolating us big time, which I understand is very common, and today I can only wonder how my sister is doing.

Communication has broken down. Judy will talk with our parents, but they don't talk about the eating disorder with her, and will not tell me anything about Judy. It is all so very sad and I miss the relationship with her and don't like the stress with our parents. I never imagined that, at age 45, my 30-year-old sister would not be my close friend anymore.

Cathy, age 35: It is hard to believe 10 years have gone by since the eating disorder took my sister Abby's life. Looking back at my high school years, my parents were conscientious enough to continue recognizing and supporting me in my own activities and successes through high school and college while dealing with Abby and her eating disorder. I never felt a lack of love and support from my parents or my other sister.

The neglect I felt mostly came from Abby because she was so self-centered as a result of her eating disorder. Four years older than me, she missed a few big occasions in my life, such as a special event I participated in the summer after high school graduation, my departure to Germany for a semester in college, and my college graduation.

Her absence at these events upset me quite a bit and took away from my enjoyment. I remember being very angry with her and feeling like I wasn't important enough for her to make the effort to be there. It was very hard because at the time I considered her my best friend and was closer to her than to my other sister.

Jennifer, age 20: Ha! No, definitely not. I'm in college now but at age 9, while my parents were handling my sister's screaming or crying or whatever her drama was that particular evening, I would be having a blast, knowing I should be in bed. I'm a second child and Sara is the cliché first child. Since the day I was born I watched her do *anything* for attention; meanwhile, I learned how to entertain myself. In fact, I hate having too much attention directed at me. It seems like my parents don't believe me sometimes but really, I loved that she took up all their energy. I got to do whatever I wanted! Luckily for my parents, that was limited to watching extra TV or being on the computer past my limit—nothing crazy.

2. When the ED first started, did you think your sister could have just stopped if she just wanted to?
Margie: At first I thought my sister could stop and could eat more/better/healthier. I started to "worry" the summer of 2007 during a visit. With each visit, my worries grew, and I finally expressed my concern in late 2007. Initially in denial about her eating disorder, Judy did then agree to see a counselor. The more phone conversations I had with her the more I realized that the eating disorder was controlling her. It was like a vice getting tighter and tighter. After she was hospitalized in spring 2008, I tried to convince her to get more help. She steadily went downhill, and the physical effects, coupled with her inability to perform her job, got the attention of her employer. Finally, in April 2009, her co-workers convinced her to get help.

Cathy: Before I knew very much about eating disorders, I did think that she could just stop it—and start viewing herself differently. I thought that she could ignore those nagging voices in her head that were telling her she was fat. After awhile, with knowledge and experience, I realized it was something she would struggle with for the rest of her life. I also realized that she would never view herself as the beautiful and successful person she really was.

Jennifer: Though I was 9 when it all began and I didn't know what was going on. I knew my sister was weird; I could have told my parents that when I was two years old and staring, bewildered, at my sister's latest antics to get attention. I don't think I knew she had an eating disorder until I was 11 or 12, when she went to get treatment. I do remember my mom standing at the bathroom door when my sister was in there sometimes. The bathroom was next to my room. Sara would run the shower, so the sound of her puking was muffled. It didn't work very well. To this day, I have a very strong aversion to anyone who is puking—mostly it's the sound that bothers me.

3. How did it generally affect your life before your older sister moved out?

Cathy: I think it affected me most at home. My parents were constantly having confrontations with Abby. It caused a lot of disruption that I was forced to deal with on my own. My oldest sister had moved out to go to college shortly after Abby's eating disorder began. I didn't feel like there was anyone on my side dealing with it and viewing it like I was. Maybe it would've been easier if my other sister had still been around.

Abby and I were on the gymnastics team in high school together. In her senior year, when I was in eighth grade, she was our team captain. Our entire team and coaches were aware of her eating disorder. It affected her performance in gymnastics and her other sports; her body didn't always have the calories and nutrients to keep going. I was constantly worrying about her health and was always afraid she was going to die.

Jennifer: I had a lot more freedom when Sara was living with us. I was used to sharing my parents with both my sister and the eating disorder. My parents got so used to always having a problem to deal with, a kid in crisis, that when Sara moved out they started worrying about me. I don't think my parents were always over-protective with me—it started after my sister moved out and the ever-blasting time bomb that is Sara wasn't ticking in the house anymore. Part of it, I'm sure, is that I became a teenager and my mom was terrified I would fall into the same hole that had sucked my sister in. When I turned 18 my parents finally relaxed and realized they didn't have to worry about me. I was the same level-headed calm kid they could always trust to take care of herself. Our relationship got exponentially better after they quit trying to parent me so much.

4. What specific things do you remember?
Cathy: It was such a long time ago, but I remember Abby always asking if her legs looked fat. Obviously they didn't. You could almost make out the shape of the bones in her knees. It was disgusting.

During high school I used to find laxatives and diet pills in her desk at home. I remember going along to an eating disorder meeting at a metro hospital and seeing girls who were worse off than Abby. It made me think maybe she wasn't that sick, but I learned that there are many levels to the illness.

I remember living with her when we both left home. Her shelf in the kitchen cupboard always had only a box of saltines and maybe some cans of soup.

Jennifer: I remember my sister eating peanut butter and raisins, together, for a few weeks. That was all she'd eat. Then there was the rice and peanut butter phase, and the teen starlet obsession phase. My sister made a goddess out of a teen TV star from a show she loved watching. She even started telling her friends at school that she knew her. Even as a kid I could tell my older sister had the brains of a younger sister and had lost touch with reality. She made up a lot of shit, and I had no problem calling her out on it, which really pissed her off, especially when she was 15 and I was 10.

5. Were you hesitant to bring friends home after school?
Jennifer: Definitely. Not because I was afraid they'd see her puking or something; I never even saw that—and we shared a bathroom. I didn't want my friends to see the large mass of sweatpants and sweatshirt wasting away on the couch, trading her precious youth for a simulated reality of her idolized teen TV stars. I would bring over a few of my close friends, just to prove to them how crazy she was. My best friend, Joe, probably saw more of her craziness than anyone except me. She used to call him a silly nickname and acted nuts around him, especially as we got older. My gut tells me it's because she had no idea how to act around men, which created a kind of paradox since she had known Joe all of his life. He would just laugh nervously until we could leave the room and she could return to her fantasyland.

6. Did you invite friends over for dinner?
Margie: When Judy visited me about a year ago it was so hard to explain to people about her ED—the bizarre behaviors, the hyper-focus on food. Now, even if she did visit me, I would not invite friends over for dinner—it's just too hard.

    Cathy: I did occasionally have friends over for lunch or dinner. I remember that mealtimes with Abby were always nerve wracking, no matter who was there. It was hard to watch her take tiny portions, then wonder whether she would even keep it in her stomach. I don't remember if the presence of one of my friends made the situation any more uncomfortable than it already was.

7. Do you fear going on a diet if you gain weight—that you too might get an eating disorder?
Margie: No, I do not feel that it is in my nature to become obsessive about my eating. It could happen . . . but I don't worry about it.

Cathy: I do have that fear. I think there have been different times in my life when I was on the verge of having a problem with eating. It is very difficult being a woman in today's society with the pressures to be thin, beautiful, and perfectly dressed. I am also a short person, so if I gain weight it is much more noticeable than if I were taller. But maybe that's just my perception.

Now I tend to notice not how I look, but how I feel in my body. I try to make healthy decisions about what I eat, but I also allow myself the luxury of pigging out, eating ice cream, and lazing around when I feel the need. I exercise on a regular basis. I'll be honest; I do not want to gain excess weight—I do the steps necessary to maintain my current weight, but I would never go the route Abby did. I don't want to jeopardize my health and well-being. I want to live life to the fullest and depriving myself of the foods I love is not the way to do it.

Jennifer: No. My sister and I are completely different people—so I don't worry that eating disorders are "hereditary." She thinks in extremes; I think in terms of balance. She never understood the concept of a grey area. That's the most annoying part of being her sister—people assume we must be alike in some way since we're related.

8. What kinds of things did your sister do that made you angry?
Margie: I am angry that she did not agree to get help earlier as this is a progressive disease. I am angry that my parents did not take a more active role in working with her to get help. I am

angry that when she did start to get help, I was, and am still, completely on the outside—there's been no family involvement yet. She has been in and out of treatment programs and does not seem to be improving.

Cathy: Abby could tend to be very manipulative and mean sometimes. I remember fighting with her a bit, but sisters do have a tendency to argue. She was just really adept at making every disagreement the other party's fault. She did it with the whole family. If any of us accused her of something, before we knew it we were the ones who had done something wrong. It was infuriating. After awhile, I tried not to have any disagreements with her. I was always agreeable, taking the path of least resistance, even if it meant giving up something I really needed.

Just the fact that Abby couldn't see or understand that she was amazingly beautiful made me angry. I just don't get it. She had been muscular and active and so very capable in all realms of her life. But she would still always ask me if she looked fat. The ironic part was that she was always the first to tell every other person how amazing and beautiful they were. She was everyone else's cheerleader, but never her own. She actually did some speaking and writing on the subject to young people. I guess after some time, her eating disorder brought her to a point where she never wanted any other woman or man to feel the way she did about herself. She wanted to help everyone else feel good about himself or herself.

She also made me angry when she wouldn't be there for me when I needed her. She often couldn't get past her own needs to be reliable. I learned not to count on her, even though I felt she was my best friend. There were so many disappointments.

Jennifer: Use too much toilet paper; get my parents in a bad mood; spend all of my parents' money; eat all of my food; be obnoxious, when she was obese and just sitting on the couch; her obsession with materialism; her absolute lack of common sense or sense for adventure; her stupidity, in general, made me really angry. I have no sympathy for her. I think she should take all the food she wasted binging and purging, figure out how much money it cost, make the money and donate it to a charity that feeds hungry kids.

9. What kinds of things did your sister do that grossed you out?
Cathy: Of course, the puking was the grossest thing ever. I also felt that she was gross because she was so skinny. The whole emaciated appearance was just disgusting. I'm amazed that anyone could have found her attractive during her bad times.

Jennifer: Walking around naked. Disgusting. I have seen more cellulite and saggy boobs than any young woman ever needs to be exposed to. Her nasty long hair was everywhere, too. She had no regard for anyone but herself.

10. How did you handle being "the other kid" during your sister's times of drama that pulled your parents in to "rescue" her?
Margie: This was not an issue since we are both adults. I do realize that much of our family "joy" has been replaced with worry and sadness, though.

Cathy: I don't remember this being an issue for me. I had my other sister so I didn't feel abandoned during Abby's more difficult times. As I have mentioned before, my parents were continually supportive of me and my other sister. We were not neglected.

Jennifer: Generally, I slept through most of her big hospital-needing outbursts and several suicide attempts, with one parent heading off to the hospital, and the other staying home with me. Other times of drama, I just shook my head and went on doing whatever I was doing.

11. What did you notice about how the illness affected your parents?

Margie: Our parents seem sad, helpless, and angry at times, but are unwilling to take more decisive action. I am saddened and angry that they have kept this "secret" from the extended family. Now Judy has lost her job at the law firm due to the illness, and our parents are paying for her apartment.

Cathy: I mostly remember their sadness and helplessness—but there was also a lot of anger. I'm sure it was very difficult on their relationship with each other. They maybe didn't always agree on how to handle Abby or what to do to help her get better or make her well. I would imagine, but do not know for sure, that they also thought that maybe they were to blame—or had questions about why their daughter ended up with this disease—like what influences in our home could have led to the progression of this disease? I only list these thoughts as speculation because if I were a parent, I would have those thoughts.

Jennifer: It turned them into worrying adults who I think had to sacrifice a lot of happy years with their kids to focus on my completely self-absorbed sister. My dad's mother was an alcoholic and had very similar episodes as my sister, so I think my dad wasn't affected as much since he'd, in a way, already been through the drama.

They probably have a lot more wrinkles and grey hairs than they would have had Sara been less crazy. My mom lost some friends over it—friends who, unbelievably, were jealous over how much attention my sister was getting and how it cut into my mom's "friend time."

My mom turned into an eating-disorder-spotting hawk, which was really annoying for a while. She got over it with me, but when diet-obsessed friends come over, I see the talons slide out again.

12. What of your sister's behaviors were the hardest for you to deal with?
Margie: The hardest part for me is Judy's hyper-focus on food. Her misjudgments, lack of clear thinking, and lying, have also been difficult.

Jennifer: Her childishness. Oh, and her being oblivious to her childishness.

13. Did you ever wish she would behave differently at mealtimes? How did that behavior affect how you feel about sitting down to eat now?
Margie: When we were still getting together, mealtimes were hard and so different from "normal." Sometimes when I sit down with other family or friends and eat a meal, and it seems so easy compared to eating with my sister, it's sad to me.

Cathy: I always wished that Abby would just eat and enjoy her food, and then keep it in her system. It was really difficult when she was so thin; you knew that her body needed as many calories as it could get. Sometimes I wished I could just force-feed her. It was painful to watch her make decisions about what to eat. If you put a restaurant menu in front of her, she immediately gravitated to salads, soup, and sides. She was a vegetarian, but ate some fish. Her food decisions were healthy; she just lacked the appropriate portions that would really fuel her body and she didn't eat often enough.

Jennifer: I wish she would have freaked out less and chewed quieter and slower. Now when I sit down to eat, I still get agitated when people eat really fast or with their mouths open, but that's always bothered me. I wish she wouldn't have been handicapped by her knowledge, limited to celebrity gossip magazines, that inhibited her from participating in the dinner conversations. Dinner without her is lovely, since I can have a conversation with whomever is present and not worry about them wondering why my sister, five years my senior, has no idea what the heck we're talking about.

14. Did you do your own research, maybe on the Internet, to learn more about eating disorders? And if so, what did you learn that helped you?

Margie: Yes, I have read books and read on the Internet. Also, I have talked to my personal coach for support and have learned a lot more than I ever wanted to know about ED.

Jennifer: No, not really. I kind of had the information shoved down my throat, so-to-speak, by my mom. Again, the world revolved around Sara according to Sara, so I didn't want to spend any more time than I had to on anything to do with her. I got more information living with her than any website could tell me.

15. Did you ever hear extended family members, friends, or neighbors blame your parents' "parenting" for your sister having an eating disorder?

Margie: No, because no one knows Judy's secret among family and my parent's friends. This is how my parents have handled this.

Jennifer: Anyone who has ever met my sister knows that it is all her. I mean, hi, I'm their kid, too, and I don't have thousands of addictions, disorders, diseases, and afflictions! I've heard my parents mention people they think blame them, but no, no one has ever told me they blame my parents, probably because I'm proof it's not their fault.

16. Did you keep it "secret" from friends and classmates that your sister had an eating disorder? If you did, why? If you told people, what did you tell them and how did they react?

Margie: I have told my closest friends. It is challenging as it goes on and on, and they don't ask me about her as much now. They see the toll this has taken on me, and are protective of me. I find it difficult now to talk about it to anyone, really, as it is so chronic, sad—and frustrating. I have talked to two counselors, and that is helping to keep me sane. I also have the loving support of my partner.

Cathy: At first, I kept her eating disorder a secret. Abby's eating disorder had become a very big part of my life. There were days when I was extremely upset and sad, and sometimes it was hard to hide my more difficult days from close friends and classmates. I wasn't going to hide such a big part of my life. After awhile, I wanted people to know so they can be educated about eating disorders. I find people are often insensitive about eating disorders and make a joke out of them because of a lack of understanding about the disease aspect of eating disorders.

They think it's funny that someone would puke up their dinner in order to avoid gaining weight. I found that to be incredibly hard to hear, so I started telling them straight-out that I had a sister with an eating disorder. I would often be quite angry with them. Most often they were shocked, apologetic, and sympathetic. I hoped that by giving them some information, maybe they would be less inclined to joke about the matter again.

I still handle the subject in pretty much the same way. I think it now has a bigger impact because people don't realize that an eating disorder can take someone's life. I find there is probably the same amount of insensitivity as there ever was, and it's still just as hard to hear as ever.

I wonder if our social attitudes will ever change. I guess I still hope that every person I touch with my knowledge will pass it along to others and someday make a positive change.

Jennifer: When I finally was let in on what was going on with her, no, I didn't keep it a secret. I didn't go shouting it; after all, I'm not the attention-whore of this story. If they asked, I told the truth, which was different, depending on what timeframe we're talking about.

17. In school, are eating disorders talked about in any class? If so, from what you know, living with it, do you think that the information was good and that the teacher really understood the disease?

Cathy: We did have a lesson plan in health class about eating disorders. It was when I was in eighth grade. My health teacher was also Abby's and my gymnastics coach. She pulled me aside before class and informed me about the day's lesson. She said I could leave at any point if I needed to during class. I honestly don't remember how the lesson affected me, if at all. My instructor knew the information quite well. As my teacher and coach, she was always a great support in my life, both before and after Abby graduated.

Jennifer: Yeah, eating disorders were touched on in a few classes. I don't think teachers can even begin to understand the complexity that is the modern female, or male for that matter. It was at the same level as sex education: the teachers were obviously not excited but forced to teach it. Slightly informative, but if you really wanted to learn anything about it, you had to find out on your own.

18. Did you ever talk to your sister about her eating disorder?

Margie: Yes, I have talked to her at length many times—maybe too much. Now it seems there is little else to talk about as it has affected her so dramatically.

Cathy: In the beginning when we talked, it was more arguing because I didn't understand her and the disease, and I was scared. I don't believe those conversations ever accomplished very much. Toward the latter part of her life, I had come to accept that I would not be able to fix her, but I would be able to support her as fully as possible. Any conversations we had regarding her eating disorder were simply "How are you doing?" "Is there anything I can help you with?"-type conversations.

I didn't feel the need to push the "Why are you still doing this?" aspect because I knew, ultimately, that she did want to get better. She would share with me the research she had done in finding therapy groups, studies and other routes of getting help and kicking this disease. The last conversation I ever had with Abby was regarding just that. She had an interview with an outpatient treatment facility scheduled for the day after she died. She had already asked me if she could spend the weekends with me. I had, of course, excitedly said yes. I really thought that treatment program was going to be the one to help her get better.

Jennifer: Now why would I go and open a can of crazy? No!

19. What would you have liked to have said to her when she still lived at home?

Jennifer: "I want you to buy me a new birthday cake. I ate one piece on my birthday so I could keep having it for a long time, but since you don't give a shit about anyone but yourself, certainly not your 12-year-old sister, you ate it *all*. I know you hate that I'm not fat, but maybe if you had left me a crumb or two I would have put on a few pounds! You are a self-absorbed ungrateful jerk, and I have no sympathy for you. Get over yourself." Okay so that's pretty harsh, I could probably cut it down to, "Get over yourself, you jerk. You owe me a birthday cake."

20. Did you ever worry that this was "hereditary" and you'd develop an eating disorder too?

Cathy: Our family has a history of addictive behavior. Both sets of our grandparents were fairly severe alcoholics. I often thought that Abby was addicted to the control she had over her eating. It was her drug, the one thing she needed. I worry that addictive behavior is instilled in our family's genes. I try to be very careful in my life's decisions as a result. I try to let the addictive nature in me cling to healthy addictions like running and having lots of pets and plants or buying myself flowers. Unfortunately, I did pick up smoking, something Abby also did, and that is the one thing I cannot get rid of.

I don't think the eating disorder itself was hereditary; I think the control behavior in it was. Whatever the addiction, I've found it always starts with something you think you have control over, until one day you realize it has control over you. I always think of Abby's eating disorder that way. It ended up controlling her, and she wasn't really Abby anymore.

Jennifer: I'm definitely NOT having kids. I do not want to go through the hell my sister put my parents through. Whatever caused this self-hatred, this addiction and screwed-up-ness, is maybe hereditary, but I missed the gene, luckily. I'll adopt, maybe, but I will not take the chance of producing another Sara. The risk outweighs the benefits.

21. Were you ever frightened for your sister's emotional well-being?

Margie: Yes, I think she now has some obsessive behaviors that affect her ability to work and to live independently. Time will tell. Her hospitalization and seeing the reality of how this disease has affected her physically and emotionally/mentally has been frightening.

Jennifer: What emotional well-being? I don't think she was born with one; therefore, there is nothing existing to be frightened for.

22. If you had to describe the "worst" memory of how your sister's eating disorder affected you and your family, what would it be?
Jennifer: I can't pick just one. My entire memory of my sister, as you have read, is not positive. Her skin was orange from using self-tanning junk for a while, but that was more funny than sad.

23. When you talk or email her now, as sisters do, does she talk about what her life is like now related to eating and food?
Jennifer: No. We barely talk. I'm too busy being thankful she's not interfering with my life. She's too busy obsessing about herself to think about her family. She didn't even know how old I was when I asked her last Christmas. "As sisters do" strikes me as a generalization pertaining to normal sisters. We've never gotten along, we've never talked "as sisters do," and I don't plan on starting. Since she moved hundreds of miles away for college years ago, we've had little contact.

24. Since you have a lot of knowledge on the subject, what would you do if you thought one of your friends or a friend's sister had an eating disorder?
Margie: Talk to them, and offer my support and concern. But I know that I cannot really do anything as long as the person does not want help.

Jennifer: Run far, far away. Yes, these people need help, but they will also squeeze you of all happiness and energy. I have had friends with eating disorders. After outright telling them I knew what was going on, since I did experience the mind warp that is my sister, they generally chose to not be my friend over getting over the eating disorder. People choose addictions over friends all the time; I'm not going to waste my time on something that isn't my responsibility. People get help only when they're ready to, and when they're ready, I'll give them Becky's email. Until then, I will not deal with it.

25. Is there something you'd like to say that was not asked?
Margie: Worrying about my sister's health has been a very difficult thing, and it has called me to reach for inner strength, to set boundaries, and to detach with love. That is a good challenge, but is very hard to do. I have gone to Al-Anon for other reasons, which has helped me with this part of my life, too.

    Jennifer: I'd like to apologize if I come off sounding like an arrogant pretentious asshole. If you grew up with Sara as your sister, you would too. I'm a nice humble person, I swear!

26. What one word describes the emotion you held in most often during this time (annoyed, agitated, worried, etc.)?
Margie: I'm trying not to worry that Judy will die. I miss my sister a lot, and work at not being sad. If you asked me what one word describes the emotion I hold often during this time, no doubt it is SCARED!

    Jennifer: Angry and annoyed.

27. What is the one thing you would say to your sister now?
Margie: Focus on yourself and on who you really are—your inner being—not what others think of you or who you "should" be.

    Jennifer: Grow the heck up and apologize to everyone, starting with Mom and Dad.

18

Grandma Betty Tells Her Story

When I was interviewing families around the country, one woman said that her mother would really like to speak for and to grandparents of a grandchild with an eating disorder. This East Coast family's sweet granddaughter developed her eating disorder when she was 14 years old, much to the shock of all of the family.

Grandma Betty's daughter also has a younger boy and girl. She has been married over 16 years, and until the tension, drama and *fear* that surrounds an eating disorder hit, she felt like they had a wonderful life.

Q: Did your daughter tell you early on about your granddaughter's eating disorder—or did she keep it a secret for a while?

A: I don't know if she kept it a secret or if we all just slowly came to the realization that this was the problem. It evolved.

Q: What did you know about eating disorders before your granddaughter was affected?

A: I knew very little. What I did *not* know is how much destruction it could cause, and how many ways it could manifest itself.

Q: What surprised you the most about how strong an eating disorder could be?

A: I was surprised that whatever has hold of her has made her decide to distance herself from all her family and childhood friends, and start a new life.

Q: What was it like having a meal with your granddaughter? Did she eat or just move her food around her plate?

A: No, she seemed very normal, ate her food and appeared to make healthy choices—at least when she was around us, her grandparents.

Q: What was your reaction when you learned that your granddaughter was purging/vomiting what she had just eaten?

A: My granddaughter was spending a few days with us when she first started telling me that she had just vomited following a meal. She told me after each meal—and almost seemed as if she was bragging about it. She had gotten into the habit of embellishing stories so it was hard to know what was real and what was made up. It didn't dawn on me right away that she was purging. When I asked her why she was vomiting, she'd say, "I don't know. I just am." She didn't want to talk about it once it was over and I now wonder if she was reaching out.

Q: What changes did you notice in your daughter as she dealt with her daughter and the eating disorder?

A: The obvious things. She was sad, frightened for her daughter, and working to keep life as normal as possible for her two other children. She was trying to maintain relationships with family and friends while she was also trying to sort out eating disorder symptoms from other possible illnesses. She became tired, lost weight and, sadly, lost interest in many of life's fun things.

Q: Did you have a sense that their other two children were affected by the drama and tension in the house caused by the eating disorder? If so, what did you observe?

A: I wanted to first answer "Duh," but the truth is, of course, I observed how they were affected. The younger daughter was a bright girl who wasn't buying into all this drama. I know it bothered and confused her, but thankfully, she still seemed to be able to focus on school, friends and her many interests. She was clearly upset with her sister. Her younger brother was too little to really express much but I could see that the various scenes involving his sister and his parents upset him.

Q: How did you help your daughter's family during this time (babysit, respite care, drive to doctor appointments)?

A: I actually felt quite helpless. I tried to let my daughter know we were there for them and would do whatever we could to help. It was difficult not knowing what we could do.

Q: What kinds of physical effects did you see in your granddaughter?

A: She didn't take care of herself—her clothes, her room, her hair, even the common areas where the family all lived.

Q: What kinds of emotional effects did you see in your granddaughter?

A: This was so hard. She became verbally and emotionally abusive to her parents—first one, then the other, when they were trying so hard to help her. She was even verbally abusive during therapy sessions. She blamed her parents for everything that was wrong in her life.

Q: Did you sometimes get so angry at your granddaughter for what she was doing to herself, your daughter and the rest of the family that you wanted to verbally strike out at her?

A: Yes, I was quite angry with her at times for what she was doing to my own child (her mom) that I wanted to say some really strong things to her—but I didn't out of fear. Would my words destroy her more than she was destroying herself? I didn't want to undo all that her parents were doing to help her get better. I'll say those words only when and if nothing else is working, and only if I have to. Right now I have a good line of communication with her, and I feel it is important she feels she can still confide in me.

Q: Did you ever worry that this eating disorder might kill your granddaughter?

A: One word says it all: YES!

Q: Did you see any signs of depression or extreme sadness in your granddaughter?

A: No, I didn't. However, perhaps I was interpreting depression or extreme sadness as rebellion, which we all saw plenty of.

Q: Was your granddaughter ever hospitalized as a result of the eating disorder? If so, did you go visit her? How did that feel?

A: Shocking. I was so scared, wondering how this could happen. I was afraid she might actually take her own life—afraid for her and for my daughter, son-in-law and my other grandchildren. At the same time, though, I was also angry with her and suspicious that she was faking it to cause more hurt to her parents. It was difficult to sort out the eating disorder from what might be rebellion and adolescent behavior.

Q: Did other relatives have strong reactions, like not wanting your granddaughter to come to holiday parties or family get-togethers because of her odd food-related behavior or how she looked?

A: Yes, they sure did, but it wasn't so much about the food-related behavior. She had the ability to really "stir up the pot" at family events. And the way she dressed was often embarrassing to others. Even after her sister and cousin asked her to adjust her clothing and be more appropriate, she wouldn't.

Q: How would you describe what you saw your daughter going through? Did you ever really worry about her physical and emotional health?

A: She was going through *hell*, and I was so worried about her. I know she has come out of it a stronger person, but she is sad at the loss of all the years that "could have been" with her daughter. Actually we all are, and we hurt for the family that "could have been."

Q: How did your husband, her grandfather, react to his granddaughter? Could he empathize with your daughter?

A: He had such empathy for our daughter and great fear for our granddaughter's safety. He would get upset but he would do all he could to help her—even when he knew she wasn't being truthful with him.

Q: Did you ever worry about your daughter's marriage?

A: Yes, the tension, divisiveness, and financial issues all were really hard on their marriage. They have worked very hard to stay on the same page and deal with this together.

Q: What advice would you give to other grandparents on dealing with a grandchild's eating disorder?

A: Learn all you can about what is happening. Be there! Knowledge of the symptoms and the treatment will help you be understanding of the affected person and of the family trying their best to deal with it.

Grandma Betty had something she wanted to add to the questions:

"One of the most unexpected blows came from friends of our daughter and granddaughter. As they were going through this and dealing with one of the most difficult times of their lives, people they knew as friends just didn't want to deal with the trauma and tension they were experiencing and withdrew their friendship from the family. This made me very angry! Some of those relationships healed; others did not. Blessedly, the really true friendships remain and are stronger than ever.

The crowning moment of my realizing how sick our grand-daughter was, and the degree of control she was exercising over her family, came the night before we were all leaving for Disney World. It was late at night and the adults were busy packing and making plans. The attention was not on our granddaughter. She chose this moment to vomit in front of everyone, then sat there and laughed as her mother cleaned it up. It was a willful act. My deep regret is that I did not intervene and insist she clean it up herself. I guess I was just too shocked."

19

Sharon's Story

Ten-Year-Old Boys Develop Anorexia Too

Talking with Sharon, an Atlanta, Georgia, mom about her now
12-year-old son and their journey with his eating disorder, which
began when he was only 10, I learned they experienced the same
sense of isolation, frustration and lack of medical knowledge just
two years ago that we had experienced 10 years ago with our
daughter's bulimia.

I was amazed when Sharon told me that even though the
Centers For Disease Control (CDC) is right in her backyard,
they still had trouble finding help for their son. We are not talking about the dark ages in eating disorders research (although,
unfortunately, the research is still in its infancy)—this was 2008.

Since the purpose of this book is to help families by providing
information, reducing feelings of isolation and instilling hope
that full recovery is possible, I was happy to hear Sharon say,
"Hearing the stories of other families with boys facing this illness
helped us get through the recovery."

SHARON'S STORY: WE FUMBLED OUR WAY TO RECOVERY

I'm a social worker with years of experience advocating for children in foster care so I was used to working with kids in crisis.

Never did I think I would have to be an advocate for one of my own children.

My son's eating disorder caught us totally off guard. In spite of my education and experience I didn't recognize what was going on with my 10-year-old son, Ron, until he was dangerously ill.

Ron was born with a Type A personality, like his dad. From an early age he excelled in school and sports. He took sports very seriously and wanted to be more fit. When a schoolmate teased him about being faster than him, Ron became more determined to get into even better shape.

Early in 2008 Ron became pickier each day about what he would eat and he started losing weight. We witnessed our highly competent son strike out top players on the field, but when we brought home this talented baseball player, who had to be famished, he wouldn't eat a thing. In three months he went from 89 pounds to 69 pounds.

We took Ron to the pediatrician who had cared for him since birth and amazingly, and very fortunately, the doctor said right away, "This is clearly anorexia nervosa" though he had never seen it in a child so young, much less a boy. He patiently went over the food groups with Ron and told him he had to eat a certain amount each day. He also referred us to a child psychologist.

Unfortunately, the psychologist knew little about eating disorders. He felt Ron was mourning losing his childhood as he grew into adolescence [Note from Becky: This is yet another theory about the cause of eating disorders that is thrown around and doesn't help]. He could see Ron was depressed and after the third session he suggested that we put him on antidepressants. We were in the process of making a decision about medication when Ron crashed.

What we witnessed was what I called, "our son going out of his mind." Ron was increasingly argumentative, not making sense, totally irrational and he refused to eat. One morning, after he stared at a breakfast bar for hours, we took him to our local children's hospital. In the emergency room they told us his heart rate was down to 69 beats per minute and he was severely dehydrated. He was admitted to the cardiac wing of the hospital.

We were assigned a psychiatrist who wanted to do behavior modification therapy and put Ron on medication. Since Ron was in crisis and we were so scared, we went along with it.

Ron convinced the psychiatrist that his illness was all Mom and Dad's fault . . . and the psychiatrist fell for it hook, line and sinker. It was as though this man had never seen a child with a malnourished brain incapable of rational thought. He fed right into Ron's wanting to blame others and even said to our son, "I can see your mom is real controlling."

We had heard Ron tell the therapist, "My mom and dad fight all the time," which simply wasn't true. I told both the therapist and the psychiatrist, "You can ask my other son—we don't fight." I also told them that I didn't want to take the focus off of Ron but blaming us was not going to get him well.

I kept thinking that if Ron had cancer they wouldn't be wasting time with such nonsense. I finally told the psychiatrist I wouldn't sit there while my son was dying and listen to this behavior modification talk.

Ron's resistance was still strong and he continued to refuse food. Our pediatrician finally told him, "If you don't start eating right now I will be back in two hours and insert a feeding tube. You won't have any control over what you eat and you'll get as many calories as we give you." This helped and Ron slowly began eating. He gained a couple pounds during his time in the hospital.

During that time I found the one book the hospital library had on eating disorders, *Boys Get Anorexia Too,* by Jenny Langley. I read to Ron as I lay next to him in his hospital bed. In that book we heard the first promising words: we were not alone and he could get well.

After ten days, Ron was released from the hospital. I couldn't find treatment in Atlanta for a boy with anorexia, not even outpatient treatment. Before he was discharged we were told, "If you take him home and he doesn't eat three meals and two snacks, don't bring him back here; take him to the psychiatric hospital." He would have had to go into the general population of psychiatric patients at the psychiatric hospital. That was simply unacceptable.

What I read plus my background as a social worker helped me to accept the label of anorexia. My husband was slower to wrap his brain around how seriously ill our son was. He was working hard to keep a roof over our heads and pay for all of the treatment. He had no experience dealing with a serious health crisis and had difficulty understanding Ron's illness stemmed from a combination of genetic predisposition for an eating disorder, being teased by a schoolmate, and his personality.

Ron was on the medications the psychiatrist had prescribed and we were instructed to use a behavior reward system. We were told to reward him for eating just half his food. Right away we knew it wouldn't work. It would take two hours just to get through one meal. He would stall, trying to get out of eating, but still expected a reward. When I refused, he pulled the classic "pit Mom against Dad" game, pleading with his father. We soon decided behavior modification wasn't working and we'd have to go a different route.

My husband and I made a pact that he wouldn't participate in the refeeding. To reduce Ron pitting us against one another, my husband agreed that he would come home after dinner.

By this time, I was reading everything I could get my hands on and searching the Internet for all the help I could get. I liked what I learned about the Maudsley Family-Based Therapy. Their website explained that eating disorders are biologically based mental illnesses and fully treatable with a combination of nutritional, medical, and therapeutic supports. Maudsley promotes the need for parents to be their child's biggest advocates and be totally involved in their care and recovery. This made sense to me.

Through the F.E.A.S.T. (Families Empowered and Supporting Treatment of Eating Disorders) website, I found the book, *Help Your Teenager Beat an Eating Disorder* by James Lock and Daniel le Grange. Thus far we had fumbled our way through recovery with few resources; this book helped me understand what we needed to be doing. No one had given us any real plan to follow; now we had direction and a scientifically tested method to guide us through Ron's recovery.

In this book I learned the principles that eating disorder treatment specialists using the Maudsley Family-Based Therapy adhere to:

- Parents do not cause eating disorders, and patients do not choose eating disorders.
- Parents and caregivers are powerful tools for a loved one's recovery from an eating disorder.
- Blaming and marginalizing parents in the eating disorder treatment process causes harm and suffering.
- When available, patients should receive evidence-based treatment.
- Families should be supported in seeking the most appropriate treatment in the least restrictive environment possible.
- Food is medicine: all treatment should include urgent and ongoing nutritional rehabilitation.
- When the family is supported, the patient is supported.
- All family members, including siblings, are affected by a family member's illness, and deserve full attention to their needs.

• Parents have unique abilities to offer other parents support, information, and the wisdom of experience.

After learning all I could about the Maudsley Family-Based Therapy approach I decided to take a leave of absence from work to focus on being Ron's caregiver. Even though we felt fortunate that I could stop working and stay home with him, it was incredibly stressful. I couldn't help but ask myself, *What happens if this doesn't work?* The thought of the psychiatric hospital made me shudder.

We tried traditional family therapy during that first summer and Ron simply fell asleep during the sessions—his body was so worn out. Therapy was expensive and since I was no longer working, we stopped and just focused on the meals.

It was hard work just getting Ron to the table. Because of what I learned through my reading and research, I had the courage to tell the psychiatrist I wasn't going along with his instruction that Ron only needed to eat half his meal. I told him "Ron needs to eat it all." With behavior modification he would still have an illusion of control. I learned *I* needed to have control so he would eat what I put in front of him. Not long after that, though, Ron found another avenue of control. He declared himself to be a vegetarian.

We found a nutritionist through the Atlanta Center for Eating Disorders. Her specialty was working with professional baseball players and other competitive athletes. We saw her every Monday and she would plan out the meals for the week. Ron and I both needed this structure. Having such clear structure took away some of the pressure on both of us. When Ron lashed out at me I gave it right back, saying, "This is not a choice! This is not negotiable!" Having the nutritionist to blame things on helped. She was fine with me letting her be the "heavy." She was extremely helpful and worked well for us even with Ron's vegetarianism.

I learned how to structure our day, prepare meals and get food to the table from a book about the Maudsley method for refeeding. Once we finished breakfast, it was time to gear up for snacks. It took all day to get meals and snacks into Ron. I got tired but saw this as the crossroad it was and knew we had to stay in this framework to get him well. There was always a lingering fear that we'd end up back at the hospital.

One day we went out for a milkshake but he wouldn't eat it. I asked, "Do you want me to show you where you'll be going if you don't eat?" I even turned the car around to head back toward the hospital. Ron said, "I'll eat it, I'll eat it."

Ron was rarely out of my sight the whole summer. We became very close. At home we watched a lot of sports, especially baseball games, as we spent whole days transitioning from one meal to the next. I knew he liked getting so much attention from me and he needed the structure our days together provided. For example, every night he needed to drink the nutritional liquid called "Boost." I usually asked him if he drank it. If I forgot, he would remind me to ask, "Did you drink the Boost?" I think he needed me to be really tied into those rituals, focusing on him, until he could re-identify with his old self.

Even though his grandparents didn't want to hear that their grandson had anorexia, I talked openly to anyone and everyone. If you don't talk about it you aren't going to be led to people who can help you. I learned this firsthand when I told a neighbor that Ron covered his food in hot sauce. This neighbor's sister-in-law had had anorexia and helped me understand the hot sauce. She told me that for a while she needed to have her food covered in ranch dressing because she was convinced food was the enemy and she had to mask it. She reassured me that the hot sauce was really insignificant and would slowly disappear. It did.

Fortunately for me, my friends were extremely supportive. They all know Ron well and knew he would recover. They gave me a lot of support by talking and laughing with me. When my sisters came over, we would often stare at Ron's milkshakes, drooling, joking about how we couldn't take a milkshake from an anorexic. Laughing was better than crying.

It was interesting to see how hard it was for Ron's 10-year-old friends to understand. One really good friend who came to visit him when we got home from the hospital looked at him like he was crazy. The look on his face said he was thinking, *YOU NEED TO EAT.* For the most part, he didn't see his friends during his recovery— their parents didn't understand the disease or what we were going through but we couldn't take the energy to worry about it; we needed everything we had to focus on helping Ron get well.

My family helped by staying with Ron if I had to leave him. We tried to normalize things as much as possible. The boys have several cousins and we made sure they had time together so Ron could just run with them for a bit and not just be the kid who was trying to recover from anorexia. I was also appreciative when someone took my older son for a while so he could have a break.

My husband's family didn't talk about the illness at all; it was very strange and reminded me of when someone is an alcoholic and no one will talk about drinking and won't drink in front of them. The family gatherings had the added stress of Ron's vegetarianism. I brought his food during that time to make it easier for everyone but family gatherings were stressful because they always involved food. The people who helped the most were those who understood the illness and were patient with the process.

When I heard comments such as "It's not like he was in a car accident," I'd try to explain, "He almost died. He became so preoccupied with not eating, something clicked and he wasn't in control." Most people could not grasp the fact that when a person is so malnourished, his actions are no longer a choice. A common response to Ron's illness was that since it was a mental illness he "did it to himself." Yes, it's a mental illness and it's serious. Maybe because we took care of him ourselves it didn't seem that serious to others.

Taking this time during the summer to really focus on getting Ron back on track paid dividends for us in the fall when it was time to go back to school. I couldn't help but think, *What if I pack his lunch and he doesn't eat it?* I'd heard that some parents choose to be with their children during school lunchtime but my intuition told me that, if we started that ritual, Ron would want it to continue. I read that if you start going to lunch with them they can become addicted to you being there.

Fortunately, Ron was attending a very small private Quaker "Friends" school that is very nurturing and his teacher was very tuned in with him. She had me over for dinner before school started and told me that she had lost her son to a drug overdose. I felt I could trust her after we talked about what to watch for.

At that point I knew I had to let it go. I decided if I learned he was throwing away his lunch, I'd give him extra food at dinnertime. All students eat in their classroom. His teacher told me she would email me if she saw he wasn't eating his lunch. I never got an email—as far as I know he always ate his lunch. We were lucky he was in that school.

Since school is where the teasing about running had started, and even though I knew we couldn't totally blame his eating disorder on the teasing, I decided to volunteer at the school answering phones so I could be close by if he needed me. Instead, soon after going back to school he became best friends with the kid who had been teasing him!

All summer we kept him on the anti-depressant. We were fine with the medicine but since he was so young we wanted to wean him off of it. Once school began, I started giving him half-doses for a few months and he did fine. The psychiatrist was supportive of weaning him off the meds and eventually stopping them and we followed his suggestion of not telling Ron. By November Ron said, "Mom I don't think I need my medicine anymore."

We also found a strength and endurance coach who helped him work out with weights and showed him how to rebuild his body. This worked well. We're grateful to the adults with anorexia at the Center for Eating Disorders in Atlanta who suggested this very helpful idea.

We have made so much progress. Ron was able to gain the weight he needed, and I am able to trust he is doing okay most of the time. Once he started getting well he realized he needed to eat meat. One day he simply asked for a burger and I didn't make a big deal out of it. He wasn't vested in vegetarianism; it was a control issue.

He is planning to switch schools this year—it's his idea. He feels he's reached his limit where he has been. This new private junior high school has high academic standards and yet is not super competitive. It has more sports plus music and art required in a very nurturing, introspective, and holistic environment where students are asked to do a lot of writing.

It took more than a year to see that he is totally back. He's doing well. I worry still—not every day but I wonder how he'll handle stressful situations during his high school and college years.

I had held everything together while Ron was so sick; once he was better and the crisis was over, I fell apart. I went through my own bout of depression after he recovered. I think it was because I had lost my purpose. I also lost my career because of the amount of time I took off from work.

I was so focused on Ron, I didn't take care of myself. Those milkshakes my sisters and I drooled over? Too often for my own good I was eating those milkshakes right along with Ron, telling my sisters I was "taking one for the team." I gained weight too.

I'm doing well now, both mentally and physically, and am going back to school for my Master's. Both of my sons understand and appreciate what I did for Ron. My older son often sat with us and helped us get through each meal and snack. On one of our toughest days he said, "Mom, if something happened to you I know Ron wouldn't eat and he would die." I know Ron will always remember that I was there for him.

SHARON'S TIPS:

1. Be an advocate to help eating disorders get appropriate funding. See the NEDA site to understand the disparity in how disease research is funded. Eating disorders receive a small fraction of the research dollars compared to other serious illnesses such as Alzheimer's.

2. Don't assume your health care providers have had specific training on eating disorders. Ask what training they have received and insist on referrals to trained providers. If you cannot find any in your area, call the nearest treatment facility or university and ask for names.

3. Take any weight loss in children seriously.

4. If you have been blamed or marginalized by treatment providers, insist that you be included or find new providers.

5. Set clear, firm boundaries with your child, even though he/she is ill. They need to know that you will guide them.

6. Don't keep the eating disorder a secret. Isolating people is one way eating disorders manipulate the whole family. Talk with others so you can learn more and get support.

7. Listen to your parental intuition when making decisions. Each situation and person is different and the professionals can't have all the answers.

20

Carolyn Costin's Story

Complete Recovery Is Possible

Interviewing Carolyn and writing her story gave me so much hope for all who are in recovery and for their families. I found so much encouragement in her story and wish that you too can know that, for many people, complete recovery is indeed truly possible. Everyone has his/her own definition of complete recovery.

Carolyn embodies the hope that all who are affected by eating disorders cling to. She has been recovered for over 30 years and now runs a successful residential eating disorder treatment center, Monte Nido, in Malibu, California, as well as a private therapy practice. Carolyn is a firm believer that complete recovery is possible and that is the message she wants everyone to hear.

An excerpt from the Monte Nido website states Carolyn's belief: "Our eating disorder treatment philosophy is that you can be 'recovered' where the goal is not only the absence of symptoms, but the resolution of whatever problems or needs your eating disorder behaviors are trying to express."

About her treatment center Carolyn says, "Monte Nido offers treatment settings I would have liked to attend when I was suffering from my own eating disorder. I wanted a beautiful environment and a loving, empathetic staff, who would know when to challenge and when to nurture."

ABOUT CAROLYN

Carolyn Costin, MFT, who recovered from anorexia, has specialized in the treatment of eating disorders and exercise addiction since 1977.

In the early 1980s, Carolyn established The Eating Disorder Center of California, which continues to provide outpatient and day-treatment services in several locations throughout Southern California. In 1996, Carolyn's dream of opening her own residential treatment center came true when she founded Monte Nido.

Despite several opportunities for growth, Carolyn has insisted on keeping only 6 to 10 clients in a small home-like atmosphere, which allows clients the opportunity to build a strong community with each other and practice necessary skills for lasting recovery, such as grocery shopping, and preparing and cooking meals just as they will have to do upon discharge. Many of the highly trained, experienced staff are recovered themselves and serve as therapists as well as recovery coaches.

Carolyn continues to educate and train professionals on the treatment and prevention of eating disorders around the country. Her lectures and workshops range from presentations at national and international conferences, to local community organizations, high schools, and study groups for professionals.

Carolyn furnishes professionals with the latest research and techniques in therapy, nutrition, and behavior modification, as well as her personal philosophy on what facilitates successful recovery. Carolyn has written four books that are popular with both professionals and the lay public: *Your Dieting Daughter; The Eating Disorder Source Book, 3rd edition; 100 Questions and Answers about Eating Disorders (2007); and Anorexia and Bulimia, A Nutritional Approach (with co-author Alexander Schauss).*

Through her own recovery, enthusiasm and expertise, Carolyn offers hope that full recovery from an eating disorder is possible.

CAROLYN'S STORY OF RECOVERY

Driving up to Beverly Hills from Simi Valley in the early 1960s with my mom and two siblings was always a bit surreal. We were heading toward my dad and stepmother's mansion in Beverly Hills for our weekend visit, a huge change from the home my mother's teacher's salary afforded.

We were originally from Texas and our father was always dressed in a cowboy hat and boots that elevated his already 6'5" frame about 7 inches taller. He was quite a commanding figure and we looked up to him. Living in a very rural town outside of Dallas, and later in the California foothills, my brother, sister and I spent time running around, riding horses, and playing tag. We were innocent and unaffected by all that was changing in the world. Fashion and body image were unknown concepts to us.

Our lives were normal until my father left for London to direct a play. While there he fell in love with a model. When he and the model returned to the U.S., he divorced my mother and our lives were changed forever.

The message I got was pretty clear. Our dad dumped our mom for this young stick-figure woman, who was a friend of "Twiggy," the infamous model who set the tone for women in the late '60s.

My experience epitomizes what women in America were beginning to go through. We left the innocence and normalcy of the '50s for this new way of thinking: women needed to look like shadows of ourselves to be accepted as sexy and worthwhile. I saw firsthand what my dad chose, and that sent an absolutely clear message of what was important about a woman.

Our lives began changing as fast as our growing bodies—all of this happening during the time when the world was being impacted by the hippie movement. Moving from a rural Texas town to the wild and free craziness of Southern California in the early '60s was a cultural change for all of us. There were so many changes all at once, including going from being a 12-year-old living with both of my parents to living part-time with my mom in Simi Valley and spending time with my dad and my now stepmother in their rented Beverly Hills home.

Years later, after recovering from the eating disorder that inhabited me for seven years, I remembered a significant incident from my youth. It occurred shortly after my father and stepmother married. My siblings and I were at their Beverly Hills mansion for our regular visit. I walked into the large white master bedroom and saw a closet with big, mirrored sliding doors, filled with my stepmother's many clothes and interesting full-length coats, including mink and cheetah.

I saw the most beautiful pink mini-dress ever and couldn't resist trying it on. This was the height of the '60s, mini-dresses were all the rage, and I was just becoming interested in fashion.

When I tried it on I couldn't believe that it did not fit my 12-year-old body. I was so embarrassed looking in the mirror, I made a vow right then that someday I would fit into that dress. For years I had forgotten that incident; remembering it was an eye opener into a part of my past that contributed to my developing an eating disorder.

Three years passed after I tried on the mini-dress before I had a full-blown eating disorder. Neither the pink mini-dress nor my model stepmother caused my eating disorder. As a therapist I know that a genetic predisposition, having a perfectionist personality, going on a diet with all of the other girls, cultural exposures, and underlying psychological issues all contributed to my eating disorder.

As the teen body is growing and changing, it is challenging to maintain a sense of self esteem. The unintentional damaging messages from the media seep into our delicate psyches and plant seeds that can bloom into life-destroying disorders. I got the clear message: *Thinness is beauty. If you are not thin, you are not special.*

By the time I was 15 I had lost 45 pounds. The details of how I suffered with anorexia nervosa aren't what is important here; what is important is what helped me to *completely* recover.

I remember feeling like there were two parts to me: the real, healthy self, and the eating disorder. Eventually, I realized *it's not about telling the eating-disordered self that it's bad and has to go; it's about permanently strengthening the healthy part of the self.* It is a person's healthy self that heals the disordered self. This is not a quick fix but a slow process, just like developing a full-blown eating disorder is a slow process.

When I am asked how I recovered or what is the most important thing for recovery, I find it difficult to reply. It's hard to say what is best because different things work for different people. One thing I think helped me was that I never battled with my parents. They truly tried hard to understand what was going on in my mind, and I think this helped us not get into battles. Having very understanding parents who listened and talked helped me feel like they weren't trying to take control. This helped me to be honest about what was going on in me.

Control is a word that always comes up with people who have eating disorders. There are many aspects to this but one important thing to note is that collaboration is important in the treatment and not just externally focused or forced change.

Another interesting thing that helped was that my mom did a visualization technique with me about having an imaginary doctor inside of me. She would tell me to imagine that this real person was breathing inside of me and could heal me. We did this a few times during a period when I was pretty ill. She was the first person who actually taught me the concept of the inner healer and how powerful we humans genuinely are.

As it was, I did not actually get much professional help. I was ill in the late '60s and early '70s and not much was known about eating disorders yet. When my mother took me to our medical

265

doctor he took blood tests and had to admit that everything was fine. I took that as a green light to keep going. My mother then took me to a different doctor but was told that perhaps I was pregnant and trying to hide it! Undeterred, Mom took me to a psychologist, who tried to get me to drink a soda in front of him to see what I would do. I never went back.

I went to the college counseling center but the therapist there had never heard of such a thing as my being so thin, yet seeing myself as fat. I tried to explain that I felt guilty when I ate and she suggested that if I felt guilty when I ate in front of others perhaps I should eat by myself. The problem was that the guilt was my own. I felt bad eating, whether in front of others or alone. In fact, eating alone made things worse.

These experiences were so bad that I never tried to get further help. No one suggested family therapy or told my mother to try to be firmer about my eating. Most people did not even know what to call what I had.

I had the eating disorder for seven years and feel that if the professionals back then (or my parents and I) had known what we all know now, I might have recovered much sooner.

During the years between ages 17 and 22, I started reading books on spirituality. They helped me to begin thinking about being in a world where I wanted to pay attention to my soul, not just my body. This made a big difference in my life and started to help me get better. Many books were about the soul and the difference between ego and soul; many had somewhat of a Buddhist slant, and they all opened me to look at the world, myself and my soul in a new way. I use these concepts in my practice and recommend these kinds of books to my clients when I feel it is appropriate. Some examples of the books I give to clients now are: *Care of the Soul* by Thomas Moore; *Seat of the Soul* by Garry Zukoff; *When Things Fall Apart* by Pema Chodren, a Buddhist Monk; and *The Power of Now* by Eckhart Tolle.

When working with clients, I try to help them reconnect and stay connected to their soul-self, a concept that is not often talked about. I talk about how, rather than being humans who are on a soulful path, we are souls who happen to be on a human path. This gives our soul top billing. I call our bodies our "earth suits" and talk about how we need to care for them as they house our souls here on the planet. It sounds complicated but it is actually simple. I help people get connected to or reacquainted with what is most important in their lives. I help each client develop a stronger core, a healthy soul-self. I believe that once reconnected with what is truly important in life, the need for the eating disorder symptoms diminishes.

Parents can be an important part in helping us develop a strong, healthy self. As parents, it is hard to know when we are doing that. As I began to recover from the eating disorder, I began to gain back weight and I would cry. No one understood why it felt so bad to be getting "better." I always ask my clients to explain to their parents, why "getting better feels so bad." This helps family and friends understand the dynamics that keep fueling the eating disorder.

I believe families are an important part of the solution. In my practice and at Monte Nido, I do a lot of work with individual family members and multi-family groups to help them not only understand the eating disorder but also help them feel supported, with the tools they need, to continue to support their loved one in recovery. I see it as my job to teach families what I do at Monte Nido that works. I tell families that the goal of the therapy is to put myself out of business with each client, that is, making it so the client no longer needs me. This is true (or should be, at least) for all therapists.

Every person who walks in the doors of Monte Nido has a healthy core person inside of her or him—as well as the eating-disorder self they have developed. When families are included in the recovery process, they can be trained to see the eating disorder is a part of the person but that the healthy person is also still there. This helps significant others work with us to strengthen their loved one's healthy self. Instead of getting in fights with their loved one, they begin to see that they can align with him or her against the eating-disorder self.

Learning to support someone you care about who has an eating disorder is a huge task, and it takes time and guidance. It is so easy to get pulled into the fights and lose sight of how important it is to support and guide your loved one back to health. Most families feel so hopeless and overwhelmed; it is essential to learn to take care of themselves as well as how to care for the person who is in eating disorder recovery.

I find it very annoying when I hear that parents are told their loved ones will not fully recover. Although it takes a long time, studies show that in 7 to 10 years, people can be fully recovered. More recent studies are showing that with family involvement the recovery is much shorter.

Monte Nido has a very positive and hopeful outcome study that was conducted on patients from 1 to 10 years post-treatment. It shows 80–85% of our clients, after being discharged, are either fully or partially recovered in an average of 4.5 years.

Other studies also show that people with eating disorders can fully recover. I have been recovered since the early 1970s, over 37 years now, with no residual effects. I don't have any desire to restrict food, weigh myself, take laxatives, skip meals, lose weight or use any of my past eating disorder symptoms. I don't need to deal with it one day at a time.

Monte Nido and my affiliate programs have a large number of staff members who also have been fully recovered for many years, some 4, 7, 10, and 20 years.

I believe that having found a deeper purpose and meaning to

life was essential for me in order to gain a foothold on recovery. I decided I wanted to be a teacher, and becoming one helped me to have something else to care about. Going through college, I studied psychology and became a high school teacher for kids who got kicked out of regular school. I went on to become a school counselor, then after further study, I interned as a marriage and family therapist. I wanted to work with troubled teens.

As I began my psychology practice, I received a few referrals for people with eating disorders and I successfully treated them. Soon people were referring clients to me from all over, and my practice grew. Eventually I was hired to run a hospital unit for eating disorders, then another, and then a residential program.

Over time, I knew I needed to open my own center. This all evolved into three residential centers, a one-day treatment program, two halfway houses and a private practice center. It sounds overwhelming when I think about it.

It gives me great joy to see others come to Monte Nido or one of my affiliates and find their own purpose and meaning—and begin the process of shedding the eating-disorder self that prevents them from fulfilling their own life purpose.

CAROLYN SHARES MONTE NIDO'S PHILOSOPHY:

1. *We believe* that the ability to enjoy life is robbed by an eating or exercise disorder.
   - We also believe that focusing on eradicating the disorder is not enough.
   - We must find things to replace the disorder, motivating clients to get better in order to enjoy what life has to offer.

2. *We believe* that in healing eating and exercise disorders, we must engender purpose and meaning in our clients' lives.
   - We believe that is made possible by providing non-denominational spirituality and what we call "Tending The Soul."

- Once clients are reconnected to the spiritual, sacred and soulful aspects of life, the need to use the symptoms/coping behaviors diminishes.

3. *We believe* that it is difficult but important that friends and family members keep trying to reach out to a suffering loved one in order to facilitate the person getting help and to support her during her struggle.
- Your efforts, love, and support may be crucial to your loved one's recovery.
- People who have recovered from eating disorders often cite being loved, believed in, and not "given up on" as crucial factors in their getting help and getting well.

4. *We believe* that to heal you do not have to get rid of what we call your eating-disorder self but rather learn from it and integrate that knowledge into your core-healthy self.
- This way you will get rid of the symptoms but keep this part of you that is a messenger and serves to let you know when there is something you need to attend to.

5. *We do not believe* you have to be ready to give up your eating disorder or want to fully recover to come to Monte Nido.
- We understand and accept ambivalence.
- It is our job to help you work through your ambivalence.
- It is also our job to help motivate you and make recovery a choice you want to make.

RESOURCES

BOOKS

Anatomy of a Food Addiction: The Brain Chemistry of Overeating—Anne Katherine, M.A.

Andrea's Voice: Silenced by Bulimia: Her Story and Her Mother's Journey through Grief toward Understanding—Doris Smeltzer

Anorexics and Bulimics Anonymous: The Fellowship Details Its Program of Recovery for Anorexia and Bulimia

Beating Ana: How to Outsmart Your Eating Disorder and Take Your Life Back—Shannon Cutts

Beyond the Looking Glass: Daily Devotions for Overcoming Anorexia and Bulimia—Remuda Ranch

Distorted: How a Mother and Daughter Unravel the Truth, the Lies, and the Realities of an Eating Disorder—Lorri Antosz and Taryn Leigh Benson

Eating in the Light of the Moon: How Women Can Transform Their Relationship with Food through Myths, Metaphors, and Storytelling—Anita J. Johnston, Ph.D.

Eating with Your Anorexic: How My Child Recovered Through Family-Based Treatment and Yours Can Too—Laura Collins

Enrich Your Caregiving Journey—Margery Pabst and Rita Goldhammer

Full Lives: A Woman's Guide to Freedom from Obsession with Good and Weight—Lindsay Hall

Goodbye Ed, Hello Me: Recover from Your Eating Disorder and fall in Love with Your Life—Jenni Schaefer

Help Your Teenager Beat an Eating Disorder (2005)—Daniel le Grange, PhD, associate professor of psychiatry and director of the eating disorders program at the University of Chicago, and James Lock, MD, PhD, professor of child psychiatry and pediatrics at Stanford University.

Hungry: A Mother and Daughter Fight Anorexia—Sheila and Lisa Himmel

Life Without ED: How One Woman Declared Independence from Her Eating Disorder and How You Can Too—Jenni Schaefer

Locker Room Diaries: The Naked Truth about Women, Body Image, and Re-Imagining the "Perfect" Body—Leslie Goldman

Nutrition Counseling in the Treatment of Eating Disorders (Brunner-Routledge, 2002) Marcia Herrin, Ed.D., M.R.H., R.D., L.S.

Off The C.U.F.F.: A Parent Skills Book for the Management of Disordered Eating—Nancy Zucker, Ph.D. (Duke University Medical Center)

The Parent's Guide to Eating Disorders: Supporting Self-Esteem, Healthy Eating, & Positive Body Image at Home—Marcia Herrin, Ed.D., M.P.H., R.D., Nancy Matsumoto

Potatoes Not Prozac: Simple Solutions for Sugar Sensitivity—Kathleen Des Maisons www.radiantrecovery.com

Secrets Girls Keep: What Girls Hide (& Why) and How to Break the Stress of Silence—Carrie Silver-Stock

Skills-based Learning for Caring for a Loved One with an Eating Disorder: The New Maudsley Method—Janet Treasure, Grainne Smith, Anna Crane

The Starving Family: Caregiving Mothers and Fathers Share Their Eating Disorder Wisdom—Cheryl Dellasega, Ph.D.

Talking to Eating Disorders: Simple Ways to Support Someone with Anorexia, Bulimia, Binge Eating Disorder, or Body Image Issues—Jeanne Albronda Heaton, Ph.D. and Claudia J. Strauss

Treating Bulimia in Adolescents (2007)—Daniel le Grange, Ph.D., associate professor of psychiatry and director of the eating disorders program at the University of Chicago, and James Lock, M.D., Ph.D., professor of child psychiatry and pediatrics at Stanford University.

Your Dieting Daughter: Is She Dying for Attention?—Carolyn Costin, M.F.T.

TREATMENT CENTERS MENTIONED IN BOOK

ARIZONA
Remuda Ranch West
1 East Apache Street
Wickenburg, AZ 85390
(800) 445-1900
www.remudaranch.com

CALIFORNIA
Monte Nido Mountain Nest
Administrative Office

27162 Sea Vista Drive
Malibu, CA 90265
(310) 457-9958
www.montenido.com/montenido

COLORADO
Eating Recovery Center
1830 Franklin St., #500
Denver, CO 80218-1169
(303) 825-8584
http://www.eatingrecoverycenter.com/

FLORIDA
Canopy Cove Eating Disorder Treatment Center
13305 Mahan Drive
Tallahassee, FL 32309
(800) 236-7524
www.canopycove.com

MINNESOTA
Tamara Tinkham, Psy.D., L.P., and Interventionist
1313 Fifth Street SE, Suite 126B
Minneapolis, MN 55414
(612) 508-3743

OKLAHOMA
Laureate Psychiatric Clinic and Hospital
Eating Disorder Program
6655 South Yale Avenue
Tulsa, OK 74136
(800) 322-5173
www.eatingdisorders.laureate.com

OREGON
Rain Rock, a Monte Nido Affiliated Treatment Center
1863 Pioneer Parkway East, Suite 304
Springfield, OR 97477
(310) 457-9958
www.montenido.com/rainrock

WEBSITES

ARTICLES

The Huffington Post, *The Naked Truth Behind Binge Eating Disorder*, Posted October 28, 2009, by Leslie Goldman www.huffingtonpost.com/leslie-goldman-the-naked-truth-behind-bi_b_337273.html/

INFORMATION AND REFERRAL

Eating Disorder Referral and Information Center
www.edreferral.com

FAMILY SUPPORT

Families Empowered and Supporting Treatment of Eating Disorders
www.feast-ed.org

Hope Network, Inc., Becky Henry—In person, webinars, tele-classes
www.hopenetwork.info

Support Forum for Parents and Caregivers of Anorexia, Bulimia, and other Eating Disorder Patients
www.aroundthedinnertable.org

ORGANIZATIONS

Anorexics and Bulimics Anonymous (ABA)
www.anorexicsandbulimicsanonymousaba.com

Binge Eating Disorder Association (BEDA)
www.bedaonline.com

Council on Size and Weight Discrimination
www.cswd.org

Domestic Abuse Intervention Program
www.theduluthmodel.org

Eating Disorders Anonymous (EDA)
www.eatingdisordersanonymous.org

Eating Disorder Hope (EDH)
www.eatingdisorderhope.com

Family Feeding Dynamics, Katja Rowell, M.D.
www.familyfeedingdynamics.com

Health At Every Size
www.haescommunity.org

I Chose To Live
www.ichosetolive.com

National Eating Disorder Association (NEDA)
www.nationaleatingdisorders.org

Overeaters Anonymous (OA)
www.oa.org

Overeaters Anonymous Honesty, Openness, Willingness (OA HOW)
of Minnesota
www.oa.advocateoffice.com

Pivotal Crossings, Rita Goldhammer
www.pivotalcrossings.com

The Rudd Center at Yale
www.yaleruddcenter.org
The charge of the Rudd Center is "to reverse the global spread of
obesity; to reduce weight bias; and to galvanize community members,
public officials, and advocacy groups to achieve positive, lasting change."

OTHER RESOURCES

Academy of Eating Disorders
www.aedweb.org

Andrea's Voice Foundation: Disordered Eating and Related Issues
www.andreasvoice.org

Eating Disorders Coalition (EDC)
www.eatingdisorderscoalition.org

Federal Response to Eliminate Eating Disorders (F.R.E.E.D.) Act
www.freedfoundation.org

Mentor Connect: Relationships Replace Eating Disorders
www.mentorconnect-ed.org

Mindfulness via: Dialectical Behavior Therapy Training: Marsha
Linehan, Ph.D., ABPP
www.BehavioralTech.org

Something Fishy
www.something-fishy.org

ACKNOWLEDGMENTS

I want to thank Connie Anderson of Words and Deeds for being the impetus for this book. Without Connie's advice, encouragement and editing, this book would not be.

Thanks to Pat Morris of Book Architects for her generous publishing assistance in bringing this book forth.

My sincere gratitude goes to all of my family and friends for being what I call "Book Widows" for so very long. The fun diversions you all created and meals prepared for me helped make this possible. I know some of you wondered if this would ever happen so thank you for believing in me and this project. Special kudos to my husband Jay Henry for his endless and unconditional support.

To the Women of Words . . . there aren't enough words to express my gratitude for your support, love, friendship, help and faith in me and this project.

My sincere thanks to all of you who bravely shared your stories to help other families cope with these ravaging illnesses. Some of your stories are combined but you will know who you are. I was so focused on sharing stories to help families that I never anticipated that the process of telling your stories would bring you the healing many of you have told me it has. Ever since I chose to reclaim the joy in my life that the e.d. tried to take away, it has been my mission at Hope Network to help other families reclaim their joy. Seeing that happen for so many of you even before this book went to print makes my heart sing.

STAY TUNED . . . if you have a story to share, apply to be interviewed.

To contact the author
www.JustTellHerToStop.com
www.HopeNetwork.info (sign up for the free e-newsletter)
Coachbeckyhenry.blogspot.com (comment on blog posts)

twitter.com/HopeNetworkBeck
linkedin.com/in/eatingdisordercoach
http://www.facebook.com/HopeNetworkBeck

Becky Henry

In July 2008 I had the great for-
tune of being photographed by
Mary Ann Halpin, Goddess of the
Camera, Muse of Creativity. Mary
Ann photographed fearless women
expressing their power by holding a sword—a symbol of courage, for the book *Fearless Women:
Midlife Portraits* written by Nancy
Alspaugh and Marilyn Kentz. I got
to hold the same sword that was
held by all of the famous and not-
so-famous fearless women in that
book. What power that sword con-
tained. Mary Ann asked me how
I wanted to hold it and I chose to
hold the sword close to my heart to
symbolize the tenderness (that nearly broke my heart) alongside
the powerfulness and fearlessness that kept my heart from breaking as my family traveled the road to recovery.

Ironically, when the photo arrived I was surprised at how
good I looked. So I am being upfront that this photo has been
retouched. Most are.

One of the factors that many feel contribute to this worldwide eating disorders epidemic is the exposure to altered and
enhanced photos. While the media may contribute, neither they
nor the fashion industry cause eating disorders. Eating disorders
are biological brain illnesses. So, I saw my photo, I realized what
a gift I'd been given–the perfect opportunity to bring up this
important subject.